Text Translation Series: 1

Śrīmad Bhagavad Gītā

(Text with roman transliteration
and English translation)

Swami Dayananda Saraswati
Arsha Vidya

Arsha Vidya
Research and Publication Trust
Chennai

Published by :
Arsha Vidya Research and Publication Trust
' Srinidhi ' Apts 3rd Floor
Sir Desika Road, Mylapore
Chennai 600 004 INDIA
Tel : 044 2499 7023
Telefax : 2499 7131
Email : avrandpt@gmail.com
Website : www.avrpt.com

ISBN : 978 - 81 - 903636 - 8 - 6

First Edition :	April	2007	Copies : 1000
1st Reprint :	May	2009	Copies : 2000
2nd Reprint :	November	2010	Copies : 2000
3rd Reprint :	July	2012	Copies : 1000
4th Reprint :	April	2014	Copies : 1000
5th Reprint :	April	2015	Copies : 2000

Design & Layout :
Graaphic Design

Printed at :
Sudarsan Graphics Pvt. Ltd.,
27, Neelakanta Mehta Street
T. Nagar, Chennai 600 017
Email : info@sudarsan.com

CONTENTS

Preface

I am very happy to present just the English translation of *Śrīmad Bhagavad Gītā* for ready reference and daily reading of the verses with their meaning. I had taken enough care to make the meaning of each verse read in a form that would reveal to a discerning reader the relevant words in the verse. My hope is that the daily *svādhyāya* would help the reader know the general meaning of each verse in time.

Swami Dayananda Saraswati

19 March 2007

Key to Transliteration and Pronunciation of Sanskrit Letters

Sanskrit is a highly phonetic language and hence accuracy in articulation of the letters is important. For those unfamiliar with the *Devanāgari* script, the international transliteration is a guide to the proper pronunciation of Sanskrit letters.

अ	*a*	*(but)*	ट	*ṭa*	*(true)**3
आ	*ā*	*(father)*	ठ	*ṭha*	*(anthill)**3
इ	*i*	*(it)*	ड	*ḍa*	*(drum)**3
ई	*ī*	*(beat)*	ढ	*ḍha*	*(godhead)**3
उ	*u*	*(full)*	ण	*ṇa*	*(under)**3
ऊ	*ū*	*(pool)*	त	*ta*	*(path)**4
ऋ	*ṛ*	*(rhythm)*	थ	*tha*	*(thunder)**4
ॠ	*ṝ*	*(marine)*	द	*da*	*(that)**4
ऌ	*ḷ*	*(revelry)*	ध	*dha*	*(breathe)**4
ए	*e*	*(play)*	न	*na*	*(nut)**4
ऐ	*ai*	*(aisle)*	प	*pa*	*(put)* 5
ओ	*o*	*(go)*	फ	*pha*	*(loophole)**5
औ	*au*	*(loud)*	ब	*ba*	*(bin)* 5
क	*ka*	*(seek)* 1	भ	*bha*	*(abhor)**5
ख	*kha*	*(blockhead)**1	म	*ma*	*(much)* 5
ग	*ga*	*(get)* 1	य	*ya*	*(loyal)*
घ	*gha*	*(log hut)**1	र	*ra*	*(red)*
ङ	*ṅa*	*(sing)* 1	ल	*la*	*(luck)*
च	*ca*	*(chunk)* 2	व	*va*	*(vase)*
छ	*cha*	*(catch him)**2	श	*śa*	*(sure)*
ज	*ja*	*(jump)* 2	ष	*ṣa*	*(shun)*
झ	*jha*	*(hedgehog)**2	स	*sa*	*(so)*
ञ	*ña*	*(bunch)* 2	ह	*ha*	*(hum)*

•	ṁ	*anusvāra*	(nasalisation of preceding vowel)
:	ḥ	*visarga*	(aspiration of preceding vowel)
*			No exact English equivalents for these letters

1.	Guttural	–	Pronounced from throat
2.	Palatal	–	Pronounced from palate
3.	Lingual	–	Pronounced from cerebrum
4.	Dental	–	Pronounced from teeth
5.	Labial	–	Pronounced from lips

The 5th letter of each of the above class – called nasals – are also pronounced nasally.

गीता ध्यानम्

Gītā Dhyānam

In praise of Gītā

ॐ पार्थाय प्रतिबोधितां भगवता नारायणेन स्वयं
व्यासेन ग्रथितां पुराणमुनिना मध्येमहाभारतम्।
अद्वैतामृतवर्षिणीं भगवतीमष्टादशाध्यायिनीम्
अम्ब त्वाम् अनुसन्दधामि भगवद्गीते भवद्वेषिणीम्॥ १॥

om pārthāya pratibodhitāṁ bhagavatā
nārāyaṇena svayaṁ
vyāsena grathitāṁ purāṇamuninā
madhyemahābhāratam
advaitāmṛtavarṣiṇīṁ bhagavatīm
aṣṭādaśādhyāyinīm
amba tvām anusandadhāmi
bhagavadgīte bhavadveṣiṇīm (1)

Om. Goddess Mother *Bhagavadgītā*! I repeatedly invoke you who were taught by Bhagavān Nārāyaṇa himself for the sake of Arjuna, the son of Pṛthā (Kuntī), (you who were) faithfully collected and reported by the ancient sage, Vyāsa, (and placed) in the middle of the *Mahābhārata*, (you who are) in eighteen chapters, you who have the nature of showering the nectar of non-duality, and who is the destroyer of the life of becoming (*saṁsāra*).

नमोऽस्तु ते व्यास विशालबुद्धे फुल्लारविन्दायतपत्रनेत्र।
येन त्वया भारततैलपूर्णः प्रज्वालितो ज्ञानमयः प्रदीपः॥ २॥

namo'stu te vyāsa viśālabuddhe
phullāravindāyatapatranetra
yena tvayā bhāratatailapūrṇaḥ
prajvālito jñānamayaḥ pradīpaḥ (2)

Bhagavān Vyāsa! Salutation be unto you, the one who has a vast mind, whose eyes are beautiful like the soft petals of a lotus, by whom (you) was lighted the lamp of knowledge, filled with the oil of *Mahābhārata*.

प्रपन्नपारिजाताय तोत्रवेत्रैकपाणये ।
ज्ञानमुद्राय कृष्णाय गीतामृतदुहे नमः ॥ ३ ॥

prapannapārijātāya totravetraikapāṇaye
jñānamudrāya kṛṣṇāya gītāmṛtaduhe namaḥ (3)

My salutation to Lord Kṛṣṇa, who is a wish-fulfilling tree for those who surrender to him, who holds a whip in one hand and has the symbol of knowledge in the other, (and) who milks the nectar that is the *Gītā*.

सर्वोपनिषदो गावो दोग्धा गोपालनन्दनः ।
पार्थो वत्सः सुधीर्भोक्ता दुग्धं गीतामृतं महत् ॥ ४ ॥

sarvopaniṣado gāvo dogdhā gopālanandanaḥ
pārtho vatsaḥ sudhīrbhoktā dugdhaṁ gītāmṛtaṁ mahat (4)

The *Upaniṣads* are the cows; the one who milks is Kṛṣṇa, the joy of cowherds; the calf is Arjuna; the partaker (of the milk) is the one whose mind is clear; and the invaluable, timeless *Gītā* is the milk.

वसुदेवसुतं देवं कंसचाणूरमर्दनम्।
देवकीपरमानन्दं कृष्णं वन्दे जगद्गुरुम्॥ ५॥

vasudevasutaṁ devaṁ kaṁsacāṇūramardanam
devakīparamānandaṁ kṛṣṇaṁ vande jagadgurum (5)

I salute Kṛṣṇa, the Lord, the world-teacher, the son of Vasudeva, the destroyer of Kaṁsa and Cāṇūra, and the greatest joy of Devakī.

भीष्मद्रोणतटा जयद्रथजला गान्धारनीलोत्पला
शल्यग्राहवती कृपेण वहनी कर्णेन वेलाकुला।
अश्वत्थामविकर्णघोरमकरा दुर्योधनावर्त्तिनी
सोत्तीर्णा खलु पाण्डवै रणनदी कैवर्तकः केशवः॥ ६॥

bhīṣmadroṇataṭā jayadrathajalā gāndhāranīlotpalā
śalyagrāhavatī kṛpeṇa vahanī karṇena velākulā
aśvatthāmavikarṇaghoramakarā duryodhanāvarttinī
sottīrṇā khalu pāṇḍavai raṇanadī kaivartakaḥ keśavaḥ (6)

With Bhīṣma and Droṇa as its banks, Jayadratha, as its water, Gāndhāra (Śakuni) as the blue lily,[1] Śalya as the shark, Kṛpa as the force of the water, Karṇa as its breakers, Aśvatthāmā and Vikarṇa as its killer whales, and Duryodhana as its whirlpools, the river of battle was indeed crossed by the Pāṇḍavas, because the boatman was Kṛṣṇa.

पाराशर्यवचःसरोजममलं गीतार्थगन्धोत्कटं
नानाख्यानककेसरं हरिकथासम्बोधनाबोधितम्।
लोके सज्जनषट्पदैरहरहः पेपीयमानं मुदा
भूयाद्भारतपङ्कजं कलिमलप्रध्वंसि नः श्रेयसे॥ ७॥

pārāśaryavacaḥsarojam amalaṁ
gītārthagandhotkaṭaṁ
nānākhyānakakesaraṁ harikathā-
sambodhanābodhitam
loke sajjanaṣaṭpadairaharahaḥ
pepīyamānaṁ mudā
bhūyād bhāratapaṅkajaṁ kalimala-
pradhvaṁsi naḥ śreyase (7)

May the spotless lotus, *Mahābhārata*—born of the water of the words of Vyāsa, the son of Parāśara, having the meaning of the *Gītā* as its sweet fragrance, with its many stories as stamens, blossoming with the revealing stories of the Lord Hari, relished happily day after day by the honey bees who are the right thinking people of the world, and which destroys the blemishes of *kali-yuga* (may this lotus of *Mahābhārata*)—be for our good.

मूकं करोति वाचालं पङ्गुं लङ्घयते गिरिम् ।
यत्कृपा तमहं वन्दे परमानन्दमाधवम् ॥ ८ ॥

mūkaṁ karoti vācālaṁ paṅguṁ laṅghayate girim
yatkṛpā tam ahaṁ vande paramānandamādhavam (8)

I salute Kṛṣṇa, the Lord of Lakṣmī (wealth), whose nature is fullness, whose grace makes the mute eloquent and the lame scale the mountaintops.

यं ब्रह्मा वरुणेन्द्ररुद्रमरुतः स्तुन्वन्ति दिव्यैः स्तवैः
वेदैः साङ्गपदक्रमोपनिषदैर्गायन्ति यं सामगाः ।
ध्यानावस्थिततद्गतेन मनसा पश्यन्ति यं योगिनो
यस्यान्तं न विदुः सुरासुरगणा देवाय तस्मै नमः ॥ ९ ॥

yaṁ brahmā varuṇendrarudramarutaḥ
stunvanti divyaiḥ stavaiḥ
vedaiḥ sāṅgapadakramopaniṣadair-
gāyanti yaṁ sāmagāḥ
dhyānāvasthitatadgatena manasā
paśyanti yaṁ yogino
yasyāntaṁ na viduḥ surāsuragaṇā
devāya tasmai namaḥ (9)

My salutations to the Lord whom Brahmā, Varuṇa, Indra, Rudra, and the *Marut-devatā*s praise with divine hymns, the one whom the singers of the *Sāmaveda* praise by singing with the full complement of the limbs (of singing) in the order of *pada, krama* and the *Upaniṣad*s, the one whom contemplative people see with minds resolved in him in a state of meditation, and whose nature the celestials and demons do not know.

Chapter 1
अर्जुन-विषाद-योगः
Arjuna-viṣāda-yogaḥ

Topic of Arjuna's sorrow

धृतराष्ट्र उवाच ।
धर्मक्षेत्रे कुरुक्षेत्रे समवेता युयुत्सवः ।
मामकाः पाण्डवाश्चैव किमकुर्वत सञ्जय ॥ १ ॥

dhṛtarāṣṭra uvāca
dharmakṣetre kurukṣetre samavetā yuyutsavaḥ
māmakāḥ pāṇḍavāścaiva kim akurvata sañjaya (1)

Dhṛtarāṣṭra said:
Sañjaya! Desiring to fight, what did my people and the Pāṇḍavas do, assembled at Kurukṣetra,[2] the abode of *dharma*?

सञ्जय उवाच ।
दृष्ट्वा तु पाण्डवानीकं व्यूढं दुर्योधनस्तदा ।
आचार्यमुपसङ्गम्य राजा वचनमब्रवीत् ॥ २ ॥

sañjaya uvāca
dṛṣṭvā tu pāṇḍavānīkaṁ vyūḍhaṁ duryodhanastadā
ācāryam upasaṅgamya rājā vacanam abravīt (2)

Sañjaya said:
Then, seeing the army of the Pāṇḍavas in battle formation, King Duryodhana approaching his teacher, Droṇa, spoke these words.

पश्यैतां पाण्डुपुत्राणामाचार्य महतीं चमूम् ।
व्यूढां द्रुपदपुत्रेण तव शिष्येण धीमता ॥ ३ ॥

paśyaitāṁ pāṇḍuputrāṇām ācārya mahatīṁ camūm
vyūḍhāṁ drupadaputreṇa tava śiṣyeṇa dhīmatā (3)

O Teacher! Please look at this great army of the sons of Pāṇḍu, formed and led by your brilliant disciple (Dhṛṣṭadyumna), the son of Drupada.

अत्र शूरा महेष्वासा भीमार्जुनसमा युधि ।
युयुधानो विराटश्च द्रुपदश्च महारथः ॥ ४ ॥
धृष्टकेतुश्चेकितानः काशिराजश्च वीर्यवान् ।
पुरुजित्कुन्तिभोजश्च शैब्यश्च नरपुङ्गवः ॥ ५ ॥
युधामन्युश्च विक्रान्त उत्तमौजाश्च वीर्यवान् ।
सौभद्रो द्रौपदेयाश्च सर्व एव महारथाः ॥ ६ ॥

atra śūrā maheṣvāsā bhīmārjunasamā yudhi
yuyudhāno virāṭaśca drupadaśca mahārathaḥ (4)
dhṛṣṭaketuścekitānaḥ kāśirājaśca vīryavān
purujitkuntibhojaśca śaibyaśca narapuṅgavaḥ (5)
yudhāmanyuśca vikrānta uttamaujāśca vīryavān
saubhadro draupadeyāśca sarva eva mahārathāḥ (6)

Here are unrivalled experts, equal to Bhīma and Arjuna in battle, great archers (each one of them) — Sātyaki,[3] the king of Virāṭa,[4] and King Drupada, a man of great valour...
...Dhṛṣṭaketu,[5] Cekitāna,[6] the valiant king of Kāśī, Purujit,[7] Kuntibhoja[8] and Śaibya,[9] the most exalted among men...
...the powerful Yudhāmanyu, Uttamaujas,[10] a warrior of great strength, the son of Subhadrā (Abhimanyu),[11] and the sons of Draupadī, all valorous warriors.

अस्माकं तु विशिष्टा ये तान्निबोध द्विजोत्तम ।
नायका मम सैन्यस्य संज्ञार्थं तान्ब्रवीमि ते ॥ ७ ॥

asmākaṁ tu viśiṣṭā ye tānnibodha dvijottama
nāyakā mama sainyasya sañjñārthaṁ tān bravīmi te (7)

Whereas, the learned among the twice born (*brāhmaṇas*)! Please take note of those who are important amongst ourselves, the leaders of my army. I mention them in order to introduce them to you.

भवान्भीष्मश्च कर्णश्च कृपश्च समितिञ्जयः ।
अश्वत्थामा विकर्णश्च सौमदत्तिर्जयद्रथः ॥ ८ ॥
अन्ये च बहवः शूरा मदर्थे त्यक्तजीविताः ।
नानाशस्त्रप्रहरणाः सर्वे युद्धविशारदाः ॥ ९ ॥

bhavān bhīṣmaśca karṇaśca kṛpaśca samitiñjayaḥ
aśvatthāmā vikarṇaśca saumadattirjayadrathaḥ (8)
anye ca bahavaḥ śūrā madarthe tyaktajīvitāḥ
nānāśastrapraharaṇāḥ sarve yuddhaviśāradāḥ (9)

Your Honour, Bhīṣma, Karṇa, Kṛpa,[12] who is always victorious in war, Aśvatthāmā,[13] Vikarṇa,[14] Saumadatti,[15] son of Somadatta (Bhūriśravā), and Jayadratha[16]...
...and many other warriors, all experts in warfare, armed with many kinds of weapons, who are determined to give up their lives for my sake (are present on our side).

अपर्याप्तं तदस्माकं बलं भीष्माभिरक्षितम् ।
पर्याप्तं त्विदमेतेषां बलं भीमाभिरक्षितम् ॥ १० ॥

aparyāptaṁ tadasmākaṁ balaṁ bhīṣmābhirakṣitam
paryāptaṁ tvidam eteṣāṁ balaṁ bhīmābhirakṣitam (10)

Our army (being larger), well protected by Bhīṣma, cannot be overwhelmed, whereas the army of these people in front of us, even though protected by Bhīma, can be overwhelmed.

अयनेषु च सर्वेषु यथाभागमवस्थिताः।
भीष्ममेवाभिरक्षन्तु भवन्तः सर्व एव हि॥ ११॥

ayaneṣu ca sarveṣu yathābhāgam avasthitāḥ
bhīṣmam evābhirakṣantu bhavantaḥ sarva eva hi (11)

Stationed in your respective positions, in all the divisions of the army, all of you should indeed protect Bhīṣma in particular.

तस्य सञ्जनयन्हर्षं कुरुवृद्धः पितामहः।
सिंहनादं विनद्योच्चैः शङ्खं दध्मौ प्रतापवान्॥ १२॥

tasya sañjanayan harṣaṁ kuruvṛddhaḥ pitāmahaḥ
siṁhanādaṁ vinadyoccaiḥ śaṅkhaṁ dadhmau
pratāpavān (12)

Bhīṣma, the grandfather of the Kuru family, known for his valour, loudly let out a lion's roar and blew his conch in order to make Duryodhana happy.

ततः शङ्खाश्च भेर्यश्च पणवानकगोमुखाः।
सहसैवाभ्यहन्यन्त स शब्दस्तुमुलोऽभवत्॥ १३॥

tataḥ śaṅkhāśca bheryaśca paṇavānakagomukhāḥ
sahasaivābhyahanyanta sa śabdastumulo'bhavat (13)

Then, suddenly, conches, kettledrums, tabors, trumpets, and cow-horns were blasted forth and the sound was indeed earth shaking.

ततः श्वेतैर्हयैर्युक्ते महति स्यन्दने स्थितौ।
माधवः पाण्डवश्चैव दिव्यौ शङ्खौ प्रदध्मतुः॥ १४॥

tataḥ śvetairhayairyukte mahati syandane sthitau
mādhavaḥ pāṇḍavaścaiva divyau śaṅkhau pradadhmatuḥ (14)

Then, Kṛṣṇa and Arjuna, seated in the great chariot drawn by white horses, blew their divine conches.

पाञ्चजन्यं हृषीकेशो देवदत्तं धनञ्जयः।
पौण्ड्रं दध्मौ महाशङ्खं भीमकर्मा वृकोदरः॥ १५॥

pāñcajanyaṁ hṛṣīkeśo devadattaṁ dhanañjayaḥ
pauṇḍraṁ dadhmau mahāśaṅkhaṁ bhīmakarmā vṛkodaraḥ (15)

Kṛṣṇa (blew) the Pāñcajanya and Arjuna the Devadatta. Bhīma, the man of fierce deeds and one with the stomach of a wolf, blew his huge conch, Pauṇḍra.

अनन्तविजयं राजा कुन्तीपुत्रो युधिष्ठिरः।
नकुलः सहदेवश्च सुघोषमणिपुष्पकौ॥ १६॥

anantavijayaṁ rājā kuntīputro yudhiṣṭhiraḥ
nakulaḥ sahadevaśca sughoṣamaṇipuṣpakau (16)

King Yudhiṣṭhira, the son of Kuntī, blew Anantavijaya and Nakula and Sahadeva blew Sughoṣa and Maṇipuṣpaka respectively.

काश्यश्च परमेष्वासः शिखण्डी च महारथः।
धृष्टद्युम्नो विराटश्च सात्यकिश्चापराजितः॥ १७॥
द्रुपदो द्रौपदेयाश्च सर्वशः पृथिवीपते।
सौभद्रश्च महाबाहुः शङ्खान्दध्मुः पृथक्पृथक्॥ १८॥

kāśyaśca parameṣvāsaḥ śikhaṇḍī ca mahārathaḥ
dhṛṣṭadyumno virāṭaśca sātyakiścāparājitaḥ (17)
drupado draupadeyāśca sarvaśaḥ pṛthivīpate
saubhadraśca mahābāhuḥ śaṅkhān dadhmuḥ
pṛthakpṛthak (18)

O The ruler of earth (Dhṛtarāṣṭra)! The king of Kāśī, an expert archer, Śikhaṇḍī of great valour, Dhṛṣṭadyumna, and Virāṭa, and the unsurpassed Sātyaki...
...King Drupada, the sons of Draupadī and the mighty armed son of Subhadrā (Abhimanyu), all blew their own conches.

स घोषो धार्तराष्ट्राणां हृदयानि व्यदारयत्।
नभश्च पृथिवीं चैव तुमुलो व्यनुनादयन्॥ १९॥

sa ghoṣo dhārtarāṣṭrāṇāṁ hṛdayāni vyadārayat
nabhaśca pṛthivīṁ caiva tumulo vyanunādayan (19)

That terrible sound, reverberating throughout the earth and sky, pierced the very hearts of the sons of Dhṛtarāṣṭra.

अथ व्यवस्थितान्दृष्ट्वा धार्तराष्ट्रान् कपिध्वजः।
प्रवृत्ते शस्त्रसम्पाते धनुरुद्यम्य पाण्डवः॥ २०॥
हृषीकेशं तदा वाक्यमिदमाह महीपते।

atha vyavasthitān dṛṣṭvā dhārtarāṣṭrān kapidhvajaḥ
pravṛtte śastrasampāte dhanurudyamya pāṇḍavaḥ (20)
hṛṣīkeśaṁ tadā vākyam idam āha mahīpate

Then, with the battle ready to begin, O the ruler of earth! seeing the sons of Dhṛtarāṣṭra assembled (on the battlefield), Arjuna, who had Hanumān on his banner, lifting his bow, said these words to Kṛṣṇa.

अर्जुन उवाच ।
सेनयोरुभयोर्मध्ये रथं स्थापय मेऽच्युत ॥ २१ ॥
यावदेतान्निरीक्षेऽहं योद्धुकामानवस्थितान् ।
कैर्मया सह योद्धव्यमस्मिन् रणसमुद्यमे ॥ २२ ॥

arjuna uvāca
senayorubhayormadhye rathaṁ sthāpaya me'cyuta (21)
yāvadetān nirīkṣe'haṁ yoddhukāmān avasthitān
kairmayā saha yoddhavyam asmin raṇasamudyame (22)

Arjuna said:
Place my chariot, Acyuta[17] (Kṛṣṇa)! between the two armies so that I can view these people who have assembled here desirous of fighting, (and also view) with whom I should fight at the onset of this war.

योत्स्यमानानवेक्षेऽहं य एतेऽत्र समागताः ।
धार्तराष्ट्रस्य दुर्बुद्धेर्युद्धे प्रियचिकीर्षवः ॥ २३ ॥

yotsyamānān avekṣe'haṁ ya ete'tra samāgatāḥ
dhārtarāṣṭrasya durbuddheryuddhe priyacikīrṣavaḥ (23)

I wish to see those who have gathered here with the intention of fighting, who want to carry out in the war what is pleasing to the son of Dhṛtarāṣṭra (Duryodhana), the one whose thinking is distorted.

सञ्जय उवाच ।
एवमुक्तो हृषीकेशो गुडाकेशेन भारत ।
सेनयोरुभयोर्मध्ये स्थापयित्वा रथोत्तमम् ॥ २४ ॥
भीष्मद्रोणप्रमुखतः सर्वेषां च महीक्षिताम् ।
उवाच पार्थ पश्यैतान्समवेतान्कुरूनिति ॥ २५ ॥

sañjaya uvāca
evamukto hṛṣīkeśo guḍākeśena bhārata
senayorubhayormadhye sthāpayitvā rathottamam (24)
bhīṣmadroṇapramukhataḥ sarveṣāṁ ca mahīkṣitām
uvāca pārtha paśyaitān samavetān kurūn iti (25)

Sañjaya said:
Bhārata[18] (Dhṛtarāṣṭra)! Commanded thus by Guḍākeśa[19] (Arjuna), Lord Hṛṣīkeśa[20] (Kṛṣṇa) placed the great chariot in the middle of the two armies, right in front of Bhīṣma, Droṇa, and all the rulers and spoke thus: 'Pārtha[21] (Arjuna)! Please look at these Kauravas who have gathered here.'

तत्रापश्यत् स्थितान्पार्थः पितॄनथ पितामहान् ।
आचार्यान्मातुलान्भ्रातॄन्पुत्रान्पौत्रान्सखींस्तथा ॥ २६ ॥
श्वशुरान्सुहृदश्चैव सेनयोरुभयोरपि ।

tatrāpaśyat sthitān pārthaḥ pitṝnatha pitāmahān
ācāryān mātulān bhrātṝn putrān pautrān
sakhīṁstathā (26)
śvaśurān suhṛdaścaiva senayorubhayorapi

There, Arjuna saw paternal elders, grandfathers, teachers, uncles, brothers, sons, grandsons, friends, fathers-in-law and well-wishers too, assembled in the two armies.

तान्समीक्ष्य स कौन्तेयः सर्वान्बन्धूनवस्थितान् ॥ २७ ॥
कृपया परयाविष्टो विषीदन्निदमब्रवीत् ।

tānsamīkṣya sa kaunteyaḥ sarvān bandhūn avasthitān (27)
kṛpayā parayāviṣṭo viṣīdannidam abravīt

Seeing clearly all the assembled relatives, Kaunteya[22] (Arjuna), seized by deep compassion, said this[23] sorrowfully.

अर्जुन उवाच ।
दृष्ट्वेमं स्वजनं कृष्ण युयुत्सुं समुपस्थितम् ॥ २८ ॥
सीदन्ति मम गात्राणि मुखं च परिशुष्यति ।
वेपथुश्च शरीरे मे रोमहर्षश्च जायते ॥ २९ ॥

arjuna uvāca
dṛṣṭvemaṁ svajanaṁ kṛṣṇa yuyutsuṁ samupasthitam (28)
sīdanti mama gātrāṇi mukhaṁ ca pariśuṣyati
vepathuśca śarīre me romaharṣaśca jāyate (29)

Arjuna said:
Kṛṣṇa! Looking at these people, who are my own people, well stationed in battle positions and desirous to fight, my limbs are losing all their strength, my mouth is drying up, my body is trembling, and the hair (on my body) is standing on end.

गाण्डीवं स्रंसते हस्तात्त्वक् चैव परिदह्यते ।
न च शक्नोम्यवस्थातुं भ्रमतीव च मे मनः ॥ ३० ॥

gāṇḍīvaṁ sraṁsate hastāt tvakcaiva paridahyate
na ca śaknomyavasthātuṁ bhramatīva ca me manaḥ (30)

The bow, Gāṇḍīva, is slipping from my hand and (my) skin also is burning. I am not able to stand up and my mind is totally confused as it were.

निमित्तानि च पश्यामि विपरीतानि केशव ।
न च श्रेयोऽनुपश्यामि हत्वा स्वजनमाहवे ॥ ३१ ॥

nimittāni ca paśyāmi viparītāni keśava
na ca śreyo'nupaśyāmi hatvā svajanam āhave (31)

Keśava[24] (Kṛṣṇa)! I see bad omens and I do not see any good in killing one's own people in this battle.

न काङ्क्षे विजयं कृष्ण न च राज्यं सुखानि च
किं नो राज्येन गोविन्द किं भोगैर्जीवितेन वा ॥ ३२ ॥

na kāṅkṣe vijayaṁ kṛṣṇa na ca rājyaṁ sukhāni ca
kiṁ no rājyena govinda kiṁ bhogairjīvitena vā (32)

Kṛṣṇa! I want neither victory, nor the kingdom, nor comforts. Govinda[25] (Kṛṣṇa)! What is the use of a kingdom or of pleasures, or of life itself to us?

येषामर्थे काङ्क्षितं नो राज्यं भोगाः सुखानि च
त इमेऽवस्थिता युद्धे प्राणांस्त्यक्त्वा धनानि च ॥ ३३ ॥

yeṣām arthe kaṅkṣitaṁ no rājyaṁ bhogāḥ sukhāni ca
ta ime'vasthitā yuddhe prāṇāṁstyaktvā dhanāni ca (33)

Those for whose sake (alone) the kingdom, objects of enjoyments and pleasures were desired by us, they have assembled in (this) battle, having given up their wealth and their lives.

आचार्याः पितरः पुत्रास्तथैव च पितामहाः ।
मातुलाः श्वशुराः पौत्राः श्यालाः सम्बन्धिनस्तथा ॥ ३४ ॥

ācāryāḥ pitaraḥ putrāstathaiva ca pitāmahāḥ
mātulāḥ śvaśurāḥ pautrāḥ śyālāḥ sambandhinastathā (34)

These are (our) teachers, paternal uncles, sons, grandfathers, maternal uncles, in-laws, grandsons, cousins, friends and other relatives.

एतान्न हन्तुमिच्छामि घ्नतोऽपि मधुसूदन ।
अपि त्रैलोक्यराज्यस्य हेतोः किं नु महीकृते ॥ ३५ ॥

etān na hantum icchāmi ghnato'pi madhusūdana
api trailokyarājyasya hetoḥ kiṁ nu mahīkṛte (35)

Madhusūdana[26] (Kṛṣṇa)! Even for the sake of ruling over the three worlds, much less for this kingdom on earth, I do not desire to kill these (people), even if they are going to kill me.

निहत्य धार्तराष्ट्रान्नः का प्रीतिः स्याज्जनार्दन ।
पापमेवाश्रयेदस्मान्हत्वैतानाततायिनः ॥ ३६ ॥

nihatya dhārtarāṣṭrān naḥ kā prītiḥ syājjanārdana
pāpamevāśrayedasmān hatvaitān ātatāyinaḥ (36)

Janārdana[27] (Kṛṣṇa)! What kind of satisfaction would be there for us by destroying these sons of Dhṛtarāṣṭra? Sin alone would come to us by destroying these wrongdoers.

तस्मान्नार्हा वयं हन्तुं धार्तराष्ट्रान् स्वबान्धवान् ।
स्वजनं हि कथं हत्वा सुखिनः स्याम माधव ॥ ३७ ॥

tasmānnārhā vayaṁ hantuṁ dhārtarāṣṭrān svabāndhavān
svajanaṁ hi kathaṁ hatvā sukhinaḥ syāma mādhava (37)

Therefore, we should not kill our own relatives, the sons of Dhṛtarāṣṭra. Destroying our own people, Mādhava[28] (Kṛṣṇa)! how would we be happy?

यद्यप्येते न पश्यन्ति लोभोपहतचेतसः ।
कुलक्षयकृतं दोषं मित्रद्रोहे च पातकम् ॥ ३८ ॥

कथं न ज्ञेयमस्माभिः पापादस्मान्निवर्तितुम् ।
कुलक्षयकृतं दोषं प्रपश्यद्भिर्जनार्दन ॥ ३९ ॥

yadyapyete na paśyanti lobhopahatacetasaḥ
kulakṣayakṛtaṁ doṣaṁ mitradrohe ca pātakam (38)
kathaṁ na jñeyam asmābhiḥ pāpādasmānnivartitum
kulakṣayakṛtaṁ doṣaṁ prapaśyadbhirjanārdana (39)

Although these people, whose minds are overpowered by greed, do not see the defect in the destruction of (one's) family and the sins of betraying one's friends, Janārdana (Kṛṣṇa)! how come it is not considered by us, who know that sin is born of the destruction of the family, to withdraw from this sin?

कुलक्षये प्रणश्यन्ति कुलधर्माः सनातनाः ।
धर्मे नष्टे कुलं कृत्स्नमधर्मोऽभिभवत्युत ॥ ४० ॥

kulakṣaye praṇaśyanti kuladharmāḥ sanātanāḥ
dharme naṣṭe kulaṁ kṛtsnam adharmo'bhi-
bhavatyuta (40)

When the family is destroyed, the ancient *dharmas* of the family perish. When the *dharma* is lost, will not *adharma* overwhelm the entire family?

अधर्माभिभवात्कृष्ण प्रदुष्यन्ति कुलस्त्रियः ।
स्त्रीषु दुष्टासु वार्ष्णेय जायते वर्णसङ्करः ॥ ४१ ॥

adharmābhibhavāt kṛṣṇa praduṣyanti kulastriyaḥ
strīṣu duṣṭāsu vārṣṇeya jāyate varṇasaṅkaraḥ (41)

Kṛṣṇa! Due to the increase of *adharma*, the women in the family will be given to improper ways. Vārṣṇeya[29] (Kṛṣṇa)! When the women become corrupt, confusion is born in the society.

सङ्करो नरकायैव कुलघ्नानां कुलस्य च ।
पतन्ति पितरो ह्येषां लुप्तपिण्डोदकक्रियाः ॥ ४२ ॥

saṅkaro narakāyaiva kulaghnānāṁ kulasya ca
patanti pitaro hyeṣāṁ luptapiṇḍodakakriyāḥ (42)

Confusion, indeed, leads the family and the destroyers of the family to the world of pain. Their ancestors, denied of their post death rituals, indeed fall.

दोषैरेतैः कुलघ्नानां वर्णसङ्करकारकैः ।
उत्साद्यन्ते जातिधर्माः कुलधर्माश्च शाश्वताः ॥ ४३ ॥

doṣairetaiḥ kulaghnānāṁ varṇasaṅkarakārakaiḥ
utsādyante jātidharmāḥ kuladharmāśca śāśvatāḥ (43)

By these wrong actions of those who destroy the family, creating confusion in the society, the perennial *dharma*s pursued by the community and the family are destroyed.

उत्सन्नकुलधर्माणां मनुष्याणां जनार्दन ।
नरके नियतं वासो भवतीत्यनुशुश्रुम ॥ ४४ ॥

utsannakuladharmāṇāṁ manuṣyāṇāṁ janārdana
narake niyataṁ vāso bhavatītyanuśuśruma (44)

We have heard, Janārdana (Kṛṣṇa)! that a life in the world of pain is inevitable for those people who destroy the *dharma* of the family.

अहो बत महत्पापं कर्तुं व्यवसिता वयम् ।
यद्राज्यसुखलोभेन हन्तुं स्वजनमुद्यताः ॥ ४५ ॥

aho bata mahatpāpaṁ kartuṁ vyavasitā vayam
yadrājyasukhalobhena hantuṁ svajanam udyatāḥ (45)

Alas! Ready to kill our own people due to greed for a kingdom and its pleasures, we are determined to commit a grave sin!

यदि मामप्रतीकारमशस्त्रं शस्त्रपाणयः ।
धार्तराष्ट्रा रणे हन्युस्तन्मे क्षेमतरं भवेत् ॥ ४६ ॥

yadi mām apratikāram aśastraṁ śastrapāṇayaḥ
dhārtarāṣṭrā raṇe hanyustanme kṣemataraṁ bhavet (46)

It will be better for me if the sons of Dhṛtarāṣṭra, with weapons in hand, were to kill me, who is unarmed and who does not retaliate, in the battle.

सञ्जय उवाच ।
एवमुक्त्वार्जुनः सङ्ख्ये रथोपस्थ उपाविशत् ।
विसृज्य सशरं चापं शोकसंविग्नमानसः ॥ ४७ ॥

sañjaya uvāca
evam uktvārjunaḥ saṅkhye rathopastha upāviśat
visṛjya saśaraṁ cāpaṁ śokasaṁvignamānasaḥ (47)

Sañjaya said:
Having spoken in this manner in the middle of the battlefield, Arjuna, whose mind was completely overcome by sorrow, sat down on the seat of the chariot casting aside his bow and arrows.

ॐतत्सत् ।
इति श्रीमद्भगवद्गीतासूपनिषत्सु ब्रह्मविद्यायां योगशास्त्रे श्रीकृष्णार्जुन-संवादेऽर्जुन-विषाद-योगो नाम प्रथमोऽध्यायः ॥ १ ॥

omtatsat.
iti śrīmadbhagavadgītāsūpaniṣatsu brahma-vidyāyāṁ yogaśāstre śrīkṛṣṇārjuna-saṁvāde'rjuna-viṣāda-yogo nāma prathamo'dhyāyaḥ (1)

Om, Brahman, is the only reality. Thus ends the first chapter called *arjuna-viṣāda-yoga*[30]—having the topic of Arjuna's sorrow—in the *Bhagavadgītā* which is in the form of a dialogue between Śrī Kṛṣṇa and Arjuna, which is the essence of the *Upaniṣads*, whose subject matter is both the knowledge of Brahman and *yoga*.[31]

Chapter 2

साङ्ख्य-योगः

Sāṅkhya-yogaḥ

Topic of knowledge

सञ्जय उवाच ।
तं तथा कृपयाविष्टमश्रुपूर्णाकुलेक्षणम् ।
विषीदन्तमिदं वाक्यमुवाच मधुसूदनः ॥ १ ॥

sañjaya uvāca
taṁ tathā kṛpayāviṣṭam aśrupūrṇākulekṣaṇam
viṣīdantam idaṁ vākyam uvāca madhusūdanaḥ (1)

Sañjaya said:
To him—who was thus sad and overwhelmed by compassion, whose eyes were filled with tears and showed distress—Madhusūdana (Kṛṣṇa) spoke these words.

श्रीभगवानुवाच ।
कुतस्त्वा कश्मलमिदं विषमे समुपस्थितम् ।
अनार्यजुष्टमस्वर्ग्यमकीर्तिकरमर्जुन ॥ २ ॥

śrībhagavān uvāca
kutastvā kaśmalam idaṁ viṣame samupasthitam
anāryajuṣṭam asvargyam akīrtikaram arjuna (2)

Śrī Bhagavān said:
Arjuna! In such crisis from where has this despair come upon you? It is unbecoming of an upright man and does not add to (your) fame. Nor does it lead you to heaven.

क्लैब्यं मा स्म गमः पार्थ नैतत्त्वय्युपपद्यते।
क्षुद्रं हृदयदौर्बल्यं त्यक्त्वोत्तिष्ठ परन्तप॥ ३॥

klaibyaṁ mā sma gamaḥ pārtha naitattvayyupapadyate
kṣudraṁ hṛdayadaurbalyaṁ tyaktvottiṣṭha parantapa (3)

Pārtha (Arjuna)! Do not yield to unmanliness. This does not befit you. The scorcher of enemies! Give up this lowly weakness of heart and get up.

अर्जुन उवाच।
कथं भीष्ममहं सङ्ख्ये द्रोणं च मधुसूदन।
इषुभिः प्रतियोत्स्यामि पूजार्हावरिसूदन॥ ४॥

arjuna uvāca
kathaṁ bhīṣmamahaṁ saṅkhye droṇaṁ ca madhusūdana
iṣubhiḥ pratiyotsyāmi pūjārhāvarisūdana (4)

Arjuna said:
Madhusūdana (Kṛṣṇa)! The destroyer of foes! How will I, in this battle, fight with arrows against Bhīṣma and Droṇa, who are worthy of my worship?

गुरूनहत्वा हि महानुभावान् श्रेयो भोक्तुं भैक्ष्यमपीह लोके।
हत्वार्थकामांस्तु गुरूनिहैव भुञ्जीय भोगान् रुधिरप्रदिग्धान्॥ ५॥

gurūn ahatvā hi mahānubhāvān
śreyo bhoktuṁ bhaikṣyam apīha loke
hatvārthakāmāṁstu gurūn ihaiva
bhuñjīya bhogān rudhirapradigdhān (5)

It would be better indeed to eat food collected from others here in this world than to kill these most revered teachers. If I kill them, the pleasures I would experience in this world will be stained with (their) blood.

न चैतद्विद्मः कतरन्नो गरीयो यद्वा जयेम यदि वा नो जयेयुः ।
यानेव हत्वा न जिजीविषामस्तेऽवस्थिताः प्रमुखे धार्तराष्ट्राः ॥ ६ ॥

na caitadvidmaḥ kataranno garīyo
yadvā jayema yadi vā no jayeyuḥ
yāneva hatvā na jijīviṣāma-
ste'vasthitāḥ pramukhe dhārtarāṣṭrāḥ (6)

And, we do not know which of the two will be better for us—that we should conquer them or that they should conquer us. The sons of Dhṛtarāṣṭra, after slaying whom we will indeed not like to live, stand facing us (to be killed).

कार्पण्यदोषोपहतस्वभावः पृच्छामि त्वां धर्मसम्मूढचेताः ।
यच्छ्रेयः स्यान्निश्चितं ब्रूहि तन्मे शिष्यस्तेऽहं शाधि मां त्वां प्रपन्नम् ॥ ७ ॥

kārpaṇyadoṣopahatasvabhāvaḥ
pṛcchāmi tvāṁ dharmasammūḍhacetāḥ
yacchreyaḥ syānniścitaṁ brūhi tanme
śiṣyaste'haṁ śādhi māṁ tvāṁ prapannam (7)

Overcome by faint-heartedness, confused about my duty, I ask you: Please tell me that which is truly better for me. I am your student. Please teach me, who has taken refuge in you.

न हि प्रपश्यामि ममापनुद्याद् यच्छोकमुच्छोषणमिन्द्रियाणाम् ।
अवाप्य भूमावसपत्नमृद्धं राज्यं सुराणामपि चाधिपत्यम् ॥ ८ ॥

na hi prapaśyāmi mamāpanudyād
yacchokamucchoṣaṇam indriyāṇām
avāpya bhūmāvasapatnam ṛddhaṁ
rājyaṁ surāṇām api cādhipatyam (8)

Indeed, I do not see anything that would remove the sorrow that dries up my senses, even if I were to obtain an unrivalled and prosperous kingdom on earth and sovereignty over the denizens of heaven.

सञ्जय उवाच ।
एवमुक्त्वा हृषीकेशं गुडाकेशः परन्तपः ।
न योत्स्य इति गोविन्दमुक्त्वा तूष्णीं बभूव ह ॥ ९॥

sañjaya uvāca
evam uktvā hṛṣīkeśaṁ guḍākeśaḥ parantapaḥ
na yotsya iti govindam uktvā tūṣṇīṁ babhūva ha (9)

Sañjaya said:
Having spoken to Hṛṣīkeśa (Lord Kṛṣṇa) in this manner, Guḍākeśa (Arjuna), the scorcher of foes, said, 'I shall not fight.' Speaking thus to Govinda (Lord Kṛṣṇa), he became silent.

तमुवाच हृषीकेशः प्रहसन्निव भारत ।
सेनयोरुभयोर्मध्ये विषीदन्तमिदं वचः ॥ १० ॥

tamuvāca hṛṣīkeśaḥ prahasanniva bhārata
senayorubhayormadhye viṣīdantam idaṁ vacaḥ (10)

Bhārata (Dhṛtarāṣṭra)! To him who was sad in the midst of both armies, Hṛṣīkeśa (Lord Kṛṣṇa), as though smiling, said these words.

श्रीभगवानुवाच ।
अशोच्यानन्वशोचस्त्वं प्रज्ञावादांश्च भाषसे ।
गतासूनगतासूंश्च नानुशोचन्ति पण्डिताः ॥ ११ ॥

śrībhagavān uvāca
aśocyān anvaśocastvaṁ prajñāvādāṁśca bhāṣase
gatāsūn agatāsūṁśca nānuśocanti paṇḍitāḥ (11)

Śrī Bhagavān said:
You grieve for those who are not be grieved for. Yet you speak words of wisdom. The wise do not grieve for those who are gone and who are not yet gone.

न त्वेवाहं जातु नासं न त्वं नेमे जनाधिपाः ।
न चैव न भविष्यामः सर्वे वयमतः परम् ॥ १२ ॥

na tvevāhaṁ jātu nāsaṁ na tvaṁ neme janādhipāḥ
na caiva na bhaviṣyāmaḥ sarve vayam ataḥ param (12)

There was never a time I did not exist, neither you nor these kings. Nor will any of us cease to exist in the future.

देहिनोऽस्मिन्यथा देहे कौमारं यौवनं जरा ।
तथा देहान्तरप्राप्तिर्धीरस्तत्र न मुह्यति ॥ १३ ॥

dehino'smin yathā dehe kaumāraṁ yauvanaṁ jarā
tathā dehāntaraprāptirdhīrastatra na muhyati (13)

Just as, for the *jīva*, the indweller of this body, there is childhood, youth and old age, similar is the gaining of another body. With reference to that, a wise person does not come to grief.

मात्रास्पर्शास्तु कौन्तेय शीतोष्णसुखदुःखदाः ।
आगमापायिनोऽनित्यास्तांस्तितिक्षस्व भारत ॥ १४ ॥

mātrāsparśāstu kaunteya śītoṣṇasukhaduḥkhadāḥ
āgamāpāyino'nityāstāṁstitikṣasva bhārata (14)

Kaunteya (Arjuna)! The contacts of the sense organs with the sensory world that give rise to cold and heat, pleasure and pain, which have the nature of coming and going, are not constant. Endure them, Bhārata (Arjuna)!

यं हि न व्यथयन्त्येते पुरुषं पुरुषर्षभ ।
समदुःखसुखं धीरं सोऽमृतत्वाय कल्पते ॥ १५ ॥

yaṁ hi na vyathayantyete puruṣaṁ puruṣarṣabha
samaduḥkhasukhaṁ dhīraṁ so'mṛtatvāya kalpate (15)

Arjuna, the prominent among men! The person whom these (*sukha* and *duḥkha*) do not affect, who is the same in pleasure and pain, and who is discriminative, is indeed fit for gaining liberation.

नासतो विद्यते भावो नाभावो विद्यते सतः ।
उभयोरपि दृष्टोऽन्तस्त्वनयोस्तत्त्वदर्शिभिः ॥ १६ ॥

nāsato vidyate bhāvo nābhāvo vidyate sataḥ
ubhayorapi dṛṣṭo'ntastvanayostattvadarśibhiḥ (16)

For the unreal (*mithyā*), there is never any being. For the real, there is never any non-being. The ultimate truth of both (the real and the unreal) is seen by the knowers of the truth.

अविनाशि तु तद्विद्धि येन सर्वमिदं ततम् ।
विनाशमव्ययस्यास्य न कश्चित्कर्तुमर्हति ॥ १७ ॥

avināśi tu tadviddhi yena sarvam idaṁ tatam
vināśam avyayasyāsya na kaścit kartum arhati (17)

Know that, by which this entire world is pervaded, to be indeed indestructible. No one can bring about the destruction of that which does not change.

अन्तवन्त इमे देहा नित्यस्योक्ताः शरीरिणः।
अनाशिनोऽप्रमेयस्य तस्माद्युध्यस्व भारत॥ १८॥

antavanta ime dehā nityasyoktāḥ śarīriṇaḥ
anāśino'prameyasya tasmādyudhyasva bhārata (18)

These bodies of the embodied one (the self), which is not subject to change and destruction, and which is not available as an object of knowledge, are said to be subject to end. Therefore, Bhārata (Arjuna)! (get up and) fight.

य एनं वेत्ति हन्तारं यश्चैनं मन्यते हतम्।
उभौ तौ न विजानीतो नायं हन्ति न हन्यते॥ १९॥

ya enaṁ vetti hantāraṁ yaścainaṁ manyate hatam
ubhau tau na vijānīto nāyaṁ hanti na hanyate (19)

The one who thinks this (self) to be the killer and the one who thinks of it as the killed, both do not know. This (self) does not kill; nor is it killed.

न जायते म्रियते वा कदाचिन्नायं भूत्वा भविता वा न भूयः।
अजो नित्यः शाश्वतोऽयं पुराणो न हन्यते हन्यमाने शरीरे॥२०॥

na jāyate mriyate vā kadācin-
nāyaṁ bhūtvā bhavitā vā na bhūyaḥ
ajo nityaḥ śāśvato'yaṁ purāṇo
na hanyate hanyamāne śarīre (20)

This (self) is never born; nor does it die. It is not that, having been, it ceases to exist again. It is unborn, eternal, undergoes no change whatsoever, and is ever new. When the body is destroyed, the self is not destroyed.

वेदाविनाशिनं नित्यं य एनमजमव्ययम्।
कथं स पुरुषः पार्थ कं घातयति हन्ति कम्॥ २१॥

vedāvināśinaṁ nityaṁ ya enam ajam avyayam
kathaṁ sa puruṣaḥ pārtha kaṁ ghātayati hanti kam (21)

Pārtha (Arjuna)! The one who knows this (self) to be indestructible, timeless, unborn, and not subject to decline, how and whom does that person kill? Whom does he cause to kill?

वासांसि जीर्णानि यथा विहाय नवानि गृह्णाति नरोऽपराणि ।
तथा शरीराणि विहाय जीर्णान्यन्यानि संयाति नवानि देही ॥२२ ॥

vāsāṁsi jīrṇāni yathā vihāya
navāni gṛhṇāti naro'parāṇi
tathā śarīrāṇi vihāya jīrṇān-
yanyāni saṁyāti navāni dehī (22)

Just as a person gives up old clothes and takes up new ones, so does the self, the one who dwells in the body, gives up old bodies[32] and takes others which are new.

नैनं छिन्दन्ति शस्त्राणि नैनं दहति पावकः ।
न चैनं क्लेदयन्त्यापो न शोषयति मारुतः ॥ २३ ॥

nainaṁ chindanti śastrāṇi nainaṁ dahati pāvakaḥ
na cainaṁ kledayantyāpo na śoṣayati mārutaḥ (23)

Weapons do not slay this (self); nor does fire burn it. Water does not wet (or drown) nor does wind dry it.

अच्छेद्योऽयमदाह्योऽयमक्लेद्योऽशोष्य एव च ।
नित्यः सर्वगतः स्थाणुरचलोऽयं सनातनः ॥ २४ ॥

acchedyo'yam adāhyo'yam akledyo'śoṣya eva ca
nityaḥ sarvagataḥ sthāṇuracalo'yaṁ sanātanaḥ (24)

This (self) cannot be slain, burnt, drowned, or dried. It is changeless, all-pervading, stable, immovable, and eternal.

अव्यक्तोऽयमचिन्त्योऽयमविकार्योऽयमुच्यते ।
तस्मादेवं विदित्वैनं नानुशोचितुमर्हसि ॥ २५ ॥

avyakto'yam acintyo'yam avikāryo'yam ucyate
tasmādevaṁ viditvainaṁ nānuśocitum arhasi (25)

This (self) is said to be unmanifest, not an object of thought, and not subject to change. Therefore, knowing this, you ought not to grieve.

अथ चैनं नित्यजातं नित्यं वा मन्यसे मृतम् ।
तथापि त्वं महाबाहो नैवं शोचितुमर्हसि ॥ २६ ॥

atha cainaṁ nityajātaṁ nityaṁ vā manyase mṛtam
tathāpi tvaṁ mahābāho naivaṁ śocitum arhasi (26)

And if you take this (*ātman*) to have constant birth and death, even then, Arjuna, the mighty armed! you ought not to grieve (for the *ātman*) in this manner.

जातस्य हि ध्रुवो मृत्युर्ध्रुवं जन्म मृतस्य च ।
तस्मादपरिहार्येऽर्थे न त्वं शोचितुमर्हसि ॥ २७ ॥

jātasya hi dhruvo mṛtyurdhruvaṁ janma mṛtasya ca
tasmādaparihārye'rthe na tvaṁ śocitum arhasi (27)

For that which is born, death is certain and for that which is dead, birth is certain. Therefore, you ought not to grieve over that which cannot be altered.

अव्यक्तादीनि भूतानि व्यक्तमध्यानि भारत ।
अव्यक्तनिधनान्येव तत्र का परिदेवना ॥ २८ ॥

avyaktādīni bhūtāni vyaktamadhyāni bhārata
avyaktanidhanānyeva tatra kā paridevanā (28)

Bhārata (Arjuna)! All beings are unmanifest in the beginning, manifest in the middle, and (again) unmanifest in the end. What indeed is there to grieve about?

आश्चर्यवत्पश्यति कश्चिदेनमाश्चर्यवद्वदति तथैव चान्यः।
आश्चर्यवच्चैनमन्यः शृणोति श्रुत्वाप्येनं वेद न चैव कश्चित्॥२९॥

āścaryavat paśyati kaścidenam
āścaryavadvadati tathaiva cānyaḥ
āścaryavaccainam anyaḥ śṛṇoti
śrutvāpyenaṁ veda na caiva kaścit (29)

One looks upon the self as a wonder. Similarly, another speaks of it as a wonder and another hears it as a wonder. Still another, even after hearing about this (self), does not understand it at all.

देही नित्यमवध्योऽयं देहे सर्वस्य भारत।
तस्मात्सर्वाणि भूतानि न त्वं शोचितुमर्हसि॥ ३०॥

dehī nityam avadhyo'yaṁ dehe sarvasya bhārata
tasmāt sarvāṇi bhūtāni na tvaṁ śocitum arhasi (30)

Bhārata (Arjuna)! This *ātman*, the indweller of the bodies of all beings, is ever indestructible. Therefore, you ought not to grieve for all these people.

स्वधर्ममपि चावेक्ष्य न विकम्पितुमर्हसि।
धर्म्याद्धि युद्धाच्छ्रेयोऽन्यत् क्षत्रियस्य न विद्यते॥ ३१॥

svadharmam api cāvekṣya na vikampitum arhasi
dharmyāddhi yuddhācchreyo'nyat kṣatriyasya na vidyate (31)

And also, from the standpoint of your own duty, you cannot waver. For, there is nothing greater to a *kṣatriya* than a battle for the cause of *dharma*.

यदृच्छया चोपपन्नं स्वर्गद्वारमपावृतम् ।
सुखिनः क्षत्रियाः पार्थ लभन्ते युद्धमीदृशम् ॥ ३२ ॥

yadṛcchayā copapannaṁ svargadvāram apāvṛtam
sukhinaḥ kṣatriyāḥ pārtha labhante yuddham īdṛśam (32)

Pārtha (Arjuna)! Only lucky *kṣatriyas* get this kind of battle, which has come by chance and which is an open gate to heaven.

अथ चेत्त्वमिमं धर्म्यं सङ्ग्रामं न करिष्यसि ।
ततः स्वधर्मं कीर्तिं च हित्वा पापमवाप्स्यसि ॥ ३३ ॥

atha cettvam imaṁ dharmyaṁ saṅgrāmaṁ na kariṣyasi
tataḥ svadharmaṁ kīrtiṁ ca hitvā pāpam avāpsyasi (33)

But, if you refuse to engage in this war that is in keeping with *dharma*, then, forfeiting your own duty and honour, you will gain only sin.

अकीर्तिं चापि भूतानि कथयिष्यन्ति तेऽव्ययाम् ।
सम्भावितस्य चाकीर्तिर्मरणादतिरिच्यते ॥ ३४ ॥

akīrtiṁ cāpi bhūtāni kathayiṣyanti te'vyayām
sambhāvitasya cākīrtirmaraṇād atiricyate (34)

Also, people will speak of your unending infamy. For the honoured, dishonour is surely worse than death.

भयाद्रणादुपरतं मंस्यन्ते त्वां महारथाः ।
येषां च त्वं बहुमतो भूत्वा यास्यसि लाघवम् ॥ ३५ ॥

bhayādraṇāduparataṁ maṁsyante tvāṁ mahārathāḥ
yeṣāṁ ca tvaṁ bahumato bhūtvā yāsyasi lāghavam (35)

The great warriors will consider you as having retreated from the battle due to fear. And you, having been so highly esteemed by them, will fall in their esteem.

अवाच्यवादांश्च बहून्वदिष्यन्ति तवाहिताः ।
निन्दन्तस्तव सामर्थ्यं ततो दुःखतरं नु किम् ॥ ३६ ॥

avācyavādāṁśca bahūn vadiṣyanti tavāhitāḥ
nindantastava sāmarthyaṁ tato duḥkhataraṁ nu kim (36)

And belittling your prowess, your enemies will say many unutterable things about (you). Is there anything more painful than that?

हतो वा प्राप्स्यसि स्वर्गं जित्वा वा भोक्ष्यसे महीम् ।
तस्मादुत्तिष्ठ कौन्तेय युद्धाय कृतनिश्चयः ॥ ३७ ॥

hato vā prāpsyasi svargaṁ jitvā vā bhokṣyase mahīm
tasmād uttiṣṭha kaunteya yuddhāya kṛtaniścayaḥ (37)

Destroyed, you will gain heaven; victorious, you will enjoy (this) world. Therefore, Kaunteya (Arjuna)! get up, having resolved to fight.

सुखदुःखे समे कृत्वा लाभालाभौ जयाजयौ ।
ततो युद्धाय युज्यस्व नैवं पापमवाप्स्यसि ॥ ३८ ॥

sukhaduḥkhe same kṛtvā lābhālābhau jayājayau
tato yuddhāya yujyasva naivaṁ pāpam avāpsyasi (38)

Taking pleasure and pain, gain and loss, victory and defeat to be the same, prepare for battle. Thus, you will gain no sin.

एषा तेऽभिहिता साङ्ख्ये बुद्धिर्योगे त्विमां शृणु ।
बुद्ध्या युक्तो यया पार्थ कर्मबन्धं प्रहास्यसि ॥ ३९ ॥

eṣā te'bhihitā sāṅkhye buddhiryoge tvimāṁ śṛṇu
buddhyā yukto yayā pārtha karmabandhaṁ
prahāsyasi (39)

This wisdom with reference to self-knowledge has so far been told to you. Now, Pārtha (Arjuna)! listen also to the wisdom of *yoga*, endowed with which you will get rid of the bondage of action.

नेहाभिक्रमनाशोऽस्ति प्रत्यवायो न विद्यते ।
स्वल्पमप्यस्य धर्मस्य त्रायते महतो भयात् ॥ ४० ॥

nehābhikramanāśo'sti pratyavāyo na vidyate
svalpam apyasya dharmasya trāyate mahato bhayāt (40)

In this, there is no waste of effort, nor are the opposite results produced. Even very little of this *karma-yoga* protects one from great fear.

व्यवसायात्मिका बुद्धिरेकेह कुरुनन्दन ।
बहुशाखा ह्यनन्ताश्च बुद्धयोऽव्यवसायिनाम् ॥ ४१ ॥

vyavasāyātmikā buddhirekeha kurunandana
bahuśākhā hyanantāśca buddhayo'vyavasāyinām (41)

With reference to this (*mokṣa*), Arjuna, the descendant of Kurus! there is a single, well ascertained understanding. The notions of those who lack discrimination are many branched and innumerable indeed.

यामिमां पुष्पितां वाचं प्रवदन्त्यविपश्चितः ।
वेदवादरताः पार्थ नान्यदस्तीति वादिनः ॥ ४२ ॥

कामात्मानः स्वर्गपरा जन्मकर्मफलप्रदाम् ।
क्रियाविशेषबहुलां भोगैश्वर्यगतिं प्रति ॥ ४३ ॥

yāmimāṁ puṣpitāṁ vācaṁ pravadantyavipaścitaḥ
vedavādaratāḥ pārtha nānyad astīti vādinaḥ (42)
kāmātmānaḥ svargaparā janmakarmaphalapradām
kriyāviśeṣabahulāṁ bhogaiśvaryagatiṁ prati (43)

Pārtha (Arjuna)! The non-discriminating people, who remain engrossed in *karma* enjoined by the Veda (and its results), who argue that there is nothing other than this, who are full of desires with heaven as their highest goal, utter these flowery words that talk of many special rituals meant for the attainment of pleasures and power and of results in the form of (better) births.

भोगैश्वर्यप्रसक्तानां तयापहृतचेतसाम् ।
व्यवसायात्मिका बुद्धिः समाधौ न विधीयते ॥ ४४ ॥

bhogaiśvaryaprasaktānāṁ tayāpahṛtacetasām
vyavasāyātmikā buddhiḥ samādhau na vidhīyate (44)

For those who pursue pleasure and power exclusively, whose minds are robbed away by these (flowery words), well-ascertained understanding does not take place in their mind.

त्रैगुण्यविषया वेदा निस्त्रैगुण्यो भवार्जुन ।
निर्द्वन्द्वो नित्यसत्त्वस्थो निर्योगक्षेम आत्मवान् ॥ ४५ ॥

traiguṇyaviṣyā vedā nistraiguṇyo bhavārjuna
nirdvandvo nityasattvastho niryogakṣema ātmavān (45)

The subject matter of the Vedas is related to the three variable qualities. Arjuna! Be one who is free from the hold of these three-fold qualities, from (the sorrow of) the pairs of opposites; be one who is ever established in *sattva-guṇa*, who is free from the anxieties of acquiring and protecting, and who is a master of oneself.

यावानर्थ उदपाने सर्वतः सम्प्लुतोदके ।
तावान्सर्वेषु वेदेषु ब्राह्मणस्य विजानतः ॥ ४६ ॥

yāvānartha udapāne sarvataḥ samplutodake
tāvān sarveṣu vedeṣu brāhmaṇasya vijānataḥ (46)

For the *brāhmaṇa* who knows the self, all the Vedas are of only so much use as a small reservoir is when there is flood everywhere.

कर्मण्येवाधिकारस्ते मा फलेषु कदाचन ।
मा कर्मफलहेतुर्भूर्मा ते सङ्गोऽस्त्वकर्मणि ॥ ४७ ॥

karmaṇyevādhikāraste mā phaleṣu kadācana
mā karmaphalaheturbhūrmā te saṅgo'stvakarmaṇi (47)

Your choice is in action only, never in the results thereof. Do not think you are the author of the results of action. Let your attachment not be to inaction.

योगस्थः कुरु कर्माणि सङ्गं त्यक्त्वा धनञ्जय ।
सिद्ध्यसिद्ध्योः समो भूत्वा समत्वं योग उच्यते ॥ ४८ ॥

yogasthaḥ kuru karmāṇi saṅgaṁ tyaktvā dhanañjaya
siddhyasiddhyoḥ samo bhūtvā samatvaṁ yoga ucyate (48)

Remaining steadfast in *yoga*, Dhanañjaya[33] (Arjuna)! perform actions abandoning attachment and remaining the same to success and failure. This evenness of mind is called *yoga*.

दूरेण ह्यवरं कर्म बुद्धियोगाद्धनञ्जय ।
बुद्धौ शरणमन्विच्छ कृपणाः फलहेतवः ॥ ४९ ॥

dūreṇa hyavaraṁ karma buddhiyogāddhanañjaya
buddhau śaraṇam anviccha kṛpaṇāḥ phalahetavaḥ (49)

Action (based on desire) is, therefore, far inferior to that performed with the proper attitude of *karma-yoga*. Seek refuge in this *buddhi-yoga* (of proper attitude), Dhanañjaya (Arjuna)! Those who perform action only for the results are misers.

बुद्धियुक्तो जहातीह उभे सुकृतदुष्कृते ।
तस्माद्योगाय युज्यस्व योगः कर्मसु कौशलम् ॥ ५० ॥

buddhiyukto jahātīha ubhe sukṛtaduṣkṛte
tasmād yogāya yujyasva yogaḥ karmasu kauśalam (50)

One who is endowed with the sameness of mind, gives up both *puṇya* and *pāpa* here, in this world. Therefore, commit yourself to *karma-yoga*. *Karma-yoga* is discretion in action.

कर्मजं बुद्धियुक्ता हि फलं त्यक्त्वा मनीषिणः ।
जन्मबन्धविनिर्मुक्ताः पदं गच्छन्त्यनामयम् ॥ ५१ ॥

karmajaṁ buddhiyuktā hi phalaṁ tyaktvā manīṣiṇaḥ
janmabandhavinirmuktāḥ padaṁ gacchantyanāmayam (51)

The wise, endowed with the attitude of *karma-yoga*, having given up the results of action, free from the bondage of birth, indeed accomplish the end that is free from all afflictions.

यदा ते मोहकलिलं बुद्धिर्व्यतितरिष्यति ।
तदा गन्तासि निर्वेदं श्रोतव्यस्य श्रुतस्य च ॥ ५२ ॥

yadā te mohakalilaṁ buddhirvyatitariṣyati
tadā gantāsi nirvedaṁ śrotavyasya śrutasya ca (52)

When your intellect crosses over the impurity of delusion, then you shall gain a dispassion towards what has been heard and what is yet to be heard.

श्रुतिविप्रतिपन्ना ते यदा स्थास्यति निश्चला ।
समाधावचला बुद्धिस्तदा योगमवाप्स्यसि ॥ ५३ ॥

śrutivipratipannā te yadā sthāsyati niścalā
samādhāvacalā buddhistadā yogam avāpsyasi (53)

When your mind is no longer distracted by the Vedas (which present various means and ends to be gained) it will remain steady, firmly established in the self. Then you will gain self-knowledge.

अर्जुन उवाच ।
स्थितप्रज्ञस्य का भाषा समाधिस्थस्य केशव ।
स्थितधीः किं प्रभाषेत किमासीत व्रजेत किम् ॥ ५४ ॥

arjuna uvāca
sthitaprajñasya kā bhāṣā samādhisthasya keśava
sthitadhīḥ kiṁ prabhāṣeta kimāsīta vrajeta kim (54)

Arjuna said:
Keśava (Kṛṣṇa)! What is the description of a person of firm wisdom, one whose mind abides in the self? How does such a person, whose mind is not shaken by anything, speak, sit, and walk?

श्रीभगवानुवाच ।
प्रजहाति यदा कामान्सर्वान्पार्थ मनोगतान् ।
आत्मन्येवात्मना तुष्टः स्थितप्रज्ञस्तदोच्यते ॥ ५५ ॥

śrībhagavān uvāca
prajahāti yadā kāmān sarvān pārtha manogatān
ātmanyevātmanā tuṣṭaḥ sthitaprajñastadocyate (55)

Śrī Bhagavān said:
When a person gives up all the desires, as they appear in the mind, happy in oneself with oneself alone, Pārtha (Arjuna)! that person is said to be one of ascertained knowledge.

दुःखेष्वनुद्विग्नमनाः सुखेषु विगतस्पृहः ।
वीतरागभयक्रोधः स्थितधीर्मुनिरुच्यते ॥ ५६ ॥

duḥkheṣvanudvignamanāḥ sukheṣu vigataspṛhaḥ
vītarāgabhayakrodhaḥ sthitadhīrmunirucyate (56)

The one who is not affected by adversities, who is without yearning for pleasures, and is free from longing, fear and anger, is said to be a wise person whose knowledge stays (unshaken).

यः सर्वत्रानभिस्नेहस्तत्तत्प्राप्य शुभाशुभम् ।
नाभिनन्दति न द्वेष्टि तस्य प्रज्ञा प्रतिष्ठिता ॥ ५७ ॥

yaḥ sarvatrānabhisnehastattat prāpya śubhāśubham
nābhinandati na dveṣṭi tasya prajñā pratiṣṭhitā (57)

The one who is unattached in all situations, who neither rejoices on gaining the pleasant nor hates the unpleasant, his knowledge is well established.

यदा संहरते चायं कूर्मोऽङ्गानीव सर्वशः ।
इन्द्रियाणीन्द्रियार्थेभ्यस्तस्य प्रज्ञा प्रतिष्ठिता ॥ ५८ ॥

yadā saṁharate cāyaṁ kūrmo'ṅgānīva sarvaśaḥ
indriyāṇīndriyārthebhyastasya prajñā pratiṣṭhitā (58)

When, like the turtle that withdraws its limbs, this person is able to completely withdraw the sense organs from their objects, his knowledge is steady.

विषया विनिवर्तन्ते निराहारस्य देहिनः ।
रसवर्जं रसोऽप्यस्य परं दृष्ट्वा निवर्तते ॥ ५९ ॥

viṣayā vinivartante nirāhārasya dehinaḥ
rasavarjaṁ raso'pyasya paraṁ dṛṣṭvā nivartate (59)

For the one who does not feed the senses, the senses come back to oneself, with the longing remaining behind. Having seen Brahman (when the self is known) even the longing goes away.

यततो ह्यपि कौन्तेय पुरुषस्य विपश्चितः ।
इन्द्रियाणि प्रमाथीनि हरन्ति प्रसभं मनः ॥ ६० ॥

yatato hyapi kaunteya puruṣasya vipaścitaḥ
indriyāṇi pramāthīni haranti prasabhaṁ manaḥ (60)

Indeed, the powerful senses forcefully take the mind away, Kaunteya (Arjuna)! of even the person who makes effort, who sees clearly.

तानि सर्वाणि संयम्य युक्त आसीत मत्परः ।
वशे हि यस्येन्द्रियाणि तस्य प्रज्ञा प्रतिष्ठिता ॥ ६१ ॥

tāni sarvāṇi saṁyamya yukta āsīta matparaḥ
vaśe hi yasyendriyāṇi tasya prajñā pratiṣṭhitā (61)

May one who is endowed with discrimination, keeping all the sense organs in one's hands, sit in contemplation of Me. For the one who has all the sense organs under control, the knowledge is well established.

ध्यायतो विषयान्पुंसः सङ्गस्तेषूपजायते ।
सङ्गात्सञ्जायते कामः कामात्क्रोधोऽभिजायते ॥ ६२ ॥
क्रोधाद्भवति सम्मोहः सम्मोहात्स्मृतिविभ्रमः ।
स्मृतिभ्रंशाद् बुद्धिनाशो बुद्धिनाशात्प्रणश्यति ॥ ६३ ॥

dhyāyato viṣayān puṁsaḥ saṅgasteṣūpajāyate
saṅgāt sañjāyate kāmaḥ kāmāt krodho'bhijāyate (62)
krodhād bhavati sammohaḥ sammohāt smṛtivibhramaḥ
smṛtibhraṁśād buddhināśo buddhināśāt praṇaśyati (63)

In the person who dwells upon objects, an attachment is born with reference to them. From attachment is born desire and from desire, anger is born.

From anger comes delusion and from delusion comes the loss of memory. Because of the loss of memory, the mind becomes incapacitated and when the mind is incapacitated, the person is destroyed.

रागद्वेषवियुक्तैस्तु विषयानिन्द्रियैश्चरन् ।
आत्मवश्यैर्विधेयात्मा प्रसादमधिगच्छति ॥ ६४ ॥

rāgadveṣaviyuktaistu viṣayān indriyaiścaran
ātmavaśyairvidheyātmā prasādam adhigacchati (64)

Whereas, one whose mind is controlled, moving in the world of objects with the sense organs that are under his or her control, free from likes and dislikes, attains tranquility.

प्रसादे सर्वदुःखानां हानिरस्योपजायते ।
प्रसन्नचेतसो ह्याशु बुद्धिः पर्यवतिष्ठते ॥ ६५ ॥

prasāde sarvaduḥkhānāṁ hānirasyopajāyate
prasannacetaso hyāśu buddhiḥ paryavatiṣṭhate (65)

For the person whose mind is tranquil, destruction of all pain and sorrow happens. The knowledge of one whose mind is tranquil soon becomes well established.

नास्ति बुद्धिरयुक्तस्य न चायुक्तस्य भावना ।
न चाभावयतः शान्तिरशान्तस्य कुतः सुखम् ॥ ६६ ॥

nāsti buddhirayuktasya na cāyuktasya bhāvanā
na cābhāvayataḥ śāntiraśāntasya kutaḥ sukham (66)

For the one who is not tranquil, there is no knowledge. For the one who is not tranquil, there is no contemplation also. For the one who is not contemplative, there is no peace. For the one who has no peace, how can there be happiness?

इन्द्रियाणां हि चरतां यन्मनोऽनुविधीयते ।
तदस्य हरति प्रज्ञां वायुर्नावमिवाम्भसि ॥ ६७ ॥

indriyāṇāṁ hi caratāṁ yanmano'nuvidhīyate
tadasya harati prajñāṁ vāyurnāvam ivāmbhasi (67)

The mind that follows the wandering senses indeed robs the person of his knowledge, just as the wind carries away a small boat on the waters.

तस्माद्यस्य महाबाहो निगृहीतानि सर्वशः ।
इन्द्रियाणीन्द्रियार्थेभ्यस्तस्य प्रज्ञा प्रतिष्ठिता ॥ ६८ ॥

tasmād yasya mahābāho nigṛhītāni sarvaśaḥ
indriyāṇīndriyārthebhyastasya prajñā pratiṣṭhitā (68)

Therefore, Arjuna, the mighty armed! the knowledge of one whose senses are completely withdrawn (mastered) from their respective objects is steady.

या निशा सर्वभूतानां तस्यां जागर्ति संयमी ।
यस्यां जाग्रति भूतानि सा निशा पश्यतो मुनेः ॥ ६९ ॥

yā niśā sarvabhūtānāṁ tasyāṁ jāgarti saṁyamī
yasyāṁ jāgrati bhūtāni sā niśā paśyato muneḥ (69)

In that which is night for all beings, the one who is wise, who has mastery over oneself, is awake. That in which beings are awake, is night for the wise one who sees.

आपूर्यमाणमचलप्रतिष्ठं समुद्रमापः प्रविशन्ति यद्वत् ।
तद्वत्कामा यं प्रविशन्ति सर्वे स शान्तिमाप्नोति न कामकामी ॥७० ॥

āpūryamāṇam acalapratiṣṭhaṁ
samudram āpaḥ praviśanti yadvat
tadvatkāmā yaṁ praviśanti sarve
sa śāntim āpnoti na kāmakāmī (70)

Just as water flows into the ocean that is brimful and still, so too, the wise person into whom all objects enter, gains peace, (remains unchanged) whereas, the desirer of objects does not gain peace.

विहाय कामान्यः सर्वान्पुमांश्चरति निःस्पृहः ।
निर्ममो निरहङ्कारः स शान्तिमधिगच्छति ॥ ७१ ॥

vihāya kāmān yaḥ sarvān pumāṁścarati niḥspṛhaḥ
nirmamo nirahaṅkāraḥ sa śāntim adhigacchati (71)

Having given up all binding desires, the person who moves around, devoid of longing, without the sense of limited 'I' and 'mine,' gains peace.

एषा ब्राह्मी स्थितिः पार्थ नैनां प्राप्य विमुह्यति ।
स्थित्वास्यामन्तकालेऽपि ब्रह्मनिर्वाणमृच्छति ॥ ७२ ॥

eṣā brāhmī sthitiḥ pārtha naināṁ prāpya vimuhyati
sthitvāsyām antakāle'pi brahmanirvāṇam ṛcchati (72)

Pārtha (Arjuna)! This is (what is meant by) one's being in Brahman. Having gained this, one is not deluded. Remaining therein, even at the end of one's life, one gains liberation.

ॐतत्सत् ।

इति श्रीमद्भगवद्गीतासूपनिषत्सु ब्रह्मविद्यायां योगशास्त्रे श्रीकृष्णार्जुन-संवादे साङ्ख्य-योगो नाम द्वितीयोऽध्यायः ॥ २ ॥

omtatsat.

iti śrīmadbhagavadgītāsūpaniṣatsu brahma-vidyāyāṁ yoga-śāstre śrīkṛṣṇārjunasaṁvāde sāṅkhya-yogo nāma dvitīyo'dhyāyaḥ (2)

Om, Brahman, is the only reality. Thus ends the second chapter called *sāṅkhya-yoga*—having the topic of knowledge—in the *Bhagavadgītā* which is in the form of a dialogue between Śrī Kṛṣṇa and Arjuna, which is the essence of the *Upaniṣads*, whose subject matter is both the knowledge of Brahman and *yoga*.

Chapter 3
कर्म-योगः
Karma-yogaḥ
Topic of karma

अर्जुन उवाच ।
ज्यायसी चेत्कर्मणस्ते मता बुद्धिर्जनार्दन ।
तत्किं कर्मणि घोरे मां नियोजयसि केशव ॥ १ ॥

arjuna uvāca
jyāyasī cetkarmaṇaste matā buddhirjanārdana
tatkiṁ karmaṇi ghore māṁ niyojayasi keśava (1)

Arjuna said:
Janārdana (Kṛṣṇa)! If in your contention knowledge is better than action, why then do you impel me into this gruesome action, Keśava (Kṛṣṇa)?

व्यामिश्रेणेव वाक्येन बुद्धिं मोहयसीव मे ।
तदेकं वद निश्चित्य येन श्रेयोऽहमाप्नुयाम् ॥ २ ॥

vyāmiśreṇeva vākyena buddhiṁ mohayasīva me
tadekaṁ vada niścitya yena śreyo'hamāpnuyām (2)

With words that are seemingly contradictory, you seem to confuse my mind. Deciding for good, which is better, tell me the one thing by which I shall gain liberation.

श्रीभगवानुवाच ।
लोकेऽस्मिन्द्विविधा निष्ठा पुरा प्रोक्ता मयानघ ।
ज्ञानयोगेन साङ्ख्यानां कर्मयोगेन योगिनाम् ॥ ३ ॥

śrībhagavān uvāca
loke'smin dvividhā niṣṭhā purā proktā mayānagha
jñānayogena sāṅkhyānāṁ karmayogena yogināṁ (3)

Śrī Bhagavān said:
The sinless one (Arjuna)! The two-fold committed life style in this world, was told by Me in the beginning[34]—the pursuit of knowledge for the renunciates and the pursuit of *karma-yoga* for those who pursue activity.

न कर्मणामनारम्भान्नैष्कर्म्यं पुरुषोऽश्नुते।
न च संन्यसनादेव सिद्धिं समधिगच्छति॥ ४॥

na karmaṇām anārambhānnaiṣkarmyaṁ puruṣo'śnute
na ca sannyasanādeva siddhiṁ samadhigacchati (4)

A person does not gain the state of actionlessness by non-performance of actions. Nor does the person attain success (liberation) out of mere renunciation, *sannyāsa*.

न हि कश्चित्क्षणमपि जातु तिष्ठत्यकर्मकृत्।
कार्यते ह्यवशः कर्म सर्वः प्रकृतिजैर्गुणैः॥ ५॥

na hi kaścit kṣaṇamapi jātu tiṣṭhatyakarmakṛt
kāryate hyavaśaḥ karma sarvaḥ prakṛtijairguṇaiḥ (5)

Indeed, no one ever remains for even a second without performing action because everyone is forced to perform action by the (three) *guṇas* (*sattva, rajas* and *tamas*) born of *prakṛti*.

कर्मेन्द्रियाणि संयम्य य आस्ते मनसा स्मरन्।
इन्द्रियार्थान्विमूढात्मा मिथ्याचारः स उच्यते॥ ६॥

karmendriyāṇi saṁyamya ya āste manasā smaran
indriyārthān vimūḍhātmā mithyācāraḥ sa ucyate (6)

The one who, controlling the organs of action, sits with the mind remembering those sense objects is deluded and is called a person of false conduct.

यस्त्विन्द्रियाणि मनसा नियम्यारभतेऽर्जुन ।
कर्मेन्द्रियैः कर्मयोगमसक्तः स विशिष्यते ॥ ७ ॥

yastvindriyāṇi manasā niyamyārabhate'rjuna
karmendriyaiḥ karmayogam asaktaḥ sa viśiṣyate (7)

Whereas, Arjuna! the one who, controlling the sense organs with the mind, remaining unattached, takes to the *yoga* of action (i.e., action performed with *yoga-buddhi*) with the organs of action, is far superior.

नियतं कुरु कर्म त्वं कर्म ज्यायो ह्यकर्मणः ।
शरीरयात्रापि च ते न प्रसिद्ध्येदकर्मणः ॥ ८ ॥

niyataṁ kuru karma tvaṁ karma jyāyo hyakarmaṇaḥ
śarīrayātrāpi ca te na prasiddhyed akarmaṇaḥ (8)

Do action that is to be done because action is superior to inaction. Even the maintenance of your body would be impossible by inaction.

यज्ञार्थात्कर्मणोऽन्यत्र लोकोऽयं कर्मबन्धनः ।
तदर्थं कर्म कौन्तेय मुक्तसङ्गः समाचर ॥ ९ ॥

yajñārthāt karmaṇo'nyatra loko'yaṁ karmabandhanaḥ
tadarthaṁ karma kaunteya muktasaṅgaḥ samācara (9)

A person is bound by *karma* if it is not done as *yajña* (i.e., as an offering to Īśvara). For this reason, Kaunteya (Arjuna)! being one free from attachment, perform action for the sake of that (*yajña*).

सहयज्ञाः प्रजाः सृष्ट्वा पुरोवाच प्रजापतिः ।
अनेन प्रसविष्यध्वमेष वोऽस्त्विष्टकामधुक् ॥ १० ॥

sahayajñāḥ prajāḥ sṛṣṭvā purovāca prajāpatiḥ
anena prasaviṣyadhvam eṣa vo'stviṣṭakāmadhuk (10)

In the beginning, the Creator, having created human beings along with *yajña*, said: "By this (*yajña*) shall you multiply. May this (*yajña*) be a wish fulfilling cow for you."

देवान्भावयतानेन ते देवा भावयन्तु वः ।
परस्परं भावयन्तः श्रेयः परमवाप्स्यथ ॥ ११ ॥

devān bhāvayatānena te devā bhāvayantu vaḥ
parasparaṁ bhāvayantaḥ śreyaḥ param avāpsyatha (11)

Propitiate the deities with this (*yajña*). May those deities propitiate you. Propitiating one another, you shall gain the highest good (*mokṣa*).

इष्टान्भोगान्हि वो देवा दास्यन्ते यज्ञभाविताः ।
तैर्दत्तानप्रदायैभ्यो यो भुङ्क्ते स्तेन एव सः ॥ १२ ॥

iṣṭān bhogān hi vo devā dāsyante yajñabhāvitāḥ
tairdattān apradāyaibhyo yo bhuṅkte stena eva saḥ (12)

The deities, propitiated by *yajña*, will give you desirable objects. One who enjoys objects given by them without offering to them in return is indeed a thief.

यज्ञशिष्टाशिनः सन्तो मुच्यन्ते सर्वकिल्बिषैः ।
भुञ्जते ते त्वघं पापा ये पचन्त्यात्मकारणात् ॥ १३ ॥

yajñaśiṣṭāśinaḥ santo mucyante sarvakilbiṣaiḥ
bhuñjate te tvaghaṁ pāpā ye pacantyātmakāraṇāt (13)

Those who eat, having first offered the food to the Lord, are released from impurities, whereas those sinful people who cook only for themselves eat *pāpa* (sin).

अन्नाद्भवन्ति भूतानि पर्जन्यादन्नसम्भवः ।
यज्ञाद्भवति पर्जन्यो यज्ञः कर्मसमुद्भवः ॥ १४ ॥

annādbhavanti bhūtāni parjanyād annasambhavaḥ
yajñādbhavati parjanyo yajñaḥ karmasamudbhavaḥ (14)

Living beings are born of food; food is born of rain; rain is born of *yajña* (*puṇya*); and *yajña* (*puṇya*) is born of action.

कर्म ब्रह्मोद्भवं विद्धि ब्रह्माक्षरसमुद्भवम् ।
तस्मात्सर्वगतं ब्रह्म नित्यं यज्ञे प्रतिष्ठितम् ॥ १५ ॥

karma brahmodbhavaṁ viddhi brahmākṣarasamudbhavam
tasmāt sarvagataṁ brahma nityaṁ yajñe pratiṣṭhitam (15)

May you understand *karma* (ritual, prayer, etc.) to be born of the Veda and the Veda to be born of the imperishable Īśvara. Therefore, the all pervasive *Brahma* (the Veda)[35] abides always in *yajña*.

एवं प्रवर्तितं चक्रं नानुवर्तयतीह यः ।
अघायुरिन्द्रियारामो मोघं पार्थ स जीवति ॥ १६ ॥

evaṁ pravartitaṁ cakraṁ nānuvartayatīha yaḥ
aghāyurindriyārāmo moghaṁ pārtha sa jīvati (16)

A person who does not follow here in this life, this cosmic wheel that is already set in motion, in this manner, and lives in sin given only to the pleasures of the senses, lives wastefully, Pārtha (Arjuna)!

यस्त्वात्मरतिरेव स्यादात्मतृप्तश्च मानवः ।
आत्मन्येव च सन्तुष्टस्तस्य कार्यं न विद्यते ॥ १७ ॥

yastvātmaratireva syād ātmatṛptaśca mānavaḥ
ātmanyeva ca santuṣṭastasya kāryaṁ na vidyate (17)

Whereas, for the person who is delighted in the self, who is satisfied with the self, contented in the self alone, (for him) there is nothing to be done.

नैव तस्य कृतेनार्थो नाकृतेनेह कश्चन ।
न चास्य सर्वभूतेषु कश्चिदर्थव्यपाश्रयः ॥ १८ ॥

naiva tasya kṛtenārtho nākṛteneha kaścana
na cāsya sarvabhūteṣu kaścid arthavyapāśrayaḥ (18)

For that person (who revels in the self), there is indeed no purpose here in this world for doing or not doing action. Nor does such a person depend on any being for any object whatsoever.

तस्मादसक्तः सततं कार्यं कर्म समाचर ।
असक्तो ह्याचरन्कर्म परमाप्नोति पूरुषः ॥ १९ ॥

tasmād asaktaḥ satataṁ kāryaṁ karma samācara
asakto hyācaran karma param āpnoti pūruṣaḥ (19)

Therefore, always perform well the action that is to be done without attachment because, by performing action without attachment, a person attains the highest.

कर्मणैव हि संसिद्धिमास्थिता जनकादयः ।
लोकसङ्ग्रहमेवापि सम्पश्यन्कर्तुमर्हसि ॥ २० ॥

karmaṇaiva hi saṁsiddhim āsthitā janakādayaḥ
lokasaṅgraham evāpi sampaśyan kartum arhasi (20)

Indeed, by action alone, Janaka and others gained liberation. Also, by merely seeing the desirability of protecting the people from falling into unbecoming ways you ought to perform action.

यद्यदाचरति श्रेष्ठस्तत्तदेवेतरो जनः ।
स यत्प्रमाणं कुरुते लोकस्तदनुवर्तते ॥ २१ ॥

yadyad ācarati śreṣṭhastattadevetaro janaḥ
sa yatpramāṇaṁ kurute lokastad anuvartate (21)

Whatsoever an important person does, that alone the other people do. Whatever that person sets as proper, the world of people follows that.

न मे पार्थास्ति कर्तव्यं त्रिषु लोकेषु किञ्चन ।
नानवाप्तमवाप्तव्यं वर्त एव च कर्मणि ॥ २२ ॥

na me pārthāsti kartavyaṁ triṣu lokeṣu kiñcana
nānavāptam avāptavyaṁ varta eva ca karmaṇi (22)

Pārtha (Arjuna)! For me, there is nothing to be done. In the three worlds, there is nothing to be gained by me, which is not yet gained. Yet, I remain engaged in action.

यदि ह्यहं न वर्तेयं जातु कर्मण्यतन्द्रितः ।
मम वर्त्मानुवर्तन्ते मनुष्याः पार्थ सर्वशः ॥ २३ ॥

yadi hyahaṁ na varteyaṁ jātu karmaṇyatandritaḥ
mama vartmānuvartante manuṣyāḥ pārtha sarvaśaḥ (23)

For, should I not ever engage myself in action, without being lazy, Pārtha (Arjuna)! people would follow my example in every way.

उत्सीदेयुरिमे लोका न कुर्यां कर्म चेदहम्।
सङ्करस्य च कर्ता स्यामुपहन्यामिमाः प्रजाः॥ २४॥

utsīdeyurime lokā na kuryāṁ karma ced aham
saṅkarasya ca kartā syām upahanyām imāḥ prajāḥ (24)

If I were not to perform action, these people would perish. I would be the author of confusion (in the society) and I would destroy these beings.

सक्ताः कर्मण्यविद्वांसो यथा कुर्वन्ति भारत।
कुर्याद्विद्वांस्तथाऽसक्तश्चिकीर्षुर्लोकसङ्ग्रहम्॥ २५॥

saktāḥ karmaṇyavidvāṁso yathā kurvanti bhārata
kuryādvidvāṁstathā'saktaścikīrṣurloka saṅgraham (25)

Bhārata (Arjuna)! Just as the unwise, who are attached to the results, perform action, so too would the wise perform action, (but) without attachment, desirous of doing that which is for the protection of the people.

न बुद्धिभेदं जनयेदज्ञानां कर्मसङ्गिनाम्।
जोषयेत्सर्वकर्माणि विद्वान्युक्तः समाचरन्॥ २६॥

na buddhibhedaṁ janayed ajñānāṁ karmasaṅginām
joṣayet sarvakarmāṇi vidvān yuktaḥ samācaran (26)

The one who knows (the *ātman*) should not create any disturbance in the understanding of the ignorant who are attached to the results of action. The wise person, steadfast in the knowledge, himself performing all the actions well, should encourage (the ignorant) into performing (all actions).

प्रकृतेः क्रियमाणानि गुणैः कर्माणि सर्वशः ।
अहङ्कारविमूढात्मा कर्ताहमिति मन्यते ॥ २७ ॥

prakṛteḥ kriyamāṇāni guṇaiḥ karmāṇi sarvaśaḥ
ahaṅkāravimūḍhātmā kartāham iti manyate (27)

Actions are performed in various ways impelled by the *guṇas*[36] of *prakṛti*—the body, mind, and senses. Deluded by the I notion, one thinks, 'I am the doer.'

तत्त्ववित्तु महाबाहो गुणकर्मविभागयोः ।
गुणा गुणेषु वर्तन्त इति मत्वा न सज्जते ॥ २८ ॥

tattvavit tu mahābāho guṇakarmavibhāgayoḥ
guṇā guṇeṣu vartanta iti matvā na sajjate (28)

Whereas, Arjuna, the mighty armed! the knower of the truth of *guṇa*s and actions is not bound, knowing that the *guṇa*s express themselves in *guṇa*s (body-mind-sense-complex).

प्रकृतेर्गुणसम्मूढाः सज्जन्ते गुणकर्मसु ।
तानकृत्स्नविदो मन्दान्कृत्स्नविन्न विचालयेत् ॥ २९ ॥

prakṛterguṇasammūḍhāḥ sajjante guṇakarmasu
tān akṛtsnavido mandān kṛtsnavinna vicālayet (29)

Those who are deluded by the modifications of the *prakṛti* become bound in terms of the body-mind-sense-complex (*guṇa*s) and actions. One who knows (the self) should not disturb those who do not know (the self), who are not discriminative.

मयि सर्वाणि कर्माणि संन्यस्याध्यात्मचेतसा ।
निराशीर्निर्ममो भूत्वा युध्यस्व विगतज्वरः ॥ ३० ॥

mayi sarvāṇi karmāṇi sannyasyādhyātmacetasā
nirāśīrnirmamo bhūtvā yudhyasva vigatajvaraḥ (30)

Renouncing all actions unto Me, with a mind that is discriminating, devoid of expectations with reference to the future and any sense of 'mine-ness,' without any anger or frustration whatsoever, fight (act).

ये मे मतमिदं नित्यमनुतिष्ठन्ति मानवाः ।
श्रद्धावन्तोऽनसूयन्तो मुच्यन्ते तेऽपि कर्मभिः ॥ ३१ ॥

ye me matam idaṁ nityam anutiṣṭhanti mānavāḥ
śraddhāvanto'nasūyanto mucyante te'pi karmabhiḥ (31)

Those people who constantly follow this teaching of Mine, full of faith, without finding fault with the teaching or the teacher (*asūyā*), they too are freed from the hold of the *karma-phala*s. (They gain *mokṣa*.)

ये त्वेतदभ्यसूयन्तो नानुतिष्ठन्ति मे मतम् ।
सर्वज्ञानविमूढांस्तान्विद्धि नष्टानचेतसः ॥ ३२ ॥

ye tvetad abhyasūyanto nānutiṣṭhanti me matam
sarvajñānavimūḍhāṁstān viddhi naṣṭān acetasaḥ (32)

Whereas those who, being critical of this (teaching) without reason, do not follow my vision, who are deluded in all realms of knowledge, and devoid of discrimination, know them as lost.

सदृशं चेष्टते स्वस्याः प्रकृतेर्ज्ञानवानपि ।
प्रकृतिं यान्ति भूतानि निग्रहः किं करिष्यति ॥ ३३ ॥

sadṛśaṁ ceṣṭate svasyāḥ prakṛterjñānavānapi
prakṛtiṁ yānti bhūtāni nigrahaḥ kiṁ kariṣyati (33)

Even a wise person acts in keeping with his or her own nature. Because all beings follow their own nature, of what use is control?

इन्द्रियस्येन्द्रियस्यार्थे रागद्वेषौ व्यवस्थितौ।
तयोर्न वशमागच्छेत्तौ ह्यस्य परिपन्थिनौ॥ ३४॥

indriyasyendriyasyārthe rāgadveṣau vyavasthitau
tayorna vaśam āgacchettau hyasya paripanthinau (34)

There are longing and aversion (potential) in every sense object. May one not come under the spell of these two because they are one's enemies.

श्रेयान्स्वधर्मो विगुणः परधर्मात्स्वनुष्ठितात्।
स्वधर्मे निधनं श्रेयः परधर्मो भयावहः॥ ३५॥

śreyān svadharmo viguṇaḥ paradharmāt svanuṣṭhitāt
svadharme nidhanaṁ śreyaḥ paradharmo bhayāvahaḥ (35)

Better is one's own imperfectly performed *dharma* than the well performed *dharma* of another. Death in one's own *dharma* is better. The *dharma* of another is fraught with fear.

अर्जुन उवाच।
अथ केन प्रयुक्तोऽयं पापं चरति पूरुषः।
अनिच्छन्नपि वार्ष्णेय बलादिव नियोजितः॥ ३६॥

arjuna uvāca
atha kena prayukto'yaṁ pāpaṁ carati pūruṣaḥ
anicchannapi vārṣṇeya balādiva niyojitaḥ (36)

Arjuna said:
Vārṣṇeya (Kṛṣṇa)! Impelled by what, does a person commit sin, as though pushed by some force even though not desiring to?

श्रीभगवानुवाच ।
काम एष क्रोध एष रजोगुणसमुद्भवः ।
महाशनो महापाप्मा विद्ध्येनमिह वैरिणम् ॥ ३७ ॥

śrībhagavān uvāca
kāma eṣa krodha eṣa rajoguṇasamudbhavaḥ
mahāśano mahāpāpmā viddhyenam iha vairiṇam (37)

Śrī Bhagavān said:
This desire, this anger, born of the *guṇa rajas*, is a glutton and a great sinner. Know that to be the enemy here in this world.

धूमेनाव्रियते वह्निर्यथादर्शो मलेन च ।
यथोल्बेनावृतो गर्भस्तथा तेनेदमावृतम् ॥ ३८ ॥

dhūmenāvriyate vahniryathādarśo malena ca
yatholbenāvṛto garbhastathā tenedam āvṛtam (38)

Just as the fire is covered by clouds of smoke, just as a mirror is covered by dust, and just as a foetus is covered by the womb, so too, knowledge is covered by (binding) desire.

आवृतं ज्ञानमेतेन ज्ञानिनो नित्यवैरिणा ।
कामरूपेण कौन्तेय दुष्पूरेणानलेन च ॥ ३९ ॥

āvṛtaṁ jñānam etena jñānino nityavairiṇā
kāmarūpeṇa kaunteya duṣpūreṇānalena ca (39)

Knowledge is covered by this insatiable fire of desire, the constant enemy of the wise, Kaunteya (Arjuna)!

इन्द्रियाणि मनो बुद्धिरस्याधिष्ठानमुच्यते ।
एतैर्विमोहयत्येष ज्ञानमावृत्य देहिनम् ॥ ४० ॥

indriyāṇi mano buddhirasyādhiṣṭhānam ucyate
etairvimohayatyeṣa jñānam āvṛtya dehinam (40)

Its location is said to be the senses, mind, and intellect. With these, it (*kāma*) deludes the person by covering his (or her) wisdom.

तस्मात्त्वमिन्द्रियाण्यादौ नियम्य भरतर्षभ ।
पाप्मानं प्रजहि ह्येनं ज्ञानविज्ञाननाशनम् ॥ ४१ ॥

tasmāt tvam indriyāṇyādau niyamya bharatarṣabha
pāpmānaṁ prajahi hyenaṁ jñānavijñānanāśanam (41)

Therefore, Arjuna, the foremost in the clan of Bharata! controlling the senses at the outset, destroy indeed this sinner, the destroyer of knowledge and wisdom.

इन्द्रियाणि पराण्याहुरिन्द्रियेभ्यः परं मनः ।
मनसस्तु परा बुद्धिर्यो बुद्धेः परतस्तु सः ॥ ४२ ॥

indriyāṇi parāṇyāhurindriyebhyaḥ paraṁ manaḥ
manasastu parā buddhiryo buddheḥ paratastu saḥ (42)

They say that the sense organs are superior (to the body); the mind is superior to the sense organs; the intellect is superior to the mind. Whereas the one who is superior to the intellect is he (the *ātman*).

एवं बुद्धेः परं बुद्ध्वा संस्तभ्यात्मानमात्मना ।
जहि शत्रुं महाबाहो कामरूपं दुरासदम् ॥ ४३ ॥

evaṁ buddheḥ paraṁ buddhvā saṁstabhyātmānam ātmanā
jahi śatruṁ mahābāho kāmarūpaṁ durāsadam (43)

Arjuna, the mighty armed! Knowing that which is superior to the intellect in this way, having made the mind steady with the *buddhi*, destroy the enemy, that is in the form of (binding) desire, that which is so difficult to understand.

ॐतत्सत् ।
इति श्रीमद्भगवद्गीतासूपनिषत्सु ब्रह्मविद्यायां योगशास्त्रे श्रीकृष्णार्जुन-संवादे कर्म-योगो नाम तृतीयोऽध्यायः ॥ ३ ॥

omtatsat.
iti śrīmadbhagavadgītāsūpaniṣatsu brahma-vidyāyāṁ yoga-śāstre śrīkṛṣṇārjuna-saṁvāde karma-yogo nāma tṛtīyo'dhyāyaḥ (3)

Om, Brahman, is the only reality. Thus ends the third chapter called *karma-yoga*—having the topic of *karma*—in the *Bhagavadgītā* which is in the form of a dialogue between Śrī Kṛṣṇa and Arjuna, which is the essence of the *Upaniṣads*, whose subject matter is both the knowledge of Brahman and *yoga*.

Chapter 4

ज्ञान-कर्मसंन्यास-योगः

Jñāna-karmasannyāsa-yogaḥ

Topic of renunciation of action through knowledge

श्रीभगवानुवाच ।
इमं विवस्वते योगं प्रोक्तवानहमव्ययम् ।
विवस्वान्मनवे प्राह मनुरिक्ष्वाकवेऽब्रवीत् ॥ १ ॥
एवं परम्पराप्राप्तमिमं राजर्षयो विदुः ।
स कालेनेह महता योगो नष्टः परन्तप ॥ २ ॥

śrībhagavān uvāca
imaṁ vivasvate yogaṁ proktavān aham avyayam
vivasvān manave prāha manurikṣvākave'bravīt (1)
evaṁ paramparāprāptam imaṁ rājarṣayo viduḥ
sa kāleneha mahatā yogo naṣṭaḥ parantapa (2)

Śrī Bhagavān said:
I taught this imperishable *yoga* to Vivasvān, Vivasvān taught it to Manu, (and) Manu taught it to Ikṣvāku.
Handed down from generation to generation in this way, the kings who were sages knew it. (But) with the long lapse of time, Arjuna, the scorcher of foes! this *yoga* has declined in the world.

स एवायं मया तेऽद्य योगः प्रोक्तः पुरातनः ।
भक्तोऽसि मे सखा चेति रहस्यं ह्येतदुत्तमम् ॥ ३ ॥

sa evāyaṁ mayā te'dya yogaḥ proktaḥ purātanaḥ
bhakto'si me sakhā ceti rahasyaṁ hyetad uttamam (3)

Today, that same ancient *yoga* has been told to you by Me because you are My devotee and My friend. This is indeed a profound secret.

अर्जुन उवाच ।
अपरं भवतो जन्म परं जन्म विवस्वतः ।
कथमेतद्विजानीयां त्वमादौ प्रोक्तवानिति ॥ ४ ॥

arjuna uvāca
aparaṁ bhavato janma paraṁ janma vivasvataḥ
katham etad vijānīyāṁ tvamādau proktavān iti (4)

Arjuna said:
Your birth was not so long ago; (whereas) Vivasvān's birth was long time ago. How am I to know that you told this (to Vivasvān) in the beginning?

श्रीभगवानुवाच ।
बहूनि मे व्यतीतानि जन्मानि तव चार्जुन ।
तान्यहं वेद सर्वाणि न त्वं वेत्थ परन्तप ॥ ५ ॥

śrībhagavān uvāca
bahūni me vyatītāni janmāni tava cārjuna
tānyahaṁ veda sarvāṇi na tvaṁ vettha parantapa (5)

Śrī Bhagavān said:
Many births have passed for Me and for you too, Arjuna! I know them all (whereas) you, (Arjuna) the scorcher of foes! do not know.

अजोऽपि सन्नव्ययात्मा भूतानामीश्वरोऽपि सन् ।
प्रकृतिं स्वामधिष्ठाय सम्भवाम्यात्ममायया ॥ ६ ॥

ajo'pi sannavyayātmā bhūtānām īśvaro'pi san
prakṛtiṁ svām adhiṣṭhāya sambhavāmyātmamāyayā (6)

Even though, being one who is unborn, one whose knowledge does not wane, and also being the Lord of all living beings, still, wielding My own *prakṛti*, I, 'as though,' come into being by My own creative power.

यदा यदा हि धर्मस्य ग्लानिर्भवति भारत ।
अभ्युत्थानमधर्मस्य तदात्मानं सृजाम्यहम् ॥ ७ ॥

yadā yadā hi dharmasya glānirbhavati bhārata
abhyutthānam adharmasya tadātmānaṁ sṛjāmyaham (7)

Bhārata (Arjuna)! Whenever there is a decline in right living and an increase in wrong living (everywhere), I bring Myself into being (assume a physical body).

परित्राणाय साधूनां विनाशाय च दुष्कृताम् ।
धर्मसंस्थापनार्थाय सम्भवामि युगे युगे ॥ ८ ॥

paritrāṇāya sādhūnāṁ vināśāya ca duṣkṛtām
dharmasaṁsthāpanārthāya sambhavāmi yuge yuge (8)

For the protection of those who are committed to *dharma* and the destruction (conversion) of those who follow *adharma*, and for the establishment of *dharma*, I come into being in every *yuga*.

जन्म कर्म च मे दिव्यमेवं यो वेत्ति तत्त्वतः ।
त्यक्त्वा देहं पुनर्जन्म नैति मामेति सोऽर्जुन ॥ ९ ॥

janma karma ca me divyam evaṁ yo vetti tattvataḥ
tyaktvā dehaṁ punarjanma naiti mām eti so'rjuna (9)

The one who knows in reality My divine birth and action in this way, Arjuna! giving up the body, that person is not born again. He attains Me.

वीतरागभयक्रोधा मन्मया मामुपाश्रिताः ।
बहवो ज्ञानतपसा पूता मद्भावमागताः ॥ १० ॥

vītarāgabhayakrodhā manmayā mām upāśritāḥ
bahavo jñānatapasā pūtā madbhāvam āgatāḥ (10)

Free from craving, fear, and anger, totally resolved in me, taking refuge in Me, purified by the discipline of knowledge, many have come back to my nature.

ये यथा मां प्रपद्यन्ते तांस्तथैव भजाम्यहम् ।
मम वर्त्मानुवर्तन्ते मनुष्याः पार्थ सर्वशः ॥ ११ ॥

ye yathā māṁ prapadyante tāṁstathaiva bhajāmyaham
mama vartmānuvartante manuṣyāḥ pārtha sarvaśaḥ (11)

Those who worship me in whatever way, I bless them in the same way. Pārtha (Arjuna)! People follow my path in all ways.

काङ्क्षन्तः कर्मणां सिद्धिं यजन्त इह देवताः ।
क्षिप्रं हि मानुषे लोके सिद्धिर्भवति कर्मजा ॥ १२ ॥

kāṅkṣantaḥ karmaṇāṁ siddhiṁ yajanta iha devatāḥ
kṣipraṁ hi mānuṣe loke siddhirbhavati karmajā (12)

Desiring the result of actions here (in this world), they worship (different) deities. For, in the human world, result born of action comes very quickly.

चातुर्वर्ण्यं मया सृष्टं गुणकर्मविभागशः ।
तस्य कर्तारमपि मां विद्ध्यकर्तारमव्ययम् ॥ १३ ॥

cāturvarṇyaṁ mayā sṛṣṭaṁ guṇakarmavibhāgaśaḥ
tasya kartāram api māṁ viddhyakartāram avyayam (13)

The four-fold grouping (of people), a division based on duties and qualities, was created by Me. Even though I am its author, know Me to be a non-doer, ever changeless.

न मां कर्माणि लिम्पन्ति न मे कर्मफले स्पृहा ।
इति मां योऽभिजानाति कर्मभिर्न स बध्यते ॥ १४ ॥

na māṁ karmāṇi limpanti na me karmaphale spṛhā
iti māṁ yo'bhijānāti karmabhirna sa badhyate (14)

Actions do not affect Me. There is no longing with reference to the result of action for Me. The one who knows Me clearly in this way is not bound by actions.

एवं ज्ञात्वा कृतं कर्म पूर्वैरपि मुमुक्षुभिः ।
कुरु कर्मैव तस्मात्त्वं पूर्वैः पूर्वतरं कृतम् ॥ १५ ॥

evaṁ jñātvā kṛtaṁ karma pūrvairapi mumukṣubhiḥ
kuru karmaiva tasmāttvaṁ pūrvaiḥ pūrvataraṁ kṛtam (15)

Knowing (Me) in this manner, even seekers of ancient times performed action. Therefore, perform action indeed as even it was done by those who came before in the ancient past.

किं कर्म किमकर्मेति कवयोऽप्यत्र मोहिताः ।
तत्ते कर्म प्रवक्ष्यामि यज्ज्ञात्वा मोक्ष्यसेऽशुभात् ॥ १६ ॥

kiṁ karma kim akarmeti kavayo'pyatra mohitāḥ
tatte karma pravakṣyāmi yajjñātvā mokṣyase'śubhāt (16)

Even the seers (scholars) are confused with reference to what is action (and) what is actionlessness. I shall tell you about action, knowing which you will be released from what is inauspicious (*saṁsāra*).

कर्मणो ह्यपि बोद्धव्यं बोद्धव्यं च विकर्मणः।
अकर्मणश्च बोद्धव्यं गहना कर्मणो गतिः॥ १७॥

karmaṇo hyapi boddhavyaṁ boddhavyaṁ ca vikarmaṇaḥ
akarmaṇaśca boddhavyaṁ gahanā karmaṇo gatiḥ (17)

Action (enjoined by the scriptures) is to be known. Forbidden action and actionlessness must also be known. (This is) because the nature of *karma* is difficult (to understand).

कर्मण्यकर्म यः पश्येदकर्मणि च कर्म यः।
स बुद्धिमान्मनुष्येषु स युक्तः कृत्स्नकर्मकृत्॥ १८॥

karmaṇyakarma yaḥ paśyed akarmaṇi ca karma yaḥ
sa buddhimān manuṣyeṣu sa yuktaḥ kṛtsnakarmakṛt (18)

The one who sees actionlessness in action and action in actionlessness is wise among human beings. That person is a *yogin*, who has done everything that is to be done.

यस्य सर्वे समारम्भाः कामसङ्कल्पवर्जिताः।
ज्ञानाग्निदग्धकर्माणं तमाहुः पण्डितं बुधाः॥ १९॥

yasya sarve samārambhāḥ kāmasaṅkalpavarjitāḥ
jñānāgnidagdhakarmāṇaṁ tamāhuḥ paṇḍitaṁ budhāḥ (19)

The one for whom all undertakings are free from (binding) desire and will, whose actions are burnt by the fire of knowledge, the sages call him as wise.

त्यक्त्वा कर्मफलासङ्गं नित्यतृप्तो निराश्रयः ।
कर्मण्यभिप्रवृत्तोऽपि नैव किञ्चित्करोति सः ॥ २० ॥

tyaktvā karmaphalāsaṅgaṁ nityatṛpto nirāśrayaḥ
karmaṇyabhipravṛtto'pi naiva kiñcit karoti saḥ (20)

Giving up the deep attachment to the results of action, always contented, being not dependent on anything, he (or she) does not do anything even though fully engaged in action.

निराशीर्यतचित्तात्मा त्यक्तसर्वपरिग्रहः ।
शारीरं केवलं कर्म कुर्वन्नाप्नोति किल्बिषम् ॥ २१ ॥

nirāśīryatacittātmā tyaktasarvaparigrahaḥ
śārīraṁ kevalaṁ karma kurvannāpnoti kilbiṣam (21)

The person who is free of expectations, whose body, mind, and senses have been mastered, who has given up all possessions, doing only action that sustains the body, does not incur sin.

यदृच्छालाभसन्तुष्टो द्वन्द्वातीतो विमत्सरः ।
समः सिद्धावसिद्धौ च कृत्वापि न निबध्यते ॥ २२ ॥

yadṛcchālābhasantuṣṭo dvandvātīto vimatsaraḥ
samaḥ siddhāvasiddhau ca kṛtvāpi na nibadhyate (22)

The one who is happy with whatever comes by chance, who is unaffected by the opposites, free from jealousy, and even-minded with reference to success and failure, is not bound even though performing action.

गतसङ्गस्य मुक्तस्य ज्ञानावस्थितचेतसः ।
यज्ञायाचरतः कर्म समग्रं प्रविलीयते ॥ २३ ॥

gatasaṅgasya muktasya jñānāvasthitacetasaḥ
yajñāyācarataḥ karma samagraṁ pravilīyate (23)

The *karma* of one who is free from attachment, who is liberated, whose mind is rooted in self-knowledge, who performs for the sake of daily *yajña*, resolves totally.

ब्रह्मार्पणं ब्रह्म हविर्ब्रह्माग्नौ ब्रह्मणा हुतम् ।
ब्रह्मैव तेन गन्तव्यं ब्रह्मकर्मसमाधिना ॥ २४ ॥

brahmārpaṇaṁ brahma havirbrahmāgnau brahmaṇā hutam
brahmaiva tena gantavyaṁ brahmakarmasamādhinā (24)

The means of offering is Brahman. The oblation is Brahman, offered by Brahman into the fire, which is Brahman. Brahman indeed is to be reached by him who sees everything as Brahman.

दैवमेवापरे यज्ञं योगिनः पर्युपासते ।
ब्रह्माग्नावपरे यज्ञं यज्ञेनैवोपजुह्वति ॥ २५ ॥

daivam evāpare yajñaṁ yoginaḥ paryupāsate
brahmāgnāvapare yajñaṁ yajñenaivopajuhvati (25)

Karma-yogins perform only those rituals that invoke the deities, while others (*sannyāsins*) offer themselves by themselves unto the fire (knowledge) of Brahman.

श्रोत्रादीनीन्द्रियाण्यन्ये संयमाग्निषु जुह्वति ।
शब्दादीन्विषयानन्य इन्द्रियाग्निषु जुह्वति ॥ २६ ॥

śrotrādīnīndriyāṇyanye saṁyamāgniṣu juhvati
śabdādīn viṣayān anya indriyāgniṣu juhvati (26)

Others offer (their) organs of hearing and other senses into the fire of self-mastery, (while still) others offer sound and other sense objects into the fire of the senses.

सर्वाणीन्द्रियकर्माणि प्राणकर्माणि चापरे ।
आत्मसंयमयोगाग्नौ जुह्वति ज्ञानदीपिते ॥ २७ ॥

sarvāṇīndriyakarmāṇi prāṇakarmāṇi cāpare
ātmasaṁyamayogāgnau juhvati jñānadīpite (27)

Others offer all the activities of the senses and the organs of action unto the fire of self mastery lighted by knowledge.

द्रव्ययज्ञास्तपोयज्ञा योगयज्ञास्तथापरे ।
स्वाध्यायज्ञानयज्ञाश्च यतयः संशितव्रताः ॥ २८ ॥

dravyayajñāstapoyajñā yogayajñāstathāpare
svādhyāyajñānayajñāśca yatayaḥ saṁśitavratāḥ (28)

So too, there are those who share (their) wealth, those who follow prayerful disciplines, those who practise *yoga*, and those of firm vows and efforts who pursue recitation of their own Veda and self-knowledge.

अपाने जुह्वति प्राणं प्राणेऽपानं तथाऽपरे ।
प्राणापानगती रुद्ध्वा प्राणायामपरायणाः ॥ २९ ॥

apāne juhvati prāṇaṁ prāṇe'pānaṁ tathā'pare
prāṇāpānagatī ruddhvā prāṇāyāmaparāyaṇāḥ (29)

So too, others who are committed to the practice of *prāṇāyāma* (breath control), stopping the flow of inhalation and exhalation, offer the outgoing breath into the incoming breath (and) the incoming breath into the outgoing breath.

अपरे नियताहाराः प्राणान्प्राणेषु जुह्वति ।
सर्वेऽप्येते यज्ञविदो यज्ञक्षपितकल्मषाः ॥ ३० ॥

apare niyatāhārāḥ prāṇān prāṇeṣu juhvati
sarve'pyete yajñavido yajñakṣapitakalmaṣāḥ (30)

Others, who regulate their food intake, offer their desire to eat (more) unto the digestive fires. All these (people) who observe religious disciplines (become), without exception, those for whom the impurities of the mind have been destroyed by the *yajña*.

यज्ञशिष्टामृतभुजो यान्ति ब्रह्म सनातनम् ।
नायं लोकोऽस्त्ययज्ञस्य कुतोऽन्यः कुरुसत्तम ॥ ३१ ॥

yajñaśiṣṭāmṛtabhujo yānti brahma sanātanam
nāyaṁ loko'styayajñasya kuto'nyaḥ kurusattama (31)

Arjuna, the best among the Kurus! Those who partake of the nectar (the result) that is left over after the *yajña*, reach the eternal Brahman. For the one who does not perform *yajña*, nothing (is gained) in this world. How, then, (can anything be gained) in any other (world)?

एवं बहुविधा यज्ञा वितता ब्रह्मणो मुखे ।
कर्मजान्विद्धि तान्सर्वानेवं ज्ञात्वा विमोक्ष्यसे ॥ ३२ ॥

evaṁ bahuvidhā yajñā vitatā brahmaṇo mukhe
karmajān viddhi tānsarvān evaṁ jñātvā vimokṣyase (32)

In this manner, many and varied religious disciplines are very elaborately mentioned in the words of the Veda. Understand them all to be born of *karma* (and therefore, *anātman*). Knowing thus, you will be liberated.

श्रेयान्द्रव्यमयाद्यज्ञाज्ज्ञानयज्ञः परन्तप ।
सर्वं कर्माखिलं पार्थ ज्ञाने परिसमाप्यते ॥ ३३ ॥

śreyān dravyamayād yajñājjñānayajñaḥ parantapa
sarvaṁ karmākhilaṁ pārtha jñāne parisamāpyate (33)

Arjuna, the scorcher of foes! This discipline of knowledge is superior to religious disciplines performed with materials. Pārtha (Arjuna)! All actions in its entirety get resolved in knowledge.

तद्विद्धि प्रणिपातेन परिप्रश्नेन सेवया ।
उपदेक्ष्यन्ति ते ज्ञानं ज्ञानिनस्तत्त्वदर्शिनः ॥ ३४ ॥

tadviddhi praṇipātena paripraśnena sevayā
upadekṣyanti te jñānaṁ jñāninastattvadarśinaḥ (34)

Understand that (which is to be known) by prostrating (the wise), by asking proper questions, (and) by serving (them). Those wise persons, who have the vision of the truth, will teach you (this) knowledge.

यज्ज्ञात्वा न पुनर्मोहमेवं यास्यसि पाण्डव ।
येन भूतान्यशेषेण द्रक्ष्यस्यात्मन्यथो मयि ॥ ३५ ॥

yajjñātvā na punarmoham evaṁ yāsyasi pāṇḍava
yena bhūtānyaśeṣeṇa drakṣyasyātmanyatho mayi (35)

Gaining this knowledge (which was taught by them)[37] Pāṇḍava[38] (Arjuna)! you will not again be deluded in this manner (and) by this (knowledge) you will see all beings in yourself and in Me.

अपि चेदसि पापेभ्यः सर्वेभ्यः पापकृत्तमः ।
सर्वं ज्ञानप्लवेनैव वृजिनं सन्तरिष्यसि ॥ ३६ ॥

api ced asi pāpebhyaḥ sarvebhyaḥ pāpakṛttamaḥ
sarvaṁ jñānaplavenaiva vṛjinaṁ santariṣyasi (36)

Even if you are the worst sinner among all sinners, you will cross all sins with ease by the mere raft of knowledge.

यथैधांसि समिद्धोऽग्निर्भस्मसात्कुरुतेऽर्जुन ।
ज्ञानाग्निः सर्वकर्माणि भस्मसात्कुरुते तथा ॥ ३७ ॥

yathaidhāṁsi samiddho'gnirbhasmasātkurute'rjuna
jñānāgniḥ sarvakarmāṇi bhasmasātkurute tathā (37)

Just as a well lighted fire reduces wood to ashes, so too, Arjuna! the fire of knowledge reduces all actions (results of actions) to ashes.

न हि ज्ञानेन सदृशं पवित्रमिह विद्यते ।
तत्स्वयं योगसंसिद्धः कालेनात्मनि विन्दति ॥ ३८ ॥

na hi jñānena sadṛśaṁ pavitram iha vidyate
tat svayaṁ yogasaṁsiddhaḥ kālenātmani vindati (38)

In this world, there is indeed no purifier equivalent to knowledge. One who has in time attained preparedness through *karma-yoga* naturally gains (knowledge) in the mind.

श्रद्धावाँल्लभते ज्ञानं तत्परः संयतेन्द्रियः ।
ज्ञानं लब्ध्वा परां शान्तिमचिरेणाधिगच्छति ॥ ३९ ॥

śraddhāvān labhate jñānaṁ tatparaḥ saṁyatendriyaḥ
jñānaṁ labdhvā parāṁ śāntim acireṇādhigacchati (39)

One who has faith (in the *śāstra* and in the words of the teacher), who is committed to that (knowledge) and who is master of one's senses gains the knowledge.

Having gained the knowledge, one immediately gains absolute peace.

अज्ञश्चाश्रद्दधानश्च संशयात्मा विनश्यति ।
नायं लोकोऽस्ति न परो न सुखं संशयात्मनः ॥ ४० ॥

ajñaścāśraddadhānaśca saṁśayātmā vinaśyati
nāyaṁ loko'sti na paro na sukhaṁ saṁśayātmanaḥ (40)

One who has no discrimination, and who has no faith (in the *śāstra* and the teacher), and one who has a doubting mind perishes. Because, for the one with a doubting mind, this world is not there, nor the world beyond, nor happiness.

योगसंन्यस्तकर्माणं ज्ञानसञ्छिन्नसंशयम् ।
आत्मवन्तं न कर्माणि निबध्नन्ति धनञ्जय ॥ ४१ ॥

yogasannyastakarmāṇaṁ jñānasañchinnasaṁśayam
ātmavantaṁ na karmāṇi nibadhnanti dhanañjaya (41)

Dhanañjaya (Arjuna)! Actions do not bind the one who has renounced action through *yoga*, whose doubts have been completely severed by knowledge (and) the one who is together.

तस्मादज्ञानसम्भूतं हृत्स्थं ज्ञानासिनात्मनः ।
छित्त्वैनं संशयं योगमातिष्ठोत्तिष्ठ भारत ॥ ४२ ॥

tasmādajñānasambhūtaṁ hṛtsthaṁ jñānāsinātmanaḥ
chittvainaṁ saṁśayaṁ yogamātiṣṭhottiṣṭha bhārata (42)

Therefore, Bhārata (Arjuna)! slaying with the sword of knowledge this doubt about the self, which is born of ignorance, which is rooted in the mind, get up (and) take to *yoga* (*karma-yoga*).

ॐतत्सत् ।

इति श्रीमद्भगवद्गीतासूपनिषत्सु ब्रह्मविद्यायां योगशास्त्रे श्रीकृष्णार्जुन-
संवादे ज्ञानकर्मसंन्यासयोगो नाम चतुर्थोऽध्यायः ॥ ४ ॥

omtatsat.

iti śrīmadbhagavadgītāsūpaniṣatsu brahma-vidyāyāṁ yoga-śāstre śrīkṛṣṇārjunasaṁvāde jñāna-karmasannyāsa-yogo nāma caturtho'dhyāyaḥ (4)

Om, Brahman, is the only reality. Thus ends the fourth chapter called *jñāna-karmasannyāsa-yoga*—having the topic of renunciation of action through knowledge—in the *Bhagavadgītā* which is in the form of a dialogue between Śrī Kṛṣṇa and Arjuna, which is the essence of the *Upaniṣads*, whose subject matter is both the knowledge of Brahman and *yoga*.

Chapter 5
संन्यास-योगः
Sannyāsa-yogaḥ
Topic of renunciation

अर्जुन उवाच ।
संन्यासं कर्मणां कृष्ण पुनर्योगं च शंससि ।
यच्छ्रेय एतयोरेकं तन्मे ब्रूहि सुनिश्चितम् ॥ १ ॥

arjuna uvāca
sannyāsaṁ karmaṇāṁ kṛṣṇa punaryogaṁ ca śaṁsasi
yacchreya etayorekaṁ tanme brūhi suniścitam (1)

Arjuna said:
Kṛṣṇa! You praise renunciation of actions and also *karma-yoga*. Tell me definitely that which is the better of the two.

श्रीभगवानुवाच ।
संन्यासः कर्मयोगश्च निःश्रेयसकरावुभौ ।
तयोस्तु कर्मसंन्यासात्कर्मयोगो विशिष्यते ॥ २ ॥

śrībhagavān uvāca
sannyāsaḥ karmayogaśca niḥśreyasakarāvubhau
tayostu karmasannyāsāt karmayogo viśiṣyate (2)

Śrī Bhagavān said:
Both renunciation (of action) and performance of action as *yoga* lead to liberation. But, of these two, the performance of action as *yoga* is better than renunciation of action.

ज्ञेयः स नित्यसंन्यासी यो न द्वेष्टि न काङ्क्षति ।
निर्द्वन्द्वो हि महाबाहो सुखं बन्धात्प्रमुच्यते ॥ ३ ॥

jñeyaḥ sa nityasannyāsī yo na dveṣṭi na kāṅkṣati
nirdvandvo hi mahābāho sukhaṁ bandhātpramucyate (3)

The person who neither hates nor longs (for anything) should be known as always a renunciate, Arjuna, the mighty armed! One who is free from the opposites (likes and dislikes) is indeed effortlessly released from bondage.

साङ्ख्ययोगौ पृथग्बालाः प्रवदन्ति न पण्डिताः ।
एकमप्यास्थितः सम्यगुभयोर्विन्दते फलम् ॥ ४ ॥

sāṅkhyayogau pṛthagbālāḥ pravadanti na paṇḍitāḥ
ekam apyāsthitaḥ samyagubhayorvindate phalam (4)

Children (those who do not know), (but) not the wise, argue that knowledge and *karma-yoga* are different. The person who follows even one (of the two) properly, gains the result of both.

यत्साङ्ख्यैः प्राप्यते स्थानं तद्योगैरपि गम्यते ।
एकं साङ्ख्यं च योगं च यः पश्यति स पश्यति ॥ ५ ॥

yatsāṅkhyaiḥ prāpyate sthānaṁ tadyogairapi gamyate
ekaṁ sāṅkhyaṁ ca yogaṁ ca yaḥ paśyati sa paśyati (5)

The end (*mokṣa*) that is gained by the *sannyāsins* is also reached by the *karma-yogins*. The one who sees knowledge and *karma-yoga* as one, that person (alone) sees (the truth).

संन्यासस्तु महाबाहो दुःखमाप्तुमयोगतः ।
योगयुक्तो मुनिर्ब्रह्म नचिरेणाधिगच्छति ॥ ६ ॥

sannyāsastu mahābāho duḥkham āptum ayogataḥ
yogayukto munirbrahma nacireṇādhigacchati (6)

Renunciation of action, Arjuna, the mighty armed! is difficult to accomplish without *karma-yoga*. Whereas, one who is committed to a life of *karma-yoga* and is capable of reasoning, gains Brahman quickly.

योगयुक्तो विशुद्धात्मा विजितात्मा जितेन्द्रियः ।
सर्वभूतात्मभूतात्मा कुर्वन्नपि न लिप्यते ॥ ७ ॥

yogayukto viśuddhātmā vijitātmā jitendriyaḥ
sarvabhūtātmabhūtātmā kurvannapi na lipyate (7)

One whose mind is purified by being committed to a life of *karma-yoga*, who has mastered the body and the sense organs, and who knows oneself to be the self in all beings, (such a person) is not affected even while doing (actions).

नैव किञ्चित्करोमीति युक्तो मन्येत तत्त्ववित् ।
पश्यञ्शृण्वन्स्पृशञ्जिघ्रन्नश्नन्गच्छन्स्वपञ्श्वसन् ॥ ८ ॥
प्रलपन्विसृजन्गृह्णन्नुन्मिषन्निमिषन्नपि ।
इन्द्रियाणीन्द्रियार्थेषु वर्तन्त इति धारयन् ॥ ९ ॥

naiva kiñcitkaromīti yukto manyeta tattvavit
paśyañśṛṇvan spṛśañjighrannaśnan gacchan svapañśvasan (8)
pralapan visṛjan gṛhṇannunmiṣan nimiṣannapi
indriyāṇīndriyārtheṣu vartanta iti dhārayan (9)

The one who is together, who knows the truth, thinks, 'I do not do anything at all,' even while seeing, hearing, touching, smelling, eating, walking, sleeping, breathing…

...talking, releasing, grasping, opening and closing the eyes, (the person) knowing (full well that) the organs are engaged in their objects.

ब्रह्मण्याधाय कर्माणि सङ्गं त्यक्त्वा करोति यः।
लिप्यते न स पापेन पद्मपत्रमिवाम्भसा ॥ १० ॥

brahmaṇyādhāya karmāṇi saṅgaṁ tyaktvā karoti yaḥ
lipyate na sa pāpena padmapatram ivāmbhasā (10)

The one who performs actions, giving up attachment, offering (one's actions) unto Brahman, is not affected by sin, just as the leaf of a lotus (is not wetted) by water.

कायेन मनसा बुद्ध्या केवलैरिन्द्रियैरपि।
योगिनः कर्म कुर्वन्ति सङ्गं त्यक्त्वात्मशुद्धये ॥ ११ ॥

kāyena manasā buddhyā kevalairindriyairapi
yoginaḥ karma kurvanti saṅgaṁ tyaktvātmaśuddhaye (11)

Giving up attachment, *karma-yogin*s perform action purely (without being impelled by likes and dislikes) with the body, mind, intellect, and also by the senses, for the purification of the mind.

युक्तः कर्मफलं त्यक्त्वा शान्तिमाप्नोति नैष्ठिकीम्।
अयुक्तः कामकारेण फले सक्तो निबध्यते ॥ १२ ॥

yuktaḥ karmaphalaṁ tyaktvā śāntim āpnoti naiṣṭhikīm
ayuktaḥ kāmakāreṇa phale sakto nibadhyate (12)

The one who is endowed with (*karma-yoga*), giving up the result of action, gains a composure born of a commitment to a life of *karma-yoga*. (Whereas) the one who is not committed to a life of *karma-yoga*, led by desire, is bound, (being) attached to the result (of action).

सर्वकर्माणि मनसा संन्यस्यास्ते सुखं वशी ।
नवद्वारे पुरे देही नैव कुर्वन्न कारयन् ॥ १३ ॥

sarvakarmāṇi manasā sannyasyāste sukhaṁ vaśī
navadvāre pure dehī naiva kurvan na kārayan (13)

The indweller of the physical body, the one who is self-controlled, having renounced all actions mentally (by knowledge), remains happily in the nine-gated city (the body) neither performing action, nor causing (others) to act.

न कर्तृत्वं न कर्माणि लोकस्य सृजति प्रभुः ।
न कर्मफलसंयोगं स्वभावस्तु प्रवर्तते ॥ १४ ॥

na kartṛtvaṁ na karmāṇi lokasya sṛjati prabhuḥ
na karmaphalasaṁyogaṁ svabhāvastu pravartate (14)

Ātman creates neither doership nor action for any person nor the connection with the results of action. But one's own nature leads to action.

नादत्ते कस्यचित्पापं न चैव सुकृतं विभुः ।
अज्ञानेनावृतं ज्ञानं तेन मुह्यन्ति जन्तवः ॥ १५ ॥

nādatte kasyacit pāpaṁ na caiva sukṛtaṁ vibhuḥ
ajñānenāvṛtaṁ jñānaṁ tena muhyanti jantavaḥ (15)

The *ātman* takes neither *pāpa* nor *puṇya* of anyone. Knowledge is covered by ignorance and due to that (ignorance) people are deluded.

ज्ञानेन तु तदज्ञानं येषां नाशितमात्मनः ।
तेषामादित्यवज्ज्ञानं प्रकाशयति तत्परम् ॥ १६ ॥

jñānena tu tadajñānaṁ yeṣāṁ nāśitam ātmanaḥ
teṣām ādityavajjñānaṁ prakāśayati tatparam (16)

Whereas for those whose ignorance of the self is destroyed by knowledge, the knowledge reveals (the self as) that Brahman, like the sun (reveals objects previously covered in darkness).

तद्बुद्धयस्तदात्मानस्तन्निष्ठास्तत्परायणाः ।
गच्छन्त्यपुनरावृत्तिं ज्ञाननिर्धूतकल्मषाः ॥ १७ ॥

tadbuddhayastadātmānastanniṣṭhāstatparāyaṇāḥ
gacchantyapunarāvṛttiṁ jñānanirdhūtakalmaṣāḥ (17)

Those whose intellect is awake to that (Brahman), for whom the self is that (Brahman), who are committed only to that (Brahman), for whom the ultimate end is that (Brahman which is already accomplished), whose impurities have been destroyed by knowledge—they attain a state from which there is no return.

विद्याविनयसम्पन्ने ब्राह्मणे गवि हस्तिनि ।
शुनि चैव श्वपाके च पण्डिताः समदर्शिनः ॥ १८ ॥

vidyāvinayasampanne brāhmaṇe gavi hastini
śuni caiva śvapāke ca paṇḍitāḥ samadarśinaḥ (18)

Wise people are indeed those who see the same (Brahman) in a *brāhmaṇa* who is endowed with knowledge and humility, in a cow, in an elephant, in a dog, and (even) in a dog eater.

इहैव तैर्जितः सर्गो येषां साम्ये स्थितं मनः ।
निर्दोषं हि समं ब्रह्म तस्माद् ब्रह्मणि ते स्थिताः ॥ १९ ॥

ihaiva tairjitaḥ sargo yeṣāṁ sāmye sthitaṁ manaḥ
nirdoṣaṁ hi samaṁ brahma tasmād brahmaṇi te sthitāḥ (19)

The cycle of birth and death (*saṁsāra*) is won over here itself (in this life) by those whose mind is rooted in that which is the same in everything (that is in Brahman). Since Brahman, that is free from any defect, is (always) the same, they (the wise people) abide in Brahman.

न प्रहृष्येत्प्रियं प्राप्य नोद्विजेत्प्राप्य चाप्रियम् ।
स्थिरबुद्धिरसम्मूढो ब्रह्मविद् ब्रह्मणि स्थितः ॥ २० ॥

na prahṛṣyet priyaṁ prāpya nodvijet prāpya cāpriyam
sthirabuddhirasammūḍho brahmavid brahmaṇi sthitaḥ (20)

The one who knows Brahman, who is established in Brahman, whose knowledge is firm, and who is free from delusion, would not rejoice over gaining that which is desirable nor would he resent gaining that which is not likeable.

बाह्यस्पर्शेष्वसक्तात्मा विन्दत्यात्मनि यत्सुखम् ।
स ब्रह्मयोगयुक्तात्मा सुखमक्षयमश्नुते ॥ २१ ॥

bāhyasparśeṣvasaktātmā vindatyātmani yatsukham
sa brahmayogayuktātmā sukham akṣayam aśnute (21)

The one whose mind is not attached to the external (sense) objects, gains (limited) happiness in oneself, whereas, if his mind is endowed with the knowledge of Brahman, he gains that happiness that does not wane.

ये हि संस्पर्शजा भोगा दुःखयोनय एव ते ।
आद्यन्तवन्तः कौन्तेय न तेषु रमते बुधः ॥ २२ ॥

ye hi saṁsparśajā bhogā duḥkhayonaya eva te
ādyantavantaḥ kaunteya na teṣu ramate budhaḥ (22)

Because those enjoyments that are born of contact (between the sense organs and desirable objects) are the sources of pain alone, and have a beginning and an end, Kaunteya (Arjuna)! the wise person does not revel in them.

शक्नोतीहैव यः सोढुं प्राक् शरीरविमोक्षणात्।
कामक्रोधोद्भवं वेगं स युक्तः स सुखी नरः॥ २३॥

śaknotīhaiva yaḥ soḍhuṁ prāk śarīravimokṣaṇāt
kāmakrodhodbhavaṁ vegaṁ sa yuktaḥ sa sukhī naraḥ (23)

The one who is able to master the force born of anger and desire here (in this world) before release from the body is a *karma-yogin*. He (or she) indeed is a happy person.

योऽन्तः सुखोऽन्तरारामस्तथान्तर्ज्योतिरेव यः।
स योगी ब्रह्मनिर्वाणं ब्रह्मभूतोऽधिगच्छति॥ २४॥

yo'ntaḥ sukho'ntarārāmastathāntarjyotireva yaḥ
sa yogī brahmanirvāṇaṁ brahmabhūto'dhigacchati (24)

The one whose fulfilment is in oneself, the one who revels in oneself, the one whose mind is awake to oneself, that wise person alone, whose self is Brahman, gains the freedom which is Brahman.

लभन्ते ब्रह्मनिर्वाणमृषयः क्षीणकल्मषाः।
छिन्नद्वैधा यतात्मानः सर्वभूतहिते रताः॥ २५॥

labhante brahmanirvāṇam ṛṣayaḥ kṣīṇakalmaṣāḥ
chinnadvaidhā yatātmānaḥ sarvabhūtahite ratāḥ (25)

Sages whose impurities have been destroyed, whose doubts have been resolved, who have self mastery (and) who are happily engaged in the good of all beings, gain liberation.

कामक्रोधवियुक्तानां यतीनां यतचेतसाम् ।
अभितो ब्रह्मनिर्वाणं वर्तते विदितात्मनाम् ॥ २६ ॥

kāmakrodhaviyuktānāṁ yatīnāṁ yatacetasām
abhito brahmanirvāṇaṁ vartate viditātmanām (26)

For the *sannyāsins* who are free from desire and anger, whose mind is under control, (and) who know the self, there is liberation, both here and in the hereafter.

स्पर्शान्कृत्वा बहिर्बाह्यांश्चक्षुश्चैवान्तरे भ्रुवोः ।
प्राणापानौ समौ कृत्वा नासाभ्यन्तरचारिणौ ॥ २७ ॥
यतेन्द्रियमनोबुद्धिर्मुनिर्मोक्षपरायणः ।
विगतेच्छाभयक्रोधो यः सदा मुक्त एव सः ॥ २८ ॥

sparśān kṛtvā bahirbāhyāṁścakṣuścaivāntare bhruvoḥ
prāṇāpānau samau kṛtvā nāsābhyantaracāriṇau (27)
yatendriyamanobuddhirmunirmokṣaparāyaṇaḥ
vigatecchābhayakrodho yaḥ sadā mukta eva saḥ (28)

Keeping the external objects external, and the eyes between the two eyebrows (and closed), keeping the exhalation and inhalation that move in the nostrils equal, (rhythmic), the contemplative person, who has mastered his (or her) organs of action, senses, mind, and intellect, for whom *mokṣa* is the ultimate end, who is free from desire, fear, and anger, (that person) is always liberated indeed.

भोक्तारं यज्ञतपसां सर्वलोकमहेश्वरम् ।
सुहृदं सर्वभूतानां ज्ञात्वा मां शान्तिमृच्छति ॥ २९ ॥

bhoktāraṁ yajñatapasāṁ sarvalokamaheśvaram
suhṛdaṁ sarvabhūtānāṁ jñātvā māṁ śāntim ṛcchati (29)

Knowing Me as the sustainer of rituals and disciplines, the Lord of all the worlds, friend of all beings, he (or she) gains peace (liberation).

ॐतत्सत् ।

इति श्रीमद्भगवद्गीतासूपनिषत्सु ब्रह्मविद्यायां योगशास्त्रे श्रीकृष्णार्जुन-संवादे संन्यास-योगो नाम पञ्चमोऽध्यायः ॥ ५ ॥

omtatsat.

iti śrīmadbhagavadgītāsūpaniṣatsu brahma-vidyāyāṁ yogaśāstre śrīkṛṣṇārjunasaṁvāde sannyāsa-yogo nāma pañcamo'dhyāyaḥ (5)

Om, Brahman, is the only reality. Thus ends the fifth chapter called *sannyāsa-yoga*—having the topic of renunciation—in the *Bhagavadgītā* which is in the form of a dialogue between Śrī Kṛṣṇa and Arjuna, which is the essence of the *Upaniṣads*, whose subject matter is both the knowledge of Brahman and *yoga*.

Chapter 6

ध्यान-योगः

Dhyāna-yogaḥ

Topic of meditation

श्रीभगवानुवाच ।
अनाश्रितः कर्मफलं कार्यं कर्म करोति यः ।
स संन्यासी च योगी च न निरग्निर्नचाक्रियः ॥ १ ॥

śrībhagavān uvāca
anāśritaḥ karmaphalaṁ kāryaṁ karma karoti yaḥ
sa sannyāsī ca yogī ca na niragnirnacākriyaḥ (1)

Śrī Bhagavān said:
The one who performs action that is to be done, not driven by ends in view, he is a *sannyāsin* and a *yogin* as well, and not just the *sannyāsin* who has renounced all fire rituals and who does not perform any other action.

यं संन्यासमिति प्राहुर्योगं तं विद्धि पाण्डव ।
न ह्यसंन्यस्तसङ्कल्पो योगी भवति कश्चन ॥ २ ॥

yaṁ sannyāsam iti prāhuryogaṁ taṁ viddhi pāṇḍava
na hyasannyastasaṅkalpo yogī bhavati kaścana (2)

What they say as renunciation, know that to be *karma-yoga*, Pāṇḍava (Arjuna)! because, anyone who has not given up desires (for limited results like heaven, etc.) does not become a *karma-yogin*.

आरुरुक्षोर्मुनेर्योगं कर्म कारणमुच्यते ।
योगारूढस्य तस्यैव शमः कारणमुच्यते ॥ ३ ॥

āruruksormuneryogaṁ karma kāraṇam ucyate
yogārūḍhasya tasyaiva śamaḥ kāraṇam ucyate (3)

For the discriminating person wishing to attain (the contemplative disposition of the) *yoga* (of meditation), *karma-yoga* is said to be the means. For the person who has (already) attained (this) *yoga*, total renunciation alone is said to be the means.

यदा हि नेन्द्रियार्थेषु न कर्मस्वनुषज्जते ।
सर्वसङ्कल्पसंन्यासी योगारूढस्तदोच्यते ॥ ४ ॥

yadā hi nendriyārtheṣu na karmasvanuṣajjate
sarvasaṅkalpasannyāsī yogārūḍhastadocyate (4)

When one is attached neither to sense objects nor to actions, then that person is said to be one who has attained liberation, one who has renounced the cause of all desires.

उद्धरेदात्मनात्मानं नात्मानमवसादयेत् ।
आत्मैव ह्यात्मनो बन्धुरात्मैव रिपुरात्मनः ॥ ५ ॥

uddhared ātmanātmānaṁ nātmānam avasādayet
ātmaiva hyātmano bandhurātmaiva ripurātmanaḥ (5)

May one lift oneself by oneself, may one not destroy oneself. For, the self alone is one's benefactor (and) the self alone is one's enemy.

बन्धुरात्मात्मनस्तस्य येनात्मैवात्मना जितः ।
अनात्मनस्तु शत्रुत्वे वर्तेतात्मैव शत्रुवत् ॥ ६ ॥

bandhurātmātmanastasya yenātmaivātmanā jitaḥ
anātmanastu śatrutve vartetātmaiva śatruvat (6)

For that (self) who has mastered oneself by oneself, the self alone is a friend of oneself. Whereas, for the self who has not mastered oneself, the self alone would remain in the status of an enemy, like an enemy.

जितात्मनः प्रशान्तस्य परमात्मा समाहितः ।
शीतोष्णसुखदुःखेषु तथा मानापमानयोः ॥ ७ ॥

jitātmanaḥ praśāntasya paramātmā samāhitaḥ
śītoṣṇasukhaduḥkheṣu tathā mānāpamānayoḥ (7)

For the one who has mastery over oneself, whose mind is tranquil with reference to heat and cold, pleasure and pain, and praise and criticism, the mind is always in a state of composure.

ज्ञानविज्ञानतृप्तात्मा कूटस्थो विजितेन्द्रियः ।
युक्त इत्युच्यते योगी समलोष्टाश्मकाञ्चनः ॥ ८ ॥

jñānavijñānatṛptātmā kūṭastho vijitendriyaḥ
yukta ityucyate yogī samaloṣṭāśmakāñcanaḥ (8)

One whose mind is content in the knowledge of the self, who remains unchanged, who has mastered the sense organs and organs of action, for whom a clump of earth, a stone, and gold are the same, this composed person is referred to as a *yogin*.

सुहृन्मित्रार्युदासीनमध्यस्थद्वेष्यबन्धुषु ।
साधुष्वपि च पापेषु समबुद्धिर्विशिष्यते ॥ ९ ॥

suhṛnmitrāryudāsīnamadhyasthadveṣyabandhuṣu
sādhuṣvapi ca pāpeṣu samabuddhirviśiṣyate (9)

The one whose vision is the same with reference to a benefactor, a friend, an enemy, an acquaintance, an arbitrator, a person who evokes dislike, a relative, good people and even towards sinners, he (or she) is the most exalted.

योगी युञ्जीत सततमात्मानं रहसि स्थितः ।
एकाकी यतचित्तात्मा निराशीरपरिग्रहः ॥ १० ॥

yogī yuñjīta satatam ātmānaṁ rahasi sthitaḥ
ekākī yatacittātmā nirāśīraparigrahaḥ (10)

May the meditator, whose body and mind are relaxed, who is free from longing and possessions, remaining alone in a quiet place, constantly unite his (or her) mind (with the object of meditation).

शुचौ देशे प्रतिष्ठाप्य स्थिरमासनमात्मनः ।
नात्युच्छ्रितं नातिनीचं चैलाजिनकुशोत्तरम् ॥ ११ ॥
तत्रैकाग्रं मनः कृत्वा यतचित्तेन्द्रियक्रियः ।
उपविश्यासने युञ्ज्याद्योगमात्मविशुद्धये ॥ १२ ॥

śucau deśe pratiṣṭhāpya sthiram āsanam ātmanaḥ
nātyucchritaṁ nātinīcaṁ cailājinakuśottaram (11)
tatraikāgraṁ manaḥ kṛtvā yatacittendriyakriyaḥ
upaviśyāsane yuñjyād yogam ātmaviśuddhaye (12)

Having arranged one's seat (made of) a piece of soft cloth, a skin, and a grass mat layered in (reverse) order, in a clean place, firm, not too high (and) not too low…

… sitting there on the seat, making one's mind one pointed (absorbed in the object of meditation), may the one who has mastered the mind and senses practice meditation for the purification of the mind.

समं कायशिरोग्रीवं धारयन्नचलं स्थिरः ।
संप्रेक्ष्य नासिकाग्रं स्वं दिशश्चानवलोकयन् ॥ १३ ॥
प्रशान्तात्मा विगतभीर्ब्रह्मचारिव्रते स्थितः ।
मनः संयम्य मच्चित्तो युक्त आसीत मत्परः ॥ १४ ॥

samaṁ kāyaśirogrīvaṁ dhārayannacalaṁ sthiraḥ
samprekṣya nāsikāgraṁ svaṁ diśaścānavalokayan (13)
praśāntātmā vigatabhīrbrahmacārivrate sthitaḥ
manaḥ saṁyamya maccitto yukta āsīta matparaḥ (14)

Holding oneself firm without moving, keeping the body, head, and neck in one straight line, (as though) looking at the tip of one's nose (for eye position) and not looking in all directions...

...being the one whose mind is tranquil, who is free from fear, established in one's commitment to the life of a *brahmacārin*, may (that) meditator sit thinking of Me, having Me as the ultimate goal, while withdrawing the mind from everything else.

युञ्जन्नेवं सदात्मानं योगी नियतमानसः ।
शान्तिं निर्वाणपरमां मत्संस्थामधिगच्छति ॥ १५ ॥

yuñjannevaṁ sadātmānaṁ yogī niyatamānasaḥ
śāntiṁ nirvāṇaparamāṁ matsaṁsthām adhigacchati (15)

Always connecting the mind in this manner, the meditator, the one whose mind is mastered, gains the peace, which is centred on Me (which is in the form of an absorption in Me), which is the ultimate liberation.

नात्यश्नतस्तु योगोऽस्ति न चैकान्तमनश्नतः ।
न चातिस्वप्नशीलस्य जाग्रतो नैव चार्जुन ॥ १६ ॥

nātyaśnatastu yogo'sti na caikāntam anasnataḥ
na cātisvapnaśīlasya jāgrato naiva cārjuna (16)

Meditation is not for one who eats too much or for one who does not eat at all; nor indeed, Arjuna! (it is) for one who sleeps too much or who is always awake.

युक्ताहारविहारस्य युक्तचेष्टस्य कर्मसु ।
युक्तस्वप्नावबोधस्य योगो भवति दुःखहा ॥ १७ ॥

yuktāhāravihārasya yuktaceṣṭasya karmasu
yuktasvapnāvabodhasya yogo bhavati duḥkhahā (17)

For one who is moderate in eating and other activities, who is mindful in all activities, (and) to one's sleeping and waking hours, (for such a person) meditation becomes the destroyer of sorrow.

यदा विनियतं चित्तमात्मन्येवावतिष्ठते ।
निःस्पृहः सर्वकामेभ्यो युक्त इत्युच्यते तदा ॥ १८ ॥

yadā viniyataṁ cittam ātmanyevāvatiṣṭhate
niḥspṛhaḥ sarvakāmebhyo yukta ityucyate tadā (18)

When the mind has gained a certain composure (and) remains in the self alone, when one is free from longing for all the objects (of desire), then (the person) is said (to be) one who is accomplished.

यथा दीपो निवातस्थो नेङ्गते सोपमा स्मृता ।
योगिनो यतचित्तस्य युञ्जतो योगमात्मनः ॥ १९ ॥

yathā dīpo nivātastho neṅgate sopamā smṛtā
yogino yatacittasya yuñjato yogam ātmanaḥ (19)

A lamp, protected from the wind, does not tremble. This illustration is cited for the composed mind of the meditator who practices contemplation of the self.

यत्रोपरमते चित्तं निरुद्धं योगसेवया ।
यत्र चैवात्मनात्मानं पश्यन्नात्मनि तुष्यति ॥ २० ॥

yatroparamate cittaṁ niruddhaṁ yogasevayā
yatra caivātmanātmānaṁ paśyannātmani tuṣyati (20)

When the mind, mastered by the practice of meditation, abides (in *ātman*) and when, seeing oneself by oneself alone, one rejoices in oneself...

सुखमात्यन्तिकं यत्तद्बुद्धिग्राह्यमतीन्द्रियम् ।
वेत्ति यत्र न चैवायं स्थितश्चलति तत्त्वतः ॥ २१ ॥

sukham ātyantikaṁ yattad buddhigrāhyam atīndriyam
vetti yatra na caivāyaṁ sthitaścalati tattvataḥ (21)

...(and when) one recognises this absolute happiness, which is known by the intellect, which is beyond sense perception and when, being rooted (therein) one never moves away from the truth of oneself...

यं लब्ध्वा चापरं लाभं मन्यते नाधिकं ततः ।
यस्मिन् स्थितो न दुःखेन गुरुणापि विचाल्यते ॥ २२ ॥
तं विद्याद् दुःखसंयोगवियोगं योगसंज्ञितम् ।
स निश्चयेन योक्तव्यो योगोऽनिर्विण्णचेतसा ॥ २३ ॥

yaṁ labdhvā cāparaṁ lābhaṁ manyate nādhikaṁ tataḥ
yasmin sthito na duḥkhena guruṇāpi vicālyate (22)

taṁ vidyād duḥkhasaṁyogaviyogaṁ yogasaṁjñitam
sa niścayena yoktavyo yogo'nirviṇṇacetasā (23)

...and, having gained which, one does not think there is any other better gain than that, established in which, one is not affected even by a great sorrow (sorrowful event)...
...may one know that dissociation from association with sorrow, to be what is called as *yoga*. That *yoga* should be pursued with clarity of purpose with a mind that is not discouraged.

सङ्कल्पप्रभवान्कामांस्त्यक्त्वा सर्वानशेषतः ।
मनसैवेन्द्रियग्रामं विनियम्य समन्ततः ॥ २४ ॥
शनैः शनैरुपरमेद् बुद्ध्या धृतिगृहीतया ।
आत्मसंस्थं मनः कृत्वा न किञ्चिदपि चिन्तयेत् ॥ २५ ॥

saṅkalpaprabhavān kāmāṁstyaktvā sarvān aśeṣataḥ
manasaivendriyagrāmaṁ viniyamya samantataḥ (24)
śanaiḥ śanairuparamed buddhyā dhṛtigṛhītayā
ātmasaṁsthaṁ manaḥ kṛtvā na kiñcid api cintayet (25)

Giving up totally all desires, which are born of thought, completely withdrawing the group of sense organs and organs of action by the mind alone...
...with the intellect endowed with perseverance, may one slowly resolve the mind (in *ātman*). Making the mind abide in the self, may one not think of anything else.

यतो यतो निश्चरति मनश्चञ्चलमस्थिरम् ।
ततस्ततो नियम्यैतदात्मन्येव वशं नयेत् ॥ २६ ॥

yato yato niścarati manaścañcalam asthiram
tatastato niyamyaitad ātmanyeva vaśaṁ nayet (26)

For whatever reason the unsteady mind, always in a state of flux, goes away, bringing it back from that, with reference to the self alone, may one bring (the mind) into one's own hands.

प्रशान्तमनसं ह्येनं योगिनं सुखमुत्तमम् ।
उपैति शान्तरजसं ब्रह्मभूतमकल्मषम् ॥ २७ ॥

praśāntamanasaṁ hyenaṁ yoginaṁ sukham uttamam
upaiti śāntarajasaṁ brahmabhūtam akalmaṣam (27)

Indeed, the most exalted happiness reaches this meditator whose mind is tranquil, whose impurities have resolved, whose life is free from defects, who has become Brahman (through knowledge).

युञ्जन्नेवं सदात्मानं योगी विगतकल्मषः ।
सुखेन ब्रह्मसंस्पर्शमत्यन्तं सुखमश्नुते ॥ २८ ॥

yuñjannevaṁ sadātmānaṁ yogī vigatakalmaṣaḥ
sukhena brahmasaṁsparśam atyantaṁ sukham aśnute (28)

The meditator, free from the conflicts born of *adharma*, always uniting the mind with the object of contemplation in this manner, easily gains absolute happiness (born of) contact with (recognition of) Brahman.

सर्वभूतस्थमात्मानं सर्वभूतानि चात्मनि ।
ईक्षते योगयुक्तात्मा सर्वत्र समदर्शनः ॥ २९ ॥

sarvabhūtastham ātmānaṁ sarvabhūtāni cātmani
īkṣate yogayuktātmā sarvatra samadarśanaḥ (29)

One whose mind is resolved by this contemplation, who has the vision of sameness everywhere, sees the self abiding in all beings and all beings in the self.

यो मां पश्यति सर्वत्र सर्वं च मयि पश्यति ।
तस्याहं न प्रणश्यामि स च मे न प्रणश्यति ॥ ३० ॥

yo māṁ paśyati sarvatra sarvaṁ ca mayi paśyati
tasyāhaṁ na praṇaśyāmi sa ca me na praṇaśyati (30)

The one who sees Me in all beings and sees all beings in Me, for him (or her) I am not remote and he (or she) is not remote from Me.

सर्वभूतस्थितं यो मां भजत्येकत्वमास्थितः ।
सर्वथा वर्तमानोऽपि स योगी मयि वर्तते ॥ ३१ ॥

sarvabhūtasthitaṁ yo māṁ bhajatyekatvam āsthitaḥ
sarvathā vartamāno'pi sa yogī mayi vartate (31)

The one who gains (the vision), having recognised the oneness of me abiding in all beings, that *yogin* abides in Me whatever he (or she) does.

आत्मौपम्येन सर्वत्र समं पश्यति योऽर्जुन ।
सुखं वा यदि वा दुःखं स योगी परमो मतः ॥ ३२ ॥

ātmaupamyena sarvatra samaṁ paśyati yo'rjuna
sukhaṁ vā yadi vā duḥkhaṁ sa yogī paramo mataḥ (32)

One who, taking oneself as an example (basis) in all situations, sees either pleasure or pain as the same, that *yogin*, Arjuna! is regarded as the most exalted.

अर्जुन उवाच ।
योऽयं योगस्त्वया प्रोक्तः साम्येन मधुसूदन ।
एतस्याहं न पश्यामि चञ्चलत्वात् स्तिथिं स्थिराम् ॥ ३३ ॥

arjuna uvāca
yo'yaṁ yogastvayā proktaḥ sāmyena madhusūdana
etasyāhaṁ na paśyāmi cañcalutvāt stithiṁ sthirām (33)

Arjuna said:
Madhusūdana (Kṛṣṇa)! This *yoga* that you have talked about as sameness, I do not see its steady vision due to agitation (of the mind).

चञ्चलं हि मनः कृष्ण प्रमाथि बलवद्दृढम्।
तस्याहं निग्रहं मन्ये वायोरिव सुदुष्करम्॥ ३४॥

cañcalaṁ hi manaḥ kṛṣṇa pramāthi balavad dṛḍham
tasyāhaṁ nigrahaṁ manye vāyoriva suduṣkaram (34)

In fact, Kṛṣṇa! the mind is 'agitation,' a strong, well rooted tyrant. I think of it as impossible to control as the wind.

श्रीभगवानुवाच।
असंशयं महाबाहो मनो दुर्निग्रहं चलम्।
अभ्यासेन तु कौन्तेय वैराग्येण च गृह्यते॥ ३५॥

śrībhagavān uvāca
asaṁśayaṁ mahābāho mano durnigrahaṁ calam
abhyāsena tu kaunteya vairāgyeṇa ca gṛhyate (35)

Śrī Bhagavān said:
No doubt, Arjuna, the mighty armed! the mind is agitated and difficult to master. But, Kaunteya (Arjuna)! it is mastered by practice and objectivity.

असंयतात्मना योगो दुष्प्राप इति मे मतिः।
वश्यात्मना तु यतता शक्योऽवाप्तुमुपायतः॥ ३६॥

asaṁyatātmanā yogo duṣprāpa iti me matiḥ
vaśyātmanā tu yatatā śakyo'vāptum upāyataḥ (36)

Yoga is difficult to gain for the one by whom the mind is not mastered. This is My vision. Whereas it can be gained by the one whose mind is mastered, who makes effort with the proper means (i.e., practice and objectivity).

अर्जुन उवाच ।
अयतिः श्रद्धयोपेतो योगाच्चलितमानसः ।
अप्राप्य योगसंसिद्धिं कां गतिं कृष्ण गच्छति ॥ ३७ ॥

arjuna uvāca
ayatiḥ śraddhayopeto yogāccalitamānasaḥ
aprāpya yogasaṁsiddhiṁ kāṁ gatiṁ kṛṣṇa gacchati (37)

Arjuna said:
The one who is endowed with faith in the *śāstra* (but) whose effort is inadequate, and whose mind wanders away from *yoga*, having not gained success in *yoga*, Kṛṣṇa! to which end does he (or she) go?

कच्चिन्नोभयविभ्रष्टश्छिन्नाभ्रमिव नश्यति ।
अप्रतिष्ठो महाबाहो विमूढो ब्रह्मणः पथि ॥ ३८ ॥

kaccinnobhayavibhraṣṭaśchinnābhramiva naśyati
apratiṣṭho mahābāho vimūḍho brahmaṇaḥ pathi (38)

Deluded in the path (knowledge) of Brahman, is one who has fallen from both, being without any support, not destroyed, Kṛṣṇa, the mighty armed! like a cloudlet torn asunder?

एतन्मे संशयं कृष्ण छेत्तुमर्हस्यशेषतः ।
त्वदन्यः संशयस्यास्य छेत्ता न ह्युपपद्यते ॥ ३९ ॥

etanme saṁśayaṁ kṛṣṇa chettum arhasyaśeṣataḥ
tvadanyaḥ saṁśayasyāsya chettā na hyupapadyate (39)

Kṛṣṇa! You should eliminate this doubt of mine totally. For, other than you, there is no one who can be the remover of this doubt.

श्रीभगवानुवाच ।
पार्थ नैवेह नामुत्र विनाशस्तस्य विद्यते ।
न हि कल्याणकृत्कश्चिद्दुर्गतिं तात गच्छति ॥ ४० ॥

śrībhagavān uvāca
pārtha naiveha nāmutra vināśastasya vidyate
na hi kalyāṇakṛt kaścid durgatiṁ tāta gacchati (40)

Śrī Bhagavān said:
Indeed, Pārtha (Arjuna)! there is no destruction for him (or her), neither here nor in the hereafter, because any one who performs good actions never reaches a bad end.

प्राप्य पुण्यकृतां लोकानुषित्वा शाश्वतीः समाः ।
शुचीनां श्रीमतां गेहे योगभ्रष्टोऽभिजायते ॥ ४१ ॥

prāpya puṇyakṛtāṁ lokān uṣitvā śāśvatīḥ samāḥ
śucīnāṁ śrīmatāṁ gehe yogabhraṣṭo'bhijāyate (41)

Having gained the worlds belonging to those who do good actions (and) having lived (there) for countless years, the one who did not succeed in *yoga* is born in the home of the wealthy (and cultured) people who are committed to *dharma*.

अथवा योगिनामेव कुले भवति धीमताम् ।
एतद्धि दुर्लभतरं लोके जन्म यदीदृशम् ॥ ४२ ॥

athavā yogināṁ eva kule bhavati dhīmatām
etaddhi durlabhataraṁ loke janma yadīdṛśam (42)

Or he is indeed born into the family of wise *yogins*. A birth such as this is indeed very difficult to gain in this world.

तत्र तं बुद्धिसंयोगं लभते पौर्वदेहिकम् ।
यतते च ततो भूयः संसिद्धौ कुरुनन्दन ॥ ४३ ॥

tatra taṁ buddhisaṁyogaṁ labhate paurvadehikam
yatate ca tato bhūyaḥ saṁsiddhau kurunandana (43)

There, he gains a connection through the intellect with that which existed in his previous body and strives for further success (in *yoga*) than that (gained previously), Arjuna, the joy of the Kuru family!

पूर्वाभ्यासेन तेनैव ह्रियते ह्यवशोऽपि सः ।
जिज्ञासुरपि योगस्य शब्दब्रह्मातिवर्तते ॥ ४४ ॥

pūrvābhyāsena tenaiva hriyate hyavaśo'pi saḥ
jijñāsurapi yogasya śabdabrahmātivartate (44)

By this previous practice alone, he is necessarily led (to *yoga*). Even as the one who is desirous of the knowledge of *yoga* he goes beyond the Veda (the *karma-kāṇḍa* of the Veda).

प्रयत्नाद्यतमानस्तु योगी संशुद्धकिल्बिषः ।
अनेकजन्मसंसिद्धस्ततो याति परां गतिम् ॥ ४५ ॥

prayatnād yatamānastu yogī saṁśuddhakilbiṣaḥ
anekajanmasaṁsiddhastato yāti parāṁ gatim (45)

Whereas the *yogin* who makes an effort by means of the will is cleansed of all impurities gathered in many births (in the past). Then, he (or she) gains the ultimate end.

तपस्विभ्योऽधिको योगी ज्ञानिभ्योऽपि मतोऽधिकः ।
कर्मिभ्यश्चाधिको योगी तस्माद्योगी भवार्जुन ॥ ४६ ॥

tapasvibhyo'dhiko yogī jñānibhyo'pi mato'dhikaḥ
karmibhyaścādhiko yogī tasmād yogī bhavārjuna (46)

A *yogin* is considered superior to those who live a life of meditation, superior even to the scholars, and superior to those who perform action. Therefore, Arjuna! be a *yogin*.

योगिनामपि सर्वेषां मद्गतेनान्तरात्मना ।
श्रद्धावान्भजते यो मां स मे युक्ततमो मतः ॥ ४७ ॥

yogīnām api sarveṣāṁ madgatenāntarātmanā
śraddhāvānbhajate yo māṁ sa me yuktatamo mataḥ (47)

The one who has *śraddhā,* who with a mind absorbed in Me, contemplates upon Me, he is the most exalted among all *yogins*. (This is) My vision.

ॐतत्सत् ।
इति श्रीमद्भगवद्गीतासूपनिषत्सु ब्रह्मविद्यायां योगशास्त्रे श्रीकृष्णार्जुन-
संवादे ध्यान-योगो नाम षष्ठोऽध्यायः ॥ ६ ॥

omtatsat.
iti śrīmadbhagavadgītāsūpaniṣatsu brahma-vidyāyāṁ yoga-śāstre śrīkṛṣṇārjunasaṁvāde dhyāna-yogo nāma ṣaṣṭho'dhyāyaḥ (6)

Om, Brahman, is the only reality. Thus ends the sixth chapter called *dhyāna-yoga*—having the topic meditation—in the *Bhagavadgītā* which is in the form of a dialogue between Śrī Kṛṣṇa and Arjuna, which is the essence of the *Upaniṣads*, whose subject matter is both the knowledge of Brahman and *yoga*.

Chapter 7

ज्ञान-विज्ञान-योगः

Jñāna-vijñāna-yogaḥ

Topic of indirect and immediate knowledge

श्रीभगवानुवाच ।
मय्यासक्तमनाः पार्थ योगं युञ्जन्मदाश्रयः ।
असंशयं समग्रं मां यथा ज्ञास्यसि तच्छृणु ॥ १ ॥

śrībhagavān uvāca
mayyāsaktamanāḥ pārtha yogaṁ yuñjan madāśrayaḥ
asaṁśayaṁ samagraṁ māṁ yathā jñāsyasi tacchṛṇu (1)

Śrī Bhagavān said:
Pārtha (Arjuna)! With a mind committed to Me by taking to *yoga*, and having surrendered to Me, please listen to the way in which you will know Me totally, without any doubt.

ज्ञानं तेऽहं सविज्ञानमिदं वक्ष्याम्यशेषतः ।
यज्ज्ञात्वा नेह भूयोऽन्यज्ज्ञातव्यमवशिष्यते ॥ २ ॥

jñānaṁ te'haṁ savijñānam idaṁ vakṣyāmyaśeṣataḥ
yajjñātvā neha bhūyo'nyajjñātavyam avaśiṣyate (2)

I will teach you without any omission, this knowledge, along with immediate knowledge, knowing which there remains nothing else to be known here.

मनुष्याणां सहस्रेषु कश्चिद्यतति सिद्धये ।
यततामपि सिद्धानां कश्चिन्मां वेत्ति तत्त्वतः ॥ ३ ॥

manuṣyāṇāṁ sahasreṣu kaścidyatati siddhaye
yatatām api siddhānāṁ kaścinmāṁ vetti tattvataḥ (3)

Among thousands of people, a rare person makes effort for *mokṣa*. Even among those seekers making effort, (only) a rare person comes to know Me in reality.

भूमिरापोऽनलो वायुः खं मनो बुद्धिरेव च ।
अहङ्कार इतीयं मे भिन्ना प्रकृतिरष्टधा ॥ ४ ॥

bhūmirāpo'nalo vāyuḥ khaṁ mano buddhireva ca
ahaṅkāra itīyaṁ me bhinnā prakṛtiraṣṭadhā (4)

Earth, water, fire, air, space, mind, intellect and indeed the sense of doership—thus this *prakṛti* of mine is divided in an eight-fold way.

अपरेयमितस्त्वन्यां प्रकृतिं विद्धि मे पराम् ।
जीवभूतां महाबाहो ययेदं धार्यते जगत् ॥ ५ ॥

apareyam itastvanyāṁ prakṛtiṁ viddhi me parām
jīvabhūtāṁ mahābāho yayedaṁ dhāryate jagat (5)

Arjuna, the mighty armed! This is (my) lower (*prakṛti*). Whereas, please understand the one other than this, my higher *prakṛti* (my very nature), which is the essential nature of the individual, by which this world is sustained.

एतद्योनीनि भूतानि सर्वाणीत्युपधारय ।
अहं कृत्स्नस्य जगतः प्रभवः प्रलयस्तथा ॥ ६ ॥

etadyonīni bhūtāni sarvāṇītyupadhāraya
ahaṁ kṛtsnasya jagataḥ prabhavaḥ pralayastathā (6)

Understand that all beings and elements have their cause in this two-fold *prakṛti*. (Therefore,) I am the one from whom this entire world comes; so too, I am the one into whom everything resolves.

मत्तः परतरं नान्यत्किञ्चिदस्ति धनञ्जय ।
मयि सर्वमिदं प्रोतं सूत्रे मणिगणा इव ॥ ७ ॥

mattaḥ parataraṁ nānyat kiñcidasti dhanañjaya
mayi sarvam idaṁ protaṁ sūtre maṇigaṇā iva (7)

Dhanañjaya (Arjuna)! There is no other cause superior to Me. All this is woven (has its being) in Me, like the beads in a string.

रसोऽहमप्सु कौन्तेय प्रभास्मि शशिसूर्ययोः ।
प्रणवः सर्ववेदेषु शब्दः खे पौरुषं नृषु ॥ ८ ॥

raso'ham apsu kaunteya prabhāsmi śaśisūryayoḥ
praṇavaḥ sarvavedeṣu śabdaḥ khe pauruṣaṁ nṛṣu (8)

Kaunteya (Arjuna)! I am the taste (basic taste) in the water; I am the light in the moon and the sun; I am *Om* in all the Vedas; I am the sound in space; and I am the strength in human beings.

पुण्यो गन्धः पृथिव्यां च तेजश्चास्मि विभावसौ ।
जीवनं सर्वभूतेषु तपश्चास्मि तपस्विषु ॥ ९ ॥

puṇyo gandhaḥ pṛthivyāṁ ca tejaścāsmi vibhāvasau
jīvanaṁ sarvabhūteṣu tapaścāsmi tapasviṣu (9)

I am the sweet fragrance in the earth and the brilliance and heat in the fire. I am the very life in all beings and the ascetic disciplines and their results in the ascetics.

बीजं मां सर्वभूतानां विद्धि पार्थ सनातनम् ।
बुद्धिर्बुद्धिमतामस्मि तेजस्तेजस्विनामहम् ॥ १० ॥

bījaṁ māṁ sarvabhūtānāṁ viddhi pārtha sanātanam
buddhirbuddhimatām asmi tejastejasvinām aham (10)

Pārtha (Arjuna)! Understand Me as the one who is the eternal seed in all beings. I am the intellect of those that have the capacity to discriminate; I am the brilliance in the brilliant.

बलं बलवतां चाहं कामरागविवर्जितम्।
धर्माविरुद्धो भूतेषु कामोऽस्मि भरतर्षभ॥ ११॥

balaṁ balavatāṁ cāhaṁ kāmarāgavivarjitam
dharmāviruddho bhūteṣu kāmo'smi bharatarṣabha (11)

Arjuna, the foremost in the clan of Bharata! In the strong I am the strength that is free from desire and attachment. In all beings, I am the desire that is not opposed to *dharma*.

ये चैव सात्विका भावा राजसास्तामसाश्च ये।
मत्त एवेति तान्विद्धि न त्वहं तेषु ते मयि॥ १२॥

ye caiva sātvikā bhāvā rājasāstāmasāśca ye
matta eveti tān viddhi na tvahaṁ teṣu te mayi (12)

Those beings and things which are indeed born of *sattva*, *rajas*, and *tamas*, may you know them to be born from Me alone. They are in Me but I am not in them.

त्रिभिर्गुणमयैर्भावैरेभिः सर्वमिदं जगत्।
मोहितं नाभिजानाति मामेभ्यः परमव्ययम्॥ १३॥

tribhirguṇamayairbhāvairebhiḥ sarvam idaṁ jagat
mohitaṁ nābhijānāti mām ebhyaḥ param avyayam (13)

This entire world deluded by these things, which are the modifications of the three qualities, does not know Me who is changeless and distinct from these (modifications of the *guṇa*s).

दैवी ह्येषा गुणमयी मम माया दुरत्यया ।
मामेव ये प्रपद्यन्ते मायामेतां तरन्ति ते ॥ १४ ॥

daivī hyeṣā guṇamayī mama māyā duratyayā
māmeva ye prapadyante māyām etāṁ taranti te (14)

Indeed this *māyā*, which belongs to Me, (the Lord), which is the modification of the three *guṇa*s, is difficult to cross. Those who seek only Me, they cross this *māyā*.

न मां दुष्कृतिनो मूढाः प्रपद्यन्ते नराधमाः ।
माययापहृतज्ञाना आसुरं भावमाश्रिताः ॥ १५ ॥

na māṁ duṣkṛtino mūḍhāḥ prapadyante narādhamāḥ
māyayāpahṛtajñānā āsuraṁ bhāvam āśritāḥ (15)

Those who do wrong actions, who are deluded, who are the lowest among men, do not seek Me. Robbed of their discrimination by *māyā*, they have resorted to the condition of those who revel in sense pursuits.

चतुर्विधा भजन्ते मां जनाः सुकृतिनोऽर्जुन ।
आर्तो जिज्ञासुरर्थार्थी ज्ञानी च भरतर्षभ ॥ १६ ॥

caturvidhā bhajante māṁ janāḥ sukṛtino'rjuna
ārto jijñāsurarthārthī jñānī ca bharatarṣabha (16)

Arjuna, the foremost in the clan of Bharata! People given to good actions, who worship me are four-fold—the distressed, the seeker of security and pleasure, the one who desires to know (Me), and the one who knows (Me).

तेषां ज्ञानी नित्ययुक्त एकभक्तिर्विशिष्यते ।
प्रियो हि ज्ञानिनोऽत्यर्थमहं स च मम प्रियः ॥ १७ ॥

teṣāṁ jñānī nityayukta ekabhaktirviśiṣyate
priyo hi jñānino'tyartham ahaṁ sa ca mama priyaḥ (17)

Among these, the *jñānin*, always united (to me), his devotion resolved in oneness, is distinguished because I am very much dear to him and he is also dear to Me.

उदाराः सर्व एवैते ज्ञानी त्वात्मैव मे मतम्।
आस्थितः स हि युक्तात्मा मामेवानुत्तमां गतिम्॥ १८॥

udārāḥ sarva evaite jñānī tvātmaiva me matam
āsthitaḥ sa hi yuktātmā mām evānuttamāṁ gatim (18)

All these are indeed exalted, but the *jñānin*, the wise person, is myself alone. This is My vision. Because he, the one whose mind is absorbed in Me, has indeed reached Me, the end beyond which there is no other end.

बहूनां जन्मनामन्ते ज्ञानवान्मां प्रपद्यते।
वासुदेवः सर्वमिति स महात्मा सुदुर्लभः॥ १९॥

bahūnāṁ janmanām ante jñānavān māṁ prapadyate
vāsudevaḥ sarvam iti sa mahātmā sudurlabhaḥ (19)

At the end of many births, the one who has gained the knowledge 'Vāsudeva is everything,' reaches Me. That wise person is very rare.

कामैस्तैस्तैर्हृतज्ञानाः प्रपद्यन्तेऽन्यदेवताः।
तं तं नियममास्थाय प्रकृत्या नियताः स्वया॥ २०॥

kāmaistaistairhṛtajñānāḥ prapadyante'nyadevatāḥ
taṁ taṁ niyamam āsthāya prakṛtyā niyatāḥ svayā (20)

Those people whose discrimination is robbed away by their own particular desires, driven by their own dispositions, worship other deities following what is stipulated.

यो यो यां यां तनुं भक्तः श्रद्धयार्चितुमिच्छति ।
तस्य तस्याचलां श्रद्धां तामेव विदधाम्यहम् ॥ २१ ॥

yo yo yāṁ yāṁ tanuṁ bhaktaḥ śraddhayārcitum icchati
tasya tasyācalāṁ śraddhāṁ tāmeva vidadhāmyaham (21)

Whoever be the devotee and in whichever form (of a deity) he wishes to worship with faith, indeed, I make that faith firm for him.

स तया श्रद्धया युक्तस्तस्याराधनमीहते ।
लभते च ततः कामान्मयैव विहितान्हि तान् ॥ २२ ॥

sa tayā śraddhayā yuktastasyārādhanam īhate
labhate ca tataḥ kāmān mayaiva vihitān hi tān (22)

He who, endowed with that faith, engages in worship of that (deity), gains from that (deity he has worshipped) those objects of desire that are definitely ordained by me alone.

अन्तवत्तु फलं तेषां तद्भवत्यल्पमेधसाम् ।
देवान् देवयजो यान्ति मद्भक्ता यान्ति मामपि ॥ २३ ॥

antavat tu phalaṁ teṣāṁ tadbhavatyalpamedhasām
devān devayajo yānti madbhaktā yānti mām api (23)

But, for those of limited discrimination, that result is finite. The worshippers of the deities go to the deities; the worshippers of Me go to Me indeed.

अव्यक्तं व्यक्तिमापन्नं मन्यन्ते मामबुद्धयः ।
परं भावमजानन्तो ममाव्ययमनुत्तमम् ॥ २४ ॥

avyaktaṁ vyaktim āpannaṁ manyante māmabuddhayaḥ
paraṁ bhāvam ajānanto mamāvyayam anuttamam (24)

Those who lack discrimination, not knowing My limitless, changeless nature beyond which there is nothing greater, look upon Me, who is formless, as one endowed with a manifest form.

नाहं प्रकाशः सर्वस्य योगमायासमावृतः ।
मूढोऽयं नाभिजानाति लोको मामजमव्ययम् ॥ २५ ॥

nāhaṁ prakāśaḥ sarvasya yogamāyāsamāvṛtaḥ
mūḍho'yaṁ nābhijānāti loko mām ajam avyayam (25)

Completely covered by *yoga-māyā*,[39] I am not recognised by everyone. This deluded person does not know Me clearly as the one who is unborn and changeless.

वेदाहं समतीतानि वर्तमानानि चार्जुन ।
भविष्याणि च भूतानि मां तु वेद न कश्चन ॥ २६ ॥

vedāhaṁ samatītāni vartamānāni cārjuna
bhaviṣyāṇi ca bhūtāni māṁ tu veda na kaścana (26)

Arjuna! I know all beings that have gone before, that exist now and that will exist in the future. But no one knows Me.

इच्छाद्वेषसमुत्थेन द्वन्द्वमोहेन भारत ।
सर्वभूतानि सम्मोहं सर्गे यान्ति परन्तप ॥ २७ ॥

icchādveṣasamutthena dvandvamohena bhārata
sarvabhūtāni sammohaṁ sarge yānti parantapa (27)

Bhārata (Arjuna), the scorcher of the enemies! All beings, due to delusion of the opposites arising from desire and aversion, go into a state of total delusion in this creation.

येषां त्वन्तगतं पापं जनानां पुण्यकर्मणाम्।
ते द्वन्द्वमोहनिर्मुक्ता भजन्ते मां दृढव्रताः॥ २८॥

yeṣāṁ tvantagataṁ pāpaṁ janānāṁ puṇyakarmaṇām
te dvandvamohanirmuktā bhajante māṁ dṛḍhavratāḥ (28)

But people of good actions, for whom *pāpa* has come to an end, being released from the delusion of the opposites and firm in their commitment, they seek/reach Me.

जरामरणमोक्षाय मामाश्रित्य यतन्ति ये।
ते ब्रह्म तद्विदुः कृत्स्नमध्यात्मं कर्म चाखिलम्॥ २९॥

jarāmaraṇamokṣāya mām āśritya yatanti ye
te brahma tadviduḥ kṛtsnam adhyātmaṁ karma cākhilam (29)

Having taken refuge in Me, those who make effort for freedom from old age and death, they know that Brahman wholly as themselves and they also know *karma* in its entirety.

साधिभूताधिदैवं मां साधियज्ञं च ये विदुः।
प्रयाणकालेऽपि च मां ते विदुर्युक्तचेतसः॥ ३०॥

sādhibhūtādhidaivaṁ māṁ sādhiyajñaṁ ca ye viduḥ
prayāṇakāle'pi ca māṁ te viduryuktacetasaḥ (30)

Those who know Me as centred on the physical world, the *devatās* and the rituals, whose minds are absorbed in Me, even at the end of their life, they know me.

ॐतत्सत्।
इति श्रीमद्भगवद्गीतासूपनिषत्सु ब्रह्मविद्यायां योगशास्त्रे श्रीकृष्णार्जुन-संवादे ज्ञान-विज्ञान-योगो नाम सप्तमोऽध्यायः॥ ७॥

omtatsat.
iti śrīmadbhagavadgītāsūpaniṣatsu brahma-vidyāyāṁ yoga-śāstre śrīkṛṣṇārjuna-saṁvāde jñāna-vijñāna-yogo nāma saptamo'dhyāyaḥ (7)

Om, Brahman, is the only reality. Thus ends the seventh chapter called *jñāna-vijñāna-yoga*—having the topic of indirect and immediate knowledge—in the *Bhagavadgītā* which is in the form of a dialogue between Śrī Kṛṣṇa and Arjuna, which is the essence of the *Upaniṣads*, whose subject matter is both the knowledge of Brahman and *yoga*.

Chapter 8

अक्षर-ब्रह्म-योगः

Akṣara-brahma-yogaḥ

Topic of imperishable Brahman

अर्जुन उवाच।
किं तद्ब्रह्म किमध्यात्मं किं कर्म पुरुषोत्तम।
अधिभूतं च किं प्रोक्तमधिदैवं किमुच्यते॥ १॥

arjuna uvāca
kiṁ tadbrahma kim adhyātmaṁ kiṁ karma puruṣottama
adhibhūtaṁ ca kiṁ proktam adhidaivaṁ kim ucyate (1)

Arjuna said:
Puruṣottama[40] (Kṛṣṇa)! What is that Brahman? What is centred on the self? What is *karma*? What is spoken of as centred on beings? And what is said to be centred on gods?

अधियज्ञः कथं कोऽत्र देहेऽस्मिन्मधुसूदन।
प्रयाणकाले च कथं ज्ञेयोऽसि नियतात्मभिः॥ २॥

adhiyajñaḥ kathaṁ ko'tra dehe'smin madhusūdana
prayāṇakāle ca kathaṁ jñeyo'si niyatātmabhiḥ (2)

Madhusūdana (Kṛṣṇa)! How and who is that which is centred on ritual here in this body? At the time of death, how are you known by those whose minds are steady?

श्रीभगवानुवाच।
अक्षरं ब्रह्म परमं स्वभावोऽध्यात्ममुच्यते।
भूतभावोद्भवकरो विसर्गः कर्मसंज्ञितः॥ ३॥

śrībhagavān uvāca
akṣaraṁ brahma paramaṁ svabhāvo'dhyātmam ucyate
bhūtabhāvodbhavakaro visargaḥ karmasañjñitaḥ (3)

Śrī Bhagavān said:
What is limitless and not subject to change is Brahman. Its manifestation, centred on the body is called the *jīva.* What is known as *karma* is an offering, which causes the production of bodies for the beings.

अधिभूतं क्षरो भावः पुरुषश्चाधिदैवतम् ।
अधियज्ञोऽहमेवात्र देहे देहभृतां वर ॥ ४ ॥

adhibhūtaṁ kṣaro bhāvaḥ puruṣaścādhidaivatam
adhiyajño'ham evātra dehe dehabhṛtāṁ vara (4)

Arjuna, the most exalted among the embodied! What is centred on beings is that which is subject to decline. What is centred on *devatās* is *hiraṇyagarbha*. Here in this body, I alone am what is centred on ritual.

अन्तकाले च मामेव स्मरन्मुक्त्वा कलेवरम् ।
यः प्रयाति स मद्भावं याति नास्त्यत्र संशयः ॥ ५ ॥

antakāle ca mām eva smaran muktvā kalevaram
yaḥ prayāti sa madbhāvaṁ yāti nāstyatra saṁśayaḥ (5)

At the time of death, the one who departs giving up the body, remembering Me alone, he gains My nature. Regarding this, there is no doubt.

यं यं वापि स्मरन्भावं त्यजत्यन्ते कलेवरम् ।
तं तमेवैति कौन्तेय सदा तद्भावभावितः ॥ ६ ॥

yaṁ yaṁ vāpi smaran bhāvaṁ tyajatyante kalevaram
taṁ tam evaiti kaunteya sadā tadbhāvabhāvitaḥ (6)

Kaunteya (Arjuna)! At the time of death, remembering whatever thing one gives up the physical body, having thought about it always, one reaches that alone.

तस्मात्सर्वेषु कालेषु मामनुस्मर युध्य च ।
मय्यर्पितमनोबुद्धिर्मामेवैष्यस्यसंशयः ॥ ७ ॥

tasmāt sarveṣu kāleṣu mām anusmara yudhya ca
mayyarpitamanobuddhirmām evaiṣyasyasaṁśayaḥ (7)

Therefore, remember Me at all times and fight. Being one whose mind and intellect are offered unto Me, you will reach Me alone. There is no doubt (in this).

अभ्यासयोगयुक्तेन चेतसा नान्यगामिना ।
परमं पुरुषं दिव्यं याति पार्थानुचिन्तयन् ॥ ८ ॥

abhyāsayogayuktena cetasā nānyagāminā
paramaṁ puruṣaṁ divyaṁ yāti pārthānucintayan (8)

Pārtha (Arjuna)! Reflecting in keeping with the teaching, with a mind endowed with the practice of *yoga* that does not stray to anything else, he reaches the limitless self-effulgent person.

कविं पुराणमनुशासितारमणोरणीयांसमनुस्मरेद्यः ।
सर्वस्य धातारमचिन्त्यरूपमादित्यवर्णं तमसः परस्तात् ॥ ९ ॥

kaviṁ purāṇam anuśāsitāram
aṇoraṇīyāṁsam anusmared yaḥ
sarvasya dhātāram acintyarūpam
ādityavarṇaṁ tamasaḥ parastāt (9)

The one who contemplates upon the being who is omniscient, the most ancient, who is the ruler, who is subtler than the subtlest, ordainer of all, whose form cannot be conceived of, who is effulgent like the sun, who is beyond ignorance (and knowledge), (he reaches the limitless self-effulgent person.)

प्रयाणकाले मनसाचलेन भक्त्या युक्तो योगबलेन चैव ।
भ्रुवोर्मध्ये प्राणमावेश्य सम्यक् स तं परं पुरुषमुपैति दिव्यम् ॥ १० ॥

prayāṇakāle manasācalena
bhaktyā yukto yogabalena caiva
bhruvormadhye prāṇam āveśya samyak
sa taṁ paraṁ puruṣam upaiti divyam (10)

At the time of death, with a steady mind, endowed with devotion and the strength gathered by *yoga*, placing the breath properly between the brows, he indeed reaches that limitless effulgent person.

यदक्षरं वेदविदो वदन्ति विशन्ति यद्यतयो वीतरागाः ।
यदिच्छन्तो ब्रह्मचर्यं चरन्ति तत्ते पदं सङ्ग्रहेण प्रवक्ष्ये ॥ ११ ॥

yadakṣaraṁ vedavido vadanti
viśanti yad yatayo vītarāgāḥ
yadicchanto brahmacaryaṁ caranti
tatte padaṁ saṅgraheṇa pravakṣye (11)

I will tell you briefly about that end, which does not decline, about which the knowers of Veda talk about, which the renunciates, free from desire, enter, and desiring which people follow a life of study and discipline.

सर्वद्वाराणि संयम्य मनो हृदि निरुध्य च।
मूर्ध्न्याधायात्मनः प्राणमास्थितो योगधारणाम्॥ १२॥
ओमित्येकाक्षरं ब्रह्म व्याहरन्मामनुस्मरन्।
यः प्रयाति त्यजन्देहं स याति परमां गतिम्॥ १३॥

sarvadvārāṇi saṁyamya mano hṛdi nirudhya ca
mūrdhnyādhāyātmanaḥ prāṇamāsthito yogadhāraṇām (12)
omityekākṣaraṁ brahma vyāharan mām anusmaran
yaḥ prayāti tyajan dehaṁ sa yāti paramāṁ gatim (13)

Closing all the gates of perception (sense organs), withdrawing the mind into the heart, placing his breath at the top of his head, being the one who remains holding (his breath) by *yoga*, chanting the single syllable *Om*, which is Brahman, giving up the body, the one who departs remembering Me, goes to the most exalted end.

अनन्यचेताः सततं यो मां स्मरति नित्यशः।
तस्याहं सुलभः पार्थ नित्ययुक्तस्य योगिनः॥ १४॥

ananyacetāḥ satataṁ yo māṁ smarati nityaśaḥ
tasyāhaṁ sulabhaḥ pārtha nityayuktasya yoginaḥ (14)

Pārtha (Arjuna)! The one who has a mind that sees no other, who remembers Me constantly, for that *yogin* who is always united with Me, I am easily gained.

मामुपेत्य पुनर्जन्म दुःखालयमशाश्वतम्।
नाप्नुवन्ति महात्मानः संसिद्धिं परमां गताः॥ १५॥

mām upetya punarjanma duḥkhālayam aśāśvatam
nāpnuvanti mahātmānaḥ saṁsiddhiṁ paramāṁ gatāḥ (15)

Having reached Me, the wise men do not gain another birth, which is the abode of misery and is finite; they have reached the ultimate success.

आब्रह्मभुवनाल्लोकाः पुनरावर्तिनोऽर्जुन ।
मामुपेत्य तु कौन्तेय पुनर्जन्म न विद्यते ॥ १६ ॥

ābrahmabhuvanāllokāḥ punarāvartino'rjuna
mām upetya tu kaunteya punarjanma na vidyate (16)

Arjuna! All the worlds (where beings exist) up to the world of Brahmaji are subject to return. However, having reached Me, Kaunteya (Arjuna)! there is no rebirth.

सहस्रयुगपर्यन्तमहर्यद्ब्रह्मणो विदुः ।
रात्रिं युगसहस्रान्तां तेऽहोरात्रविदो जनाः ॥ १७ ॥

sahasrayugaparyantam aharyad brahmaṇo viduḥ
rātriṁ yugasahasrāntāṁ te'horātravido janāḥ (17)

Those people who know about the day and night, know that a day of Brahmaji consists of one thousand *yuga*s and a night (of Brahmaji) measuring one thousand *yuga*s.

अव्यक्ताद्व्यक्तयः सर्वाः प्रभवन्त्यहरागमे ।
रात्र्यागमे प्रलीयन्ते तत्रैवाव्यक्तसंज्ञके ॥ १८ ॥

avyaktād vyaktayaḥ sarvāḥ prabhavantyaharāgame
rātryāgame pralīyante tatraivāvyaktasañjñake (18)

At the beginning of the day, all things that are manifest arise from the unmanifest. At the beginning of the night, they resolve in that alone which is called unmanifest.

भूतग्रामः स एवायं भूत्वा भूत्वा प्रलीयते ।
रात्र्यागमेऽवशः पार्थ प्रभवत्यहरागमे ॥ १९ ॥

bhūtagrāmaḥ sa evāyaṁ bhūtvā bhūtvā pralīyate
rātryāgame'vaśaḥ pārtha prabhavatyaharāgame (19)

Pārtha (Arjuna)! The same group of beings indeed (which), having repeatedly come into being necessarily dissolves when the night (of Brahmaji) comes. When the day comes, it necessarily arises.

परस्तस्मात्तु भावोऽन्योऽव्यक्तोऽव्यक्तात्सनातनः ।
यः स सर्वेषु भूतेषु नश्यत्सु न विनश्यति ॥ २० ॥

parastasmāt tu bhāvo'nyo'vyakto'vyaktāt sanātanaḥ
yaḥ sa sarveṣu bhūteṣu naśyatsu na vinaśyati (20)

But, distinct from that unmanifest is another unmanifest, which is existent and eternal. That is not destroyed when all beings are destroyed.

अव्यक्तोऽक्षर इत्युक्तस्तमाहुः परमां गतिम् ।
यं प्राप्य न निवर्तन्ते तद्धाम परमं मम ॥ २१ ॥

avyakto'kṣara ityuktastam āhuḥ paramāṁ gatim
yaṁ prāpya na nivartante taddhāma paramaṁ mama (21)

The unmanifest that was spoken of as the one that is not subject to destruction, is the highest end, they say. That abode of mine, gaining which (people) do not return, is the highest.

पुरुषः स परः पार्थ भक्त्या लभ्यस्त्वनन्यया ।
यस्यान्तःस्थानि भूतानि येन सर्वमिदं ततम् ॥ २२ ॥

puruṣaḥ sa paraḥ pārtha bhaktyā labhyastvananyayā
yasyāntaḥsthāni bhūtāni yena sarvam idaṁ tatam (22)

That *puruṣa* who is the limitless, Pārtha (Arjuna)! can be gained by devotion in which there is no other. (He is) the one in whom all the beings have their being, the one by whom all this is pervaded.

यत्र काले त्वनावृत्तिमावृत्तिं चैव योगिनः।
प्रयाता यान्ति तं कालं वक्ष्यामि भरतर्षभ॥ २३॥

yatra kāle tvanāvṛttim āvṛttiṁ caiva yoginaḥ
prayātā yānti taṁ kālaṁ vakṣyāmi bharatarṣabha (23)

Arjuna, the foremost in the clan of Bharata! I will tell you what is the time (route) of no return and also the time (route) of return by which the departed *yogins* go.

अग्निर्ज्योतिरहः शुक्लः षण्मासा उत्तरायणम्।
तत्र प्रयाता गच्छन्ति ब्रह्म ब्रह्मविदो जनाः॥ २४॥

agnirjyotirahaḥ śuklaḥ ṣaṇmāsā uttarāyaṇam
tatra prayātā gacchanti brahma brahmavido janāḥ (24)

Departing there (through that path) in which the deity of fire, the deity of light, the deity of the day, the deity of the bright fortnight (of the waxing moon), the deity of the six months of the northern solstice (the sun's travel towards the north) are present, the meditators of Brahman go to *brahma-loka*.

धूमो रात्रिस्तथा कृष्णः षण्मासा दक्षिणायनम्।
तत्र चान्द्रमसं ज्योतिर्योगी प्राप्य निवर्तते॥ २५॥

dhūmo rātristathā kṛṣṇaḥ ṣaṇmāsā dakṣiṇāyanam
tatra cāndramasaṁ jyotiryogī prāpya nivartate (25)

The *yogin*, (travelling by the route) where the presiding deity of clouds, the deity of night, the deity of the dark fortnight (of the waning moon), and the deity of the six months of the southern solstice (the sun's travel towards the south) (are present), having gained the world of the moon, returns.

शुक्लकृष्णे गती ह्येते जगतः शाश्वते मते ।
एकया यात्यनावृत्तिमन्ययावर्तते पुनः ॥ २६ ॥

śuklakṛṣṇe gatī hyete jagataḥ śāsvate mate
ekayā yātyanāvṛttim anyayāvartate punaḥ (26)

As is well known in the *śāstra*, these two paths of the world, the bright and the dark, are considered eternal. By the one (path), one goes to a place of no return, by the other, one returns again.

नैते सृती पार्थ जानन्योगी मुह्यति कश्चन ।
तस्मात्सर्वेषु कालेषु योगयुक्तो भवार्जुन ॥ २७ ॥

naite sṛtī pārtha jānan yogī muhyati kaścana
tasmāt sarveṣu kāleṣu yogayukto bhavārjuna (27)

Knowing these two paths, Pārtha (Arjuna)! a *yogin* is not deluded. Therefore, Arjuna! at all times may you be united to *yoga*.

वेदेषु यज्ञेषु तपःसु चैव दानेषु यत्पुण्यफलं प्रदिष्टम् ।
अत्येति तत्सर्वमिदं विदित्वा योगी परं स्थानमुपैति चाद्यम् ॥२८ ॥

vedeṣu yajñeṣu tapaḥsu caiva
dāneṣu yatpuṇyaphalaṁ pradiṣṭam
atyeti tatsarvam idaṁ viditvā
yogī paraṁ sthānam upaiti cādyam (28)

The *yogin* knowing this, (the answers to Arjuna's questions here) goes beyond all things taught by the *śāstra*, with reference to the result of good actions, which abides in the (study of the) Veda, the rituals, disciplines, and charitics. And he reaches the primal cause (of creation), which is the highest state.

ॐतत्सत् ।
इति श्रीमद्भगवद्गीतासूपनिषत्सु ब्रह्मविद्यायां योगशास्त्रे श्रीकृष्णार्जुन-
संवादे अक्षर-ब्रह्म-योगो नाम अष्टमोऽध्यायः ॥ ८ ॥

omtatsat.
iti śrīmadbhagavadgītāsūpaniṣatsu brahma-vidyāyāṁ yoga-śāstre śrīkṛṣṇārjuna-saṁvāde akṣara-brahma-yogo nāma aṣṭamo'dhyāyaḥ (8)

Om, Brahman, is the only reality. Thus ends the eighth chapter called *akṣara-brahma-yoga*—having the topic of imperishable Brahman—in the *Bhagavadgītā* which is in the form of a dialogue between Śrī Kṛṣṇa and Arjuna, which is the essence of the *Upaniṣads*, whose subject matter is both the knowledge of Brahman and *yoga*.

Chapter 9

राजविद्या-राजगुह्य-योगः

Rājavidyā-rājaguhya-yogaḥ

Topic of the king of knowledge, the king of secrets

श्रीभगवानुवाच ।
इदं तु ते गुह्यतमं प्रवक्ष्याम्यनसूयवे ।
ज्ञानं विज्ञानसहितं यज्ज्ञात्वा मोक्ष्यसेऽशुभात् ॥ १ ॥

śrībhagavān uvāca
idaṁ tu te guhyatamaṁ pravakṣyāmyanasūyave
jñānaṁ vijñānasahitaṁ yajjñātvā mokṣyase'śubhāt (1)

Śrī Bhagavān said:
Now, I will clearly explain to you (who are) without calumny, this most secret knowledge together with immediate knowledge, knowing which you will be released from all that is inauspicious.

राजविद्या राजगुह्यं पवित्रमिदमुत्तमम् ।
प्रत्यक्षावगमं धर्म्यं सुसुखं कर्तुमव्ययम् ॥ २ ॥

rājavidyā rājaguhyaṁ pavitram idam uttamam
pratyakṣāvagamaṁ dharmyaṁ susukhaṁ kartum avyayam (2)

This is the king of all knowledge, the king of secrets, the greatest purifier, directly appreciated, not opposed to *dharma*, easy to accomplish and imperishable.

अश्रद्दधानाः पुरुषा धर्मस्यास्य परन्तप ।
अप्राप्य मां निवर्तन्ते मृत्युसंसारवर्त्मनि ॥ ३ ॥

aśraddadhānāḥ puruṣā dharmasyāsya parantapa
aprāpya māṁ nivartante mṛtyusaṁsāravartmani (3)

Arjuna, the scorcher of foes! Those people who have no faith in this self-knowledge, not gaining Me, they return to/ remain in the road of *saṁsāra*, which is fraught with death.

मया ततमिदं सर्वं जगदव्यक्तमूर्तिना ।
मत्स्थानि सर्वभूतानि न चाहं तेष्ववस्थितः ॥ ४ ॥

mayā tatam idaṁ sarvaṁ jagad avyaktamūrtinā
matsthāni sarvabhūtāni na cāhaṁ teṣvavasthitaḥ (4)

This entire world is pervaded by Me whose form cannot be objectified. All beings have their being in Me and I am not based in them.

न च मत्स्थानि भूतानि पश्य मे योगमैश्वरम् ।
भूतभृन्न च भूतस्थो ममात्मा भूतभावनः ॥ ५ ॥

na ca matsthāni bhūtāni paśya me yogam aiśvaram
bhūtabhṛnna ca bhūtastho mamātmā bhūtabhāvanaḥ (5)

And the beings do not exist in Me; look at this *aiśvara*, connection of Mine to the *jagat*. My Self is the creator of the beings, the sustainer of the beings and yet is not residing in the beings.

यथाकाशस्थितो नित्यं वायुः सर्वत्रगो महान् ।
तथा सर्वाणि भूतानि मत्स्थानीत्युपधारय ॥ ६ ॥

yathākāśasthito nityaṁ vāyuḥ sarvatrago mahān
tathā sarvāṇi bhūtāni matsthānītyupadhāraya (6)

Just as the vast air, which goes everywhere, always exists in space, similarly, may you understand that all beings exist in Me.

सर्वभूतानि कौन्तेय प्रकृतिं यान्ति मामिकाम् ।
कल्पक्षये पुनस्तानि कल्पादौ विसृजाम्यहम् ॥ ७ ॥

sarvabhūtāni kaunteya prakṛtiṁ yānti māmikam
kalpakṣaye punastāni kalpādau visṛjāmyaham (7)

All beings, Kaunteya (Arjuna)! go to My *prakṛti* at the dissolution of the cycle of creation. Again, at the beginning of the cycle, I create them.

प्रकृतिं स्वामवष्टभ्य विसृजामि पुनः पुनः ।
भूतग्राममिमं कृत्स्नमवशं प्रकृतेर्वशात् ॥ ८ ॥

prakṛtiṁ svām avaṣṭabhya visṛjāmi punaḥ punaḥ
bhūtagrāmam imaṁ kṛtsnam avaśaṁ prakṛtervaśāt (8)

Keeping My own *prakṛti* under control, again and again I create this entire group of beings necessarily, by the force of *prakṛti.*

न च मां तानि कर्माणि निबध्नन्ति धनञ्जय ।
उदासीनवदासीनमसक्तं तेषु कर्मसु ॥ ९ ॥

na ca māṁ tāni karmāṇi nibadhnanti dhanañjaya
udāsīnavad āsīnam asaktaṁ teṣu karmasu (9)

Dhanañjaya (Arjuna)! These *karma*s do not bind Me who is seated as though indifferent, who is unconnected with reference to these *karma*s.

मयाध्यक्षेण प्रकृतिः सूयते सचराचरम् ।
हेतुनानेन कौन्तेय जगद्विपरिवर्तते ॥ १० ॥

mayādhyakṣeṇa prakṛtiḥ sūyate sacarācaram
hetunānena kaunteya jagad viparivartate (10)

With me as the presiding presence, the *prakṛti* creates (the world of) the movables and immovables. Because of this reason, Kaunteya (Arjuna)! the world undergoes changes.

अवजानन्ति मां मूढा मानुषीं तनुमाश्रितम् ।
परं भावमजानन्तो मम भूतमहेश्वरम् ॥ ११ ॥

avajānanti māṁ mūḍhā mānuṣīṁ tanum āśritam
paraṁ bhāvam ajānanto mama bhūtamaheśvaram (11)

The deluded fail to recognise Me, the one who obtains in the human body, not knowing My limitless nature as the Lord of all beings.

मोघाशा मोघकर्माणो मोघज्ञाना विचेतसः ।
राक्षसीमासुरीं चैव प्रकृतिं मोहिनीं श्रिताः ॥ १२ ॥

moghāśā moghakarmāṇo moghajñānā vicetasaḥ
rākṣasīm āsurīṁ caiva prakṛtiṁ mohinīṁ śritāḥ (12)

Devoid of discrimination, those of vain hopes, of fruitless actions and useless knowledge, indeed, resort to the deluding disposition of *rākṣasa* and of *asura*.

महात्मानस्तु मां पार्थ दैवीं प्रकृतिमाश्रिताः ।
भजन्त्यनन्यमनसो ज्ञात्वा भूतादिमव्ययम् ॥ १३ ॥

mahātmānastu māṁ pārtha daivīṁ prakṛtim āśritāḥ
bhajantyananyamanaso jñātvā bhūtādim avyayam (13)

Pārtha (Arjuna)! Those of noble heart, on the other hand, who are given to a spiritual disposition, knowing Me as the imperishable cause of all beings and elements and being totally committed to Me, seek Me.

सततं कीर्तयन्तो मां यतन्तश्च दृढव्रताः ।
नमस्यन्तश्च मां भक्त्या नित्ययुक्ता उपासते ॥ १४ ॥

satatam̐ kīrtayanto mām̐ yatantaśca dṛḍhavratāḥ
namasyantaśca mām̐ bhaktyā nityayuktā upāsate (14)

Those who are always appreciating Me and making the necessary efforts, whose commitment is firm and who remain surrendered to Me with devotion, who are always united to Me (with a prayerful heart), seek Me.

ज्ञानयज्ञेन चाप्यन्ये यजन्तो मामुपासते ।
एकत्वेन पृथक्त्वेन बहुधा विश्वतोमुखम् ॥ १५ ॥

jñānayajñena cāpyanye yajanto mām upāsate
ekatvena pṛthaktvena bahudhā viśvatomukham (15)

There are others too worshipping Me with the ritual of knowledge. In many ways they worship Me as the one who is many faceted, as one and as distinct.

अहं क्रतुरहं यज्ञः स्वधाहमहमौषधम् ।
मन्त्रोऽहमहमेवाज्यमहमग्निरहं हुतम् ॥ १६ ॥

aham̐ kraturaham̐ yajñaḥ svadhāham aham auṣadham
mantro'ham ahamevājyam aham agniraham̐ hutam (16)

I am the ritual; I am the worship; I am the food that is offered; I am food in general; I am the chants; I alone am the ghee; I am the fire (in the ritual); I am the oblation.

पिताहमस्य जगतो माता धाता पितामहः ।
वेद्यं पवित्रमोङ्कार ऋक्साम यजुरेव च ॥ १७ ॥

pitāham asya jagato mātā dhātā pitāmahaḥ
vedyam̐ pavitram oṅkāra ṛksāma yajureva ca (17)

I am the father of this world, I am the mother, I am the one who sustains it, and I am the grandfather (the uncaused cause). I am what is to be known, I am the purifier, I am the *Oṁkāra*, and I am the Ṛk, Sāma, and Yajur Vedas.

गतिर्भर्ता प्रभुः साक्षी निवासः शरणं सुहृत्।
प्रभवः प्रलयः स्थानं निधानं बीजमव्ययम्॥ १८ ॥

gatirbhartā prabhuḥ sākṣī nivāsaḥ śaraṇaṁ suhṛt
prabhavaḥ pralayaḥ sthānaṁ nidhānaṁ bījam avyayam (18)

I am the result of all actions, the one who nourishes, the Lord, the witness. I am the abode, the refuge and I am the helpful by My very nature. I am the one from whom the whole creation has come, into whom everything is resolved, and in whom everything has its being, in whom everything is placed and the imperishable cause.

तपाम्यहमहं वर्षं निगृह्णाम्युत्सृजामि च।
अमृतं चैव मृत्युश्च सदसच्चाहमर्जुन॥ १९ ॥

tapāmyaham ahaṁ varṣaṁ nigṛhṇāmyutsṛjāmi ca
amṛtaṁ caiva mṛtyuśca sadasaccāham arjuna (19)

I heat up the world and I withhold and release the rain. I am immortal and I am also death. I am cause and effect, Arjuna!

त्रैविद्या मां सोमपाः पूतपापा यज्ञैरिष्ट्वा स्वर्गतिं प्रार्थयन्ते।
ते पुण्यमासाद्य सुरेन्द्रलोकमश्नन्ति दिव्यान्दिवि देवभोगान्॥२० ॥

traividyā māṁ somapāḥ pūtapāpā
yajñairiṣṭvā svargatiṁ prārthayante
te puṇyam āsādya surendralokam
aśnanti divyān divi devabhogān (20)

The knowers of the three Vedas, who perform the ritual in which *soma* is offered and thereby being purified of their *pāpas*, having propitiated Me with rituals, they pray to go to heaven. Gaining the world of Indra, which is a result of their *puṇya*, they enjoy the heavenly pleasures of the celestials in heaven.

ते तं भुक्त्वा स्वर्गलोकं विशालं क्षीणे पुण्ये मर्त्यलोकं विशन्ति।
एवं त्रयीधर्ममनुप्रपन्नाः गतागतं कामकामा लभन्ते॥ २१॥

te taṁ bhuktvā svargalokaṁ viśālaṁ
kṣīṇe puṇye martyalokaṁ viśanti
evaṁ trayīdharmam anuprapannāḥ
gatāgataṁ kāmakāmā labhante (21)

These people, having enjoyed that vast heaven, enter the world of mortals when their *puṇya* is exhausted. In this manner, following the rituals in the three Vedas, those who are desirous of various ends gain the condition of (repeated) going and coming, *saṁsāra.*

अनन्याश्चिन्तयन्तो मां ये जनाः पर्युपासते।
तेषां नित्याभियुक्तानां योगक्षेमं वहाम्यहम्॥ २२॥

ananyāścintayanto māṁ ye janāḥ paryupāsate
teṣāṁ nityābhiyuktānāṁ yogakṣemaṁ vahāmyaham (22)

Those people who (see themselves as) non-separate from Me, recognising Me, gain Me. For those who are always one with Me, I take care of what they want to acquire and protect.

येऽप्यन्यदेवता भक्ता यजन्ते श्रद्धयान्विताः।
तेऽपि मामेव कौन्तेय यजन्त्यविधिपूर्वकम्॥ २३॥

ye'pyanyadevatā bhaktā yajante śraddhayānvitāḥ
te'pi māmeva kaunteya yajantyavidhipūrvakam (23)

Kaunteya (Arjuna)! Even those devotees who worship other *devatās* with *śraddhā*, worship Me only, (but) backed by ignorance.

अहं हि सर्वयज्ञानां भोक्ता च प्रभुरेव च ।
न तु मामभिजानन्ति तत्त्वेनातश्च्यवन्ति ते ॥ २४ ॥

ahaṁ hi sarvayajñānāṁ bhoktā ca prabhureva ca
na tu māmabhijānanti tattvenātaścyavanti te (24)

I am indeed the recipient of all rituals and the only Lord. But they do not know Me in reality. Therefore, they fall away.

यान्ति देवव्रता देवान् पितॄन्यान्ति पितृव्रताः ।
भूतानि यान्ति भूतेज्या यान्ति मद्याजिनोऽपि माम् ॥ २५ ॥

yānti devavratā devān pitṛn yānti pitṛvratāḥ
bhūtāni yānti bhūtejyā yānti madyājino'pi mām (25)

Those who are committed to the Gods reach the world of the Gods. Those who are committed to the manes reach the plane of the manes. Those who worship the spirits go to the realm of the spirits. Whereas, those who worship Me, reach Me.

पत्रं पुष्पं फलं तोयं यो मे भक्त्या प्रयच्छति ।
तदहं भक्त्युपहृतमश्नामि प्रयतात्मनः ॥ २६ ॥

patraṁ puṣpaṁ phalaṁ toyaṁ yo me bhaktyā prayacchati
tadahaṁ bhaktyupahṛtam aśnāmi prayatātmanaḥ (26)

He who offers Me with devotion— a leaf, a flower, a fruit, water—I receive that offering imbued with the devotion of the person whose mind is pure.

यत्करोषि यदश्नासि यज्जुहोषि ददासि यत्।
यत्तपस्यसि कौन्तेय तत्कुरुष्व मदर्पणम्॥ २७॥

yatkaroṣi yadaśnāsi yajjuhoṣi dadāsi yat
yat tapasyasi kaunteya tat kuruṣva madarpaṇam (27)

Whatever you do, whatever you eat, whatever ritual you perform, whatever you give, whatever religious discipline you follow, Kaunteya (Arjuna)! please do it as an offering to me.

शुभाशुभफलैरेवं मोक्ष्यसे कर्मबन्धनैः।
संन्यासयोगयुक्तात्मा विमुक्तो मामुपैष्यसि॥ २८॥

śubhāśubhaphalairevaṁ mokṣyase karmabandhanaiḥ
sannyāsayogayuktātmā vimukto mām upaiṣyasi (28)

In this way you will be released from the bondage of *karma,* which is in the form of desirable and undesirable results. Being one whose mind is endowed with renunciation and *karma-yoga,* you will come to Me liberated.

समोऽहं सर्वभूतेषु न मे द्वेष्योऽस्ति न प्रियः।
ये भजन्ति तु मां भक्त्या मयि ते तेषु चाप्यहम्॥ २९॥

samo'haṁ sarvabhūteṣu na me dveṣyo'sti na priyaḥ
ye bhajanti tu māṁ bhaktyā mayi te teṣu cāpyaham (29)

I am the same in all beings. There is no one I dislike nor do I have a favourite. But those who seek Me with devotion exist in Me and I (exist) in them.

अपि चेत्सुदुराचारो भजते मामनन्यभाक्।
साधुरेव स मन्तव्यः सम्यग्व्यवसितो हि सः॥ ३०॥

api cetsudurācāro bhajate mām ananyabhāk
sādhureva sa mantavyaḥ samyagvyavasito hi saḥ (30)

Even if someone of highly improper conduct seeks Me without a sense of separation, he is to be considered a good person because he is one whose understanding is clear.

क्षिप्रं भवति धर्मात्मा शश्वच्छान्तिं निगच्छति ।
कौन्तेय प्रतिजानीहि न मे भक्तः प्रणश्यति ॥ ३१ ॥

kṣipraṁ bhavati dharmātmā śaśvacchāntiṁ nigacchati
kaunteya pratijānīhi na me bhaktaḥ praṇaśyati (31)

Quickly he becomes one whose mind is in conformity with *dharma* and gains eternal peace. May you know for certain, Kaunteya (Arjuna)! My devotee never gets destroyed.

मां हि पार्थ व्यपाश्रित्य येऽपि स्युः पापयोनयः ।
स्त्रियो वैश्यास्तथा शूद्रास्तेऽपि यान्ति परां गतिम् ॥ ३२ ॥

māṁ hi pārtha vyapāśritya ye'pi syuḥ pāpayonayaḥ
striyo vaiśyāstathā śūdrāste'pi yānti parāṁ gatim (32)

Indeed, Pārtha (Arjuna)! even those who are born in families given to improper conduct, and so too, women, *vaiśya*s and *śūdra*s, taking refuge in Me, they also gain the ultimate end.

किं पुनर्ब्राह्मणाः पुण्या भक्ता राजर्षयस्तथा ।
अनित्यमसुखं लोकमिमं प्राप्य भजस्व माम् ॥ ३३ ॥

kiṁ punarbrāhmaṇāḥ puṇyā bhaktā rājarṣayastathā
anityamasukhaṁ lokamimaṁ prāpya bhajasva mām (33)

Then what to talk of *brāhmaṇas* who have fortunate births and are devoted, so too, the sage kings (*kṣatriyas*)? Having gained this world, which is non-eternal and of little happiness, may you seek me.

मन्मना भव मद्भक्तो मद्याजी मां नमस्कुरु ।
मामेवैष्यसि युक्त्वैवमात्मानं मत्परायणः ॥ ३४ ॥

manmanā bhava madbhakto madyājī māṁ namaskuru
mām evaiṣyasi yuktvaivam ātmānaṁ matparāyaṇaḥ (34)

May you become one whose mind is committed to Me, who is devoted to Me, who offers rituals unto Me and may you surrender to Me. Having yourself prepared in this way and being one for whom I am the ultimate end, you will reach Me, the self alone.

ॐतत्सत् ।
इति श्रीमद्भगवद्गीतासूपनिषत्सु ब्रह्मविद्यायां योगशास्त्रे श्रीकृष्णार्जुन-संवादे राजविद्या-राजगुह्य-योगो नाम नवमोऽध्यायः ॥ ९ ॥

omtatsat.
iti śrīmadbhagavadgītāsūpaniṣatsu brahma-vidyāyāṁ yoga-śāstre śrīkṛṣṇārjunasaṁvāde rājavidyā-rājaguhya-yogo nāma navamo'dhyāyaḥ (9)

Om, Brahman, is the only reality. Thus ends the ninth chapter called *rājavidyā-rājaguhya-yoga*—having the topic of the king of knowledge, the king of secrets—in the *Bhagavadgītā* which is in the form of a dialogue between Śrī Kṛṣṇa and Arjuna, which is the essence of the *Upaniṣads*, whose subject matter is both the knowledge of Brahman and *yoga*.

Chapter 10

विभूति-योगः

Vibhūti-yogaḥ

Topic of glories (of the Lord)

श्रीभगवानुवाच ।
भूय एव महाबाहो शृणु मे परमं वचः ।
यत्तेऽहं प्रीयमाणाय वक्ष्यामि हितकाम्यया ॥ १ ॥

śrībhagavān uvāca
bhūya eva mahābāho śṛṇu me paramaṁ vacaḥ
yatte'haṁ prīyamāṇāya vakṣyāmi hitakāmyayā (1)

Śrī Bhagavān said:
Indeed, Arjuna, the mighty armed! for your benefit, listen again to My words revealing the limitless, which I will tell you, who is pleased (by My words).

न मे विदुः सुरगणाः प्रभवं न महर्षयः ।
अहमादिर्हि देवानां महर्षीणां च सर्वशः ॥ २ ॥

na me viduḥ suragaṇāḥ prabhavaṁ na maharṣayaḥ
aham ādirhi devānāṁ maharṣīṇāṁ ca sarvaśaḥ (2)

The whole host of Gods do not know My glory of coming into being as this world, nor do the sages because I am the cause of all the Gods and sages.

यो मामजमनादिं च वेत्ति लोकमहेश्वरम् ।
असम्मूढः स मर्त्येषु सर्वपापैः प्रमुच्यते ॥ ३ ॥

yo mām ajam anādiṁ ca vetti lokamaheśvaram
asammūḍhaḥ sa martyeṣu sarvapāpaiḥ pramucyate (3)

The one who knows Me as unborn (not an effect), beginningless (not a cause), and the limitless Lord of the world, he among the mortals, being no longer deluded, is released from all *pāpa*s.

बुद्धिर्ज्ञानमसम्मोहः क्षमा सत्यं दमः शमः ।
सुखं दुःखं भवोऽभावो भयं चाभयमेव च ॥ ४ ॥
अहिंसा समता तुष्टिः तपो दानं यशोऽयशः ।
भवन्ति भावा भूतानां मत्त एव पृथग्विधाः ॥ ५ ॥

buddhirjñānam asammohaḥ kṣamā satyaṁ damaḥ śamaḥ
sukhaṁ duḥkhaṁ bhavo'bhāvo bhayaṁ cābhayameva ca (4)
ahiṁsā samatā tuṣṭiḥ tapo dānaṁ yaśo'yaśaḥ
bhavanti bhāvā bhūtānāṁ matta eva pṛthagvidhāḥ (5)

The capacity to understand, knowledge, freedom from delusion, accommodation, truthfulness, restraint in behaviour, mastery over the ways of thinking, pleasure, pain, creation, destruction, fear, and fearlessness, and further...

...non-hurting, equanimity, contentment, religious discipline, charity, fame, ill-fame—these different dispositions (and things) of living beings—are all from Me alone.

महर्षयः सप्त पूर्वे चत्वारो मनवस्तथा ।
मद्भावा मानसा जाता येषां लोक इमाः प्रजाः ॥ ६ ॥

maharṣayaḥ sapta pūrve catvāro manavastathā
madbhāvā mānasā jātā yeṣāṁ loka imāḥ prajāḥ (6)

The seven *ṛṣi*s of yore as well as the four *manu*s who have their minds resolved in Me, are born of My mind, and of whom are all these living beings in the world.

एतां विभूतिं योगं च मम यो वेत्ति तत्त्वतः।
सोऽविकम्पेन योगेन युज्यते नात्र संशयः॥ ७॥

etāṁ vibhūtiṁ yogaṁ ca mama yo vetti tattvataḥ
so'vikampena yogena yujyate nātra saṁśayaḥ (7)

The one who knows, in reality, this glory of Mine and My connection with that, he is endowed with unshaken vision. There is no doubt about this.

अहं सर्वस्य प्रभवो मत्तः सर्वं प्रवर्तते।
इति मत्वा भजन्ते मां बुधा भावसमन्विताः॥ ८॥

ahaṁ sarvasya prabhavo mattaḥ sarvaṁ pravartate
iti matvā bhajante māṁ budhā bhāvasamanvitāḥ (8)

I am the creator of everything and because of Me every thing is sustained. Thus knowing, the wise men endowed with vision gain Me.

मच्चित्ता मद्गतप्राणा बोधयन्तः परस्परम्।
कथयन्तश्च मां नित्यं तुष्यन्ति च रमन्ति च॥ ९॥

maccittā madgataprāṇā bodhayantaḥ parasparam
kathayantaśca māṁ nityaṁ tuṣyanti ca ramanti ca (9)

Those whose minds are in Me, whose living is resolved in Me, teaching one another and always talking about Me, they are (ever) satisfied and they revel (always).

तेषां सततयुक्तानां भजतां प्रीतिपूर्वकम्।
ददामि बुद्धियोगं तं येन मामुपयान्ति ते॥ १०॥

teṣāṁ satatayuktānāṁ bhajatāṁ prītipūrvakam
dadāmi buddhiyogaṁ taṁ yena mām upayānti te (10)

For them who are always committed to Me, seeking Me with love, I give that vision whereby they reach Me.

तेषामेवानुकम्पार्थमहमज्ञानजं तमः ।
नाशयाम्यात्मभावस्थो ज्ञानदीपेन भास्वता ॥ ११ ॥

teṣām evānukampārtham aham ajñānajaṁ tamaḥ
nāśayāmyātmabhāvastho jñānadīpena bhāsvatā (11)

For them alone, out of compassion, I, obtaining in the thought of (their) mind, destroy the delusion born of ignorance by the shining lamp of knowledge.

अर्जुन उवाच ।
परं ब्रह्म परं धाम पवित्रं परमं भवान् ।
पुरुषं शाश्वतं दिव्यमादिदेवमजं विभुम् ॥ १२ ॥
आहुस्त्वामृषयः सर्वे देवर्षिर्नारदस्तथा ।
असितो देवलो व्यासः स्वयं चैव ब्रवीषि मे ॥ १३ ॥

arjuna uvāca
paraṁ brahma paraṁ dhāma pavitraṁ paramaṁ bhavān
puruṣaṁ śāśvataṁ divyam ādidevam ajaṁ vibhum (12)
āhustvām ṛṣayaḥ sarve devarṣirnāradastathā
asito devalo vyāsaḥ svayaṁ caiva bravīṣi me (13)

Arjuna said:
Revered One! You are limitless Brahman, the light of all lights, the most purifying. All the sages, including Nārada, the sage among Gods, Asita, Devala, and Vyāsa talk of you as the eternal being, not of this world, the cause of all the Gods, unborn and all-pervasive. And indeed, you yourself tell me so.

सर्वमेतदृतं मन्ये यन्मां वदसि केशव ।
न हि ते भगवन्व्यक्तिं विदुर्देवा न दानवाः ॥ १४ ॥

sarvam etad ṛtaṁ manye yanmāṁ vadasi keśava
na hi te bhagavan vyaktiṁ vidurdevā na dānavāḥ (14)

All this, which you have told me, Keśava (Kṛṣṇa)! I consider true. Indeed, neither the celestials nor the *rākṣasa*s know your manifestation (they do not know what you are), O Lord!

स्वयमेवात्मनात्मानं वेत्थ त्वं पुरुषोत्तम ।
भूतभावन भूतेश देवदेव जगत्पते ॥ १५ ॥

svayam evātmanātmānaṁ vettha tvaṁ puruṣottama
bhūtabhāvana bhūteśa devadeva jagatpate (15)

You yourself know yourself with your own mind, Puruṣottama (Kṛṣṇa)! The creator of all beings! The ruler of all beings! The Lord of the Gods! The Lord of creation!

वक्तुमर्हस्यशेषेण दिव्या ह्यात्मविभूतयः ।
याभिर्विभूतिभिर्लोकानिमांस्त्वं व्याप्य तिष्ठसि ॥ १६ ॥

vaktum arhasyaśeṣeṇa divyā hyātmavibhūtayaḥ
yābhirvibhūtibhirlokān imāṁstvaṁ vyāpya tiṣṭhasi (16)

You indeed are capable of telling in full the extraordinary glories of yourself, the glories by which you remain pervading these worlds.

कथं विद्यामहं योगिंस्त्वां सदा परिचिन्तयन् ।
केषु केषु च भावेषु चिन्त्योऽसि भगवन्मया ॥ १७ ॥

kathaṁ vidyām ahaṁ yogiṁstvāṁ sadā paricintayan
keṣu keṣu ca bhāveṣu cintyo'si bhagavan mayā (17)

The greatest of the *yogins*! Ever contemplating, how can I know you? In which forms are you to be meditated upon by me, O Lord!

विस्तरेणात्मनो योगं विभूतिं च जनार्दन।
भूयः कथय तृप्तिर्हि शृण्वतो नास्ति मेऽमृतम्॥ १८॥

vistareṇātmano yogaṁ vibhūtiṁ ca janārdana
bhūyaḥ kathaya tṛptirhi śṛṇvato nāsti me'mṛtam (18)

Please describe (me) again in detail the wonder and the glory of yourself, Janārdana (Kṛṣṇa)! because I, the listener of this nectar, have no satisfaction.

श्रीभगवानुवाच।
हन्त ते कथयिष्यामि दिव्या ह्यात्मविभूतयः।
प्राधान्यतः कुरुश्रेष्ठ नास्त्यन्तो विस्तरस्य मे॥ १९॥

śrībhagavān uvāca
hanta te kathayiṣyāmi divyā hyātmavibhūtayaḥ
prādhānyataḥ kuruśreṣṭha nāstyanto vistarasya me (19)

Śrī Bhagavān said:
Well now, Arjuna, the best of the Kurus! I will tell you My divine glories in keeping with their prominence; because there is no end to a detailed description of My glories.

अहमात्मा गुडाकेश सर्वभूताशयस्थितः।
अहमादिश्च मध्यं च भूतानामन्त एव च॥ २०॥

aham ātmā guḍākeśa sarvabhūtāśayasthitaḥ
aham ādiśca madhyaṁ ca bhūtānām anta eva ca (20)

Guḍākeśa (Arjuna)! I am the self, who resides in the hearts of all beings and I am the cause of the creation, sustenance, and resolution of all beings/things.

आदित्यानामहं विष्णुर्ज्योतिषां रविरंशुमान्।
मरीचिर्मरुतामस्मि नक्षत्राणामहं शशी॥ २१॥

ādityānām ahaṁ viṣṇurjyotiṣāṁ raviraṁśumān
marīcirmarutām asmi nakṣatrāṇām ahaṁ śaśī (21)

Among the *āditya*s I am Viṣṇu; among the luminaries I am the Sun, the one who has rays; among the *marut*s I am Marīci, and among the luminaries seen at night I am the Moon.

वेदानां सामवेदोऽस्मि देवानामस्मि वासवः।
इन्द्रियाणां मनश्चास्मि भूतानामस्मि चेतना॥ २२॥

vedānāṁ sāmavedo'smi devānām asmi vāsavaḥ
indriyāṇāṁ manaścāsmi bhūtānām asmi cetanā (22)

Among the Vedas I am the *Sāmaveda*; among the Gods I am Indra; among the means of knowing I am the mind, and of the embodied beings I am the faculty of cognition.

रुद्राणां शङ्करश्चास्मि वित्तेशो यक्षरक्षसाम्।
वसूनां पावकश्चास्मि मेरुः शिखरिणामहम्॥ २३॥

rudrāṇāṁ śaṅkaraścāsmi vitteśo yakṣarakṣasām
vasūnāṁ pāvakaścāsmi meruḥ śikhariṇām aham (23)

Among the *rudra*s I am Śaṅkara; I am Kubera among the *yakṣa*s and *rākṣasa*s; among the *vasu*s I am Fire, and among the snow-peaked mountains I am *Meru*.

पुरोधसां च मुख्यं मां विद्धि पार्थ बृहस्पतिम्।
सेनानीनामहं स्कन्दः सरसामस्मि सागरः॥ २४॥

purodhasāṁ ca mukhyaṁ māṁ viddhi pārtha bṛhaspatim
senānīnām ahaṁ skandaḥ sarasām asmi sāgaraḥ (24)

Pārtha (Arjuna)! May you know Me to be Bṛhaspati, the chief among the priests. Among the commanders in chief I am Skanda, and among the water reservoirs I am the ocean.

महर्षीणां भृगुरहं गिरामस्म्येकमक्षरम्।
यज्ञानां जपयज्ञोऽस्मि स्थावराणां हिमालयः॥ २५॥

maharṣīṇāṁ bhṛgurahaṁ girām asmyekam akṣaram
yajñānāṁ japayajño'smi sthāvarāṇāṁ himālayaḥ (25)

Among the sages I am Bhṛgu; among the words I am the single syllable *Om*; among the rituals I am the ritual of *japa*, and among the mountains, the Himalayas.

अश्वत्थः सर्ववृक्षाणां देवर्षीणां च नारदः।
गन्धर्वाणां चित्ररथः सिद्धानां कपिलो मुनिः॥ २६॥

aśvatthaḥ sarvavṛkṣāṇāṁ devarṣīṇāṁ ca nāradaḥ
gandharvāṇāṁ citrarathaḥ siddhānāṁ kapilo muniḥ (26)

I am the sacred ficus tree among all the trees; among the celestial sages I am Nārada; among the *gandharva*s I am Citraratha, and among the *siddha*s I am the sage Kapila.

उच्चैःश्रवसमश्वानां विद्धि माममृतोद्भवम्।
ऐरावतं गजेन्द्राणां नराणां च नराधिपम्॥ २७॥

uccaiḥśravasam aśvānāṁ viddhi mām amṛtodbhavam
airāvataṁ gajendrāṇāṁ narāṇāṁ ca narādhipam (27)

Among the horses may you know Me as Uccaiḥśravas, and among the elephants as Airāvata, (both) born of the churning for nectar, and I am the king among men.

आयुधानामहं वज्रं धेनूनामस्मि कामधुक् ।
प्रजनश्चास्मि कन्दर्पः सर्पाणामस्मि वासुकिः ॥ २८ ॥

āyudhānām ahaṁ vajraṁ dhenūnām asmi kāmadhuk
prajanaścāsmi kandarpaḥ sarpāṇām asmi vāsukiḥ (28)

Among the weapons I am *Vajra*; among the cows I am the wish fulfilling cow (Kāmadhenu). I am Kandarpa (Manmatha), the God of love, who is the cause for progeny. Among the poisonous snakes I am Vāsuki.

अनन्तश्चास्मि नागानां वरुणो यादसामहम् ।
पितृणामर्यमा चास्मि यमः संयमतामहम् । २९ ॥

anantaścāsmi nāgānāṁ varuṇo yādasām aham
pitṛṇām aryamā cāsmi yamaḥ saṁyamatām aham (29)

I am Ananta among the many-headed snakes, Varuṇa among the Gods of water, Aryamā among the manes, and among those who enforce discipline I am Yama.

प्रह्लादश्चास्मि दैत्यानां कालः कलयतामहम् ।
मृगाणां च मृगेन्द्रोऽहं वैनतेयश्च पक्षिणाम् ॥ ३० ॥

prahlādaścāsmi daityānāṁ kālaḥ kalayatām aham
mṛgāṇāṁ ca mṛgendro'haṁ vainateyaśca pakṣiṇām (30)

I am Prahlāda among the *daityas*, the *asuras* who are born of Diti. Among things that reckon, I am the Time; among the wild animals I am the lion, and I am Garuḍa among the birds.

पवनः पवतामस्मि रामः शस्त्रभृतामहम्।
झषाणां मकरश्चास्मि स्रोतसामस्मि जाह्नवी ॥ ३१ ॥

pavanaḥ pavatām asmi rāmaḥ śastrabhṛtām aham
jhaṣāṇāṁ makaraścāsmi srotasām asmi jāhnavī (31)

Among the purifiers, I am Air; I am Rāma among those who bear weapons; among the fish I am shark, and among the rivers I am Gaṅgā.

सर्गाणामादिरन्तश्च मध्यं चैवाहमर्जुन।
अध्यात्मविद्या विद्यानां वादः प्रवदतामहम्॥ ३२ ॥

sargāṇām ādirantaśca madhyaṁ caivāham arjuna
adhyātmavidyā vidyānāṁ vādaḥ pravadatām aham (32)

Arjuna! I am indeed the beginning, the middle, and the end of the creations. Among the disciplines of knowledge, I am the knowledge of the self. Of those who discuss, I am the discussion leading to truth.

अक्षराणामकारोऽस्मि द्वन्द्वः सामासिकस्य च।
अहमेवाक्षयः कालो धाताहं विश्वतोमुखः॥ ३३ ॥

akṣarāṇām akāro'smi dvandvaḥ sāmāsikasya ca
aham evākṣayaḥ kālo dhātāhaṁ viśvatomukhaḥ (33)

Among the letters I am '*a*', and I am the *dvandva* among the compounds. I am indeed the perennially eternal time. I am the giver (of *karma-phala*) who is all pervasive.

मृत्युः सर्वहरश्चाहमुद्भवश्च भविष्यताम्।
कीर्तिः श्रीर्वाक् च नारीणां स्मृतिर्मेधा धृतिः क्षमा ॥ ३४ ॥

mṛtyuḥ sarvaharaścāham udbhavaśca bhaviṣyatām
kīrtiḥ śrīrvāk ca nārīṇāṁ smṛtirmedhā dhṛtiḥ kṣamā (34)

I am Death that takes away everything, and I am the cause of prosperity of those yet to be. Among the feminine words[41] I am fame, wealth, speech, memory, intelligence, fortitude, and equanimity.

बृहत्साम तथा साम्नां गायत्री छन्दसामहम् ।
मासानां मार्गशीर्षोऽहमृतूनां कुसुमाकरः ॥ ३५ ॥

bṛhatsāma tathā sāmnāṁ gāyatrī chandasām aham
māsānāṁ mārgaśīrṣo'ham ṛtūnāṁ kusumākaraḥ (35)

So too, I am the Bṛhatsāma among the *sāmas*; Gāyatrī among the metres; among the months, Mārgaśirṣa, and among the seasons, the Spring.

द्यूतं छलयतामस्मि तेजस्तेजस्विनामहम् ।
जयोऽस्मि व्यवसायोऽस्मि सत्त्वं सत्त्ववतामहम् ॥ ३६ ॥

dyūtaṁ chalayatām asmi tejastejasvinām aham
jayo'smi vyavasāyo'smi sattvaṁ sattvavatām aham (36)

I am the game of dice among the things that deceive; of the brilliant I am the brilliance. I am the victory of the victorious. I am the clarity in thinking (of those who have that clarity). Of those whose nature is predominantly *sattva*, I am that *sattva-guṇa* (contemplative disposition).

वृष्णीनां वासुदेवोऽस्मि पाण्डवानां धनञ्जयः ।
मुनीनामप्यहं व्यासः कवीनामुशना कविः ॥ ३७ ॥

vṛṣṇīnāṁ vāsudevo'smi pāṇḍavānāṁ dhanañjayaḥ
munīnām apyahaṁ vyāsaḥ kavīnām uśanā kaviḥ (37)

Among the *yādavas*, I am Vāsudeva (Kṛṣṇa); among the *pāṇḍavas*, I am Arjuna; among the seers I am Vyāsa, and among the sages, the preceptor Uśanā.

दण्डो दमयतामस्मि नीतिरस्मि जिगीषताम्।
मौनं चैवास्मि गुह्यानां ज्ञानं ज्ञानवतामहम्॥ ३८॥

daṇḍo damayatām asmi nītirasmi jigīṣatām
maunaṁ caivāsmi guhyānāṁ jñānaṁ jñānavatām aham (38)

I am the discipline of those who enforce discipline. I am justice of those who want success and I am silence among the secrets. Of those who have knowledge, I am that knowledge.

यच्चापि सर्वभूतानां बीजं तदहमर्जुन।
न तदस्ति विना यत्स्यान्मया भूतं चराचरम्॥ ३९॥

yaccāpi sarvabhūtānāṁ bījaṁ tad aham arjuna
na tadasti vinā yatsyānmayā bhūtaṁ carācaram (39)

Arjuna! I am also that which is the cause of all things. There is no mobile/sentient or immobile/insentient thing that can exist without Me.

नान्तोऽस्ति मम दिव्यानां विभूतीनां परन्तप।
एष तूद्देशतः प्रोक्तो विभूतेर्विस्तरो मया॥ ४०॥

nānto'sti mama divyānāṁ vibhūtīnāṁ parantapa
eṣa tūddeśataḥ prokto vibhūtervistaro mayā (40)

There is no end to My extraordinary glories, Arjuna, the scorcher of foes! But this detailed narration of glories was told by Me taking into account a few important ones.

यद्यद्विभूतिमत्सत्त्वं श्रीमदूर्जितमेव वा
तत्तदेवावगच्छ त्वं मम तेजोंऽशसम्भवम्॥ ४१॥

yadyadvibhūtimatsattvaṁ śrīmadūrjitameva vā
tattadevāvagaccha tvaṁ mama tejoṁ'śasambhavam (41)

Whatever existent thing there is, which has glory, which is endowed with any form of wealth, or that which is mighty, every one of that, may you know, is born of a fraction of My glory.

अथवा बहुनैतेन किं ज्ञातेन तवार्जुन ।
विष्टभ्याहमिदं कृत्स्नमेकांशेन स्थितो जगत् ॥ ४२ ॥

athavā bahunaitena kiṁ jñātena tavārjuna
viṣṭabhyāham idaṁ kṛtsnam ekāṁśena sthito jagat (42)

On the other hand, by this (incomplete) knowledge of manifold things what is accomplished for you, Arjuna? (May you know fully that) I remain pervading this entire world with one part (of Myself).

ॐतत्सत् ।
इति श्रीमद्भगवद्गीतासूपनिषत्सु ब्रह्मविद्यायां योगशास्त्रे श्रीकृष्णार्जुन-संवादे विभूति-योगो नाम दशमोऽध्यायः ॥ १० ॥

omtatsat.
iti śrīmadbhagavadgītāsūpaniṣatsu brahma-vidyāyāṁ yoga-śāstre śrīkṛṣṇārjuna-saṁvāde vibhūti-yogo nāma daśamo'dhyāyaḥ (10)

Om, Brahman, is the only reality. Thus ends the tenth chapter called *vibhūti-yoga*— having the topic of glories (of the Lord)—in the *Bhagavadgītā* which is in the form of a dialogue between Śrī Kṛṣṇa and Arjuna, which is the essence of the *Upaniṣads*, whose subject matter is both the knowledge of Brahman and *yoga*.

Chapter 11

विश्वरूप-दर्शन-योगः

Viśvarūpa-darśana-yogaḥ

Topic of the vision of Cosmic Person

अर्जुन उवाच ।
मदनुग्रहाय परमं गुह्यमध्यात्मसंज्ञितम् ।
यत्त्वयोक्तं वचस्तेन मोहोऽयं विगतो मम ॥ १ ॥

arjuna uvāca
madanugrahāya paramaṁ guhyam adhyātmasañjñitam
yattvayoktaṁ vacastena moho'yaṁ vigato mama (1)

Arjuna said:
As a result of the words taught by you (Lord!) in order to bless me with the greatest secret known as (knowledge) centred on the self, this delusion of mine is gone.

भवाप्ययौ हि भूतानां श्रुतौ विस्तरशो मया ।
त्वत्तः कमलपत्राक्ष माहात्म्यमपि चाव्ययम् ॥ २ ॥

bhavāpyayau hi bhūtānāṁ śrutau vistaraśo mayā
tvattaḥ kamalapatrākṣa māhātmyam api cāvyayam (2)

Indeed the creation and dissolution of things (and beings) have been heard in detail by me from you, Kṛṣṇa, you whose eyes are like the lotus petal! and also (your) perennial glory (was heard).

एवमेतद्यथात्थ त्वमात्मानं परमेश्वर ।
द्रष्टुमिच्छामि ते रूपमैश्वरं पुरुषोत्तम ॥ ३ ॥

evam etad yathāttha tvam ātmānaṁ parameśvara
draṣṭum icchāmi te rūpam aiśvaraṁ puruṣottama (3)

Just as you have been telling about yourself, Lord! in the same manner I long to see the form of yours as the Lord, Puruṣottama (Kṛṣṇa)!

मन्यसे यदि तच्छक्यं मया द्रष्टुमिति प्रभो ।
योगेश्वर ततो मे त्वं दर्शयात्मानमव्ययम् ॥ ४ ॥

manyase yadi tacchakyaṁ mayā draṣṭum iti prabho
yogeśvara tato me tvaṁ darśayātmānam avyayam (4)

If you think it is possible for me Lord! to see that (form of yours), then, Lord of the *yogins*! you please show me your perennially eternal self.

श्रीभगवानुवाच ।
पश्य मे पार्थ रूपाणि शतशोऽथ सहस्रशः ।
नानाविधानि दिव्यानि नानावर्णाकृतीनि च ॥ ५ ॥

śrībhagavān uvāca
paśya me pārtha rūpāṇi śataśo'tha sahasraśaḥ
nānāvidhāni divyāni nānāvarṇākṛtīni ca (5)

Śrī Bhagavān said:
See, Pārtha (Arjuna)! hundreds, and thousands of My forms of many varieties, effulgent and of many colours and shapes.

पश्यादित्यान्वसून् रुद्रानश्विनौ मरुतस्तथा ।
बहून्यदृष्टपूर्वाणि पश्याश्चर्याणि भारत ॥ ६ ॥

paśyādityān vasūn rudrān aśvinau marutastathā
bahūnyadṛṣṭapūrvāṇi paśyāścaryāṇi bhārata (6)

Bhārata (Arjuna)! See the *ādityas, vasus, rudras*, two *aśvins* as well as the *maruts*. See (also) many (other) wondrous (forms) never seen before.

इहैकस्थं जगत्कृत्स्नं पश्याद्य सचराचरम्।
मम देहे गुडाकेश यच्चान्यद् द्रष्टुमिच्छसि॥ ७॥

ihaikasthaṁ jagat kṛtsnaṁ paśyādya sacarācaram
mama dehe guḍākeśa yaccānyad draṣṭum icchasi (7)

Today, here, in My body, please see the entire world, movable and immovable, in one place, and anything else, Guḍākeśa (Arjuna)! which you wish to see.

न तु मां शक्यसे द्रष्टुमनेनैव स्वचक्षुषा।
दिव्यं ददामि ते चक्षुः पश्य मे योगमैश्वरम्॥ ८॥

na tu māṁ śakyase draṣṭum anenaiva svacakṣuṣā
divyaṁ dadāmi te cakṣuḥ paśya me yogam aiśvaram (8)

But it is not possible for you to see Me merely with your own eyes alone. I will give you a divine eye. Please see My wondrous power.

सञ्जय उवाच।
एवमुक्त्वा ततो राजन्महायोगेश्वरो हरिः।
दर्शयामास पार्थाय परमं रूपमैश्वरम्॥ ९॥

sañjaya uvāca
evam uktvā tato rājan mahāyogeśvaro hariḥ
darśayāmāsa pārthāya paramaṁ rūpam aiśvaram (9)

Sañjaya said:
Having spoken thus, O King! then, the limitless Lord of all *yogins*, whose grace destroys all *pāpa*, showed to Arjuna his wondrous all inclusive form.

अनेकवक्त्रनयनमनेकाद्भुतदर्शनम् ।
अनेकदिव्याभरणं दिव्यानेकोद्यतायुधम् ॥ १० ॥
दिव्यमाल्याम्बरधरं दिव्यगन्धानुलेपनम् ।
सर्वाश्चर्यमयं देवमनन्तं विश्वतोमुखम् ॥ ११ ॥

anekavaktranayanam anekādbhutadarśanam
anekadivyābharaṇaṁ divyānekodyatāyudham (10)
divyamālyāmbaradharaṁ divyagandhānulepanam
sarvāścaryamayaṁ devam anantaṁ viśvatomukham (11)

That form consisted of countless mouths and eyes, countless wondrous objects, countless celestial ornaments, and countless extraordinary weapons in a raised state (for use).
Wearing celestial garlands and garments, anointed with special sandal paste, it was all wonder, was endless, and was one that spanned all the directions.

दिवि सूर्यसहस्रस्य भवेद्युगपदुत्थिता ।
यदि भाः सदृशी सा स्याद्भासस्तस्य महात्मनः ॥ १२ ॥

divi sūryasahasrasya bhaved yugapad utthitā
yadi bhāḥ sadṛśī sā syād bhāsastasya mahātmanaḥ (12)

If one thousand effulgent suns should simultaneously rise in the sky, that (effulgence) would be equal to the effulgence of that great Lord.

तत्रैकस्थं जगत्कृत्स्नं प्रविभक्तमनेकधा ।
अपश्यद् देवदेवस्य शरीरे पाण्डवस्तदा ॥ १३ ॥

tatraikasthaṁ jagat kṛtsnaṁ pravibhaktam anekadhā
apaśyad devadevasya śarīre pāṇḍavastadā (13)

Then, there in the body of the Lord of all Gods, Pāṇḍava (Arjuna) saw the entire world remaining in a single form (but) distinctly divided in a manifold way.

ततः स विस्मयाविष्टो हृष्टरोमा धनञ्जयः ।
प्रणम्य शिरसा देवं कृताञ्जलिरभाषत ॥ १४ ॥

tataḥ sa vismayāviṣṭo hṛṣṭaromā dhanañjayaḥ
praṇamya śirasā devaṁ kṛtāñjalirabhāṣata (14)

Then, overwhelmed with awe, with his hair standing on end, Arjuna, saluting the Lord with his head, hands folded together, said:

अर्जुन उवाच ।
पश्यामि देवांस्तव देव देहे सर्वांस्तथा भूतविशेषसङ्घान् ।
ब्रह्माणमीशं कमलासनस्थं ऋषींश्च सर्वानुरगांश्च दिव्यान् ॥ १५ ॥

arjuna uvāca
paśyāmi devāṁstava deva dehe
sarvāṁstathā bhūtaviśeṣasaṅghān
brahmāṇam īśaṁ kamalāsanasthaṁ
ṛṣīṁśca sarvān uragāṁśca divyān (15)

Arjuna said:
In your body, O Lord! I see all the celestials as well as hosts of different types of beings, the Lord Brahmā (residing in *brahma-loka*), seated on the lotus, and all the *ṛṣi*s and celestial snakes.

अनेकबाहूदरवक्त्रनेत्रं पश्यामि त्वां सर्वतोऽनन्तरूपम् ।
नान्तं न मध्यं न पुनस्तवादिं पश्यामि विश्वेश्वर विश्वरूप ॥१६ ॥

anekabāhūdaravaktranetraṁ
paśyāmi tvāṁ sarvato'nantarūpam

nāntaṁ na madhyaṁ na punastavādiṁ
paśyāmi viśveśvara viśvarūpa (16)

I see you having countless arms, stomachs, mouths, and eyes; from every quarter (you have) endless forms. I see that you have no end, no middle, and again no beginning, O Lord of creation! Lord of the cosmic form!

किरीटिनं गदिनं चक्रिणं च तेजोराशिं सर्वतो दीप्तिमन्तम् ।
पश्यामि त्वां दुर्निरीक्ष्यं समन्ताद् दीप्तानलार्कद्युतिमप्रमेयम् ॥ १७ ॥

kirīṭinaṁ gadinaṁ cakriṇaṁ ca
tejorāśiṁ sarvato dīptimantam
paśyāmi tvāṁ durnirīkṣyaṁ samantād
dīptānalārkadyutim aprameyam (17)

I see you as one who has a crown, a mace and a disc, as a mass of brilliance with light on all sides and (therefore,) difficult to see from every angle, as one who is having the brilliance of a conflagration and the blazing sun, and as one who is not knowable as a limited object.

त्वमक्षरं परमं वेदितव्यं त्वमस्य विश्वस्य परं निधानम् ।
त्वमव्ययः शाश्वतधर्मगोप्ता सनातनस्त्वं पुरुषो मतो मे ॥ १८ ॥

tvam akṣaraṁ paramaṁ veditavyaṁ
tvam asya viśvasya paraṁ nidhānam
tvam avyayaḥ śāśvatadharmagoptā
sanātanastvaṁ puruṣo mato me (18)

It is my appreciation that you (are) imperishable, limitless, the one who is to be known; you are the ultimate basis (cause) of this world; you are not subject to change; you are the protector of the perennially eternal laws; you are eternal, and you are the complete being.

अनादिमध्यान्तमनन्तवीर्यमनन्तबाहुं शशिसूर्यनेत्रम्।
पश्यामि त्वां दीप्तहुताशवक्त्रं स्वतेजसा विश्वमिदं तपन्तम्॥ १९॥

anādimadhyāntam anantavīryam
anantabāhuṁ śaśisūryanetram
paśyāmi tvāṁ dīptahutāśavaktraṁ
svatejasā viśvam idaṁ tapantam (19)

I see you as one who has no beginning, middle or end, with limitless power and endless arms, and the moon and the sun for your eyes, and a mouth like the blazing fire, who heats/energises this world by his own light.

द्यावापृथिव्योरिदमन्तरं हि व्याप्तं त्वयैकेन दिशश्च सर्वाः।
दृष्ट्वाद्भुतं रूपमुग्रं तवेदं लोकत्रयं प्रव्यथितं महात्मन्॥ २०॥

dyāvāpṛthivyoridam antaraṁ hi
vyāptaṁ tvayaikena diśaśca sarvāḥ
dṛṣṭvādbhutaṁ rūpam ugraṁ tavedaṁ
lokatrayaṁ pravyathitaṁ mahātman (20)

Indeed, this (space) in between heaven and earth and all the quarters are pervaded by you as one (form). Lord! Seeing this wondrous, frightening form of yours, the three worlds would tremble.

अमी हि त्वां सुरसङ्घा विशन्ति
केचिद्भीताः प्राञ्जलयो गृणन्ति।
स्वस्तीत्युक्त्वा महर्षिसिद्धसङ्घाः
स्तुवन्ति त्वां स्तुतिभिः पुष्कलाभिः॥ २१॥

amī hi tvāṁ surasaṅghā viśanti
kecid bhītāḥ prāñjalayo gṛṇanti

svastītyuktvā maharṣisiddhasaṅghāḥ
stuvanti tvāṁ stutibhiḥ puṣkalābhiḥ (21)

Indeed, these hosts of good people are entering into you. Some who are frightened pray with hands folded. The group of *ṛṣi*s and *siddha*s (*yogin*s), having said, 'Let there be well being,' worship you with praises full of meaning.

रुद्रादित्या वसवो ये च साध्याः विश्वेऽश्विनौ मरुतश्चोष्मपाश्च ।
गन्धर्वयक्षासुरसिद्धसङ्घाः वीक्षन्ते त्वां विस्मिताश्चैव सर्वे ॥ २२ ॥

rudrādiyā vasavo ye ca sādhyāḥ
viśve'śvinau marutaścoṣmapāśca
gandharvayakṣāsurasiddhasaṅghāḥ
vīkṣante tvāṁ vismitāścaiva sarve (22)

The *rudra*s, the *āditya*s, the *vasus*, the *sādhya*s, the *viśve-deva*s, *aśvin*s, the *maruts*, the *ūṣmapā*s, and the host of *gandharva*s, *yakṣa*s, *asura*s and *siddha*s are looking at you being struck with great wonder indeed.

रूपं महत्ते बहुवक्त्रनेत्रं महाबाहो बहुबाहूरुपादम् ।
बहूदरं बहुदंष्ट्राकरालं दृष्ट्वा लोकाः प्रव्यथितास्तथाहम् ॥ २३ ॥

rūpaṁ mahatte bahuvaktranetraṁ
mahābāho bahubāhūrupādam
bahūdaraṁ bahudaṁṣṭrākarālaṁ
dṛṣṭvā lokāḥ pravyathitāstathāham (23)

Kṛṣṇa, the mighty armed! Seeing your immeasurable form of many mouths and eyes, of many arms, thighs, feet and stomachs, and of many protruding teeth, the people are afraid and so am I.

नभःस्पृशं दीप्तमनेकवर्णं
व्यात्ताननं दीप्तविशालनेत्रम्।
दृष्ट्वा हि त्वां प्रव्यथितान्तरात्मा
धृतिं न विन्दामि शमं च विष्णो॥ २४॥

nabhaḥspṛśaṁ dīptam anekavarṇaṁ
vyāttānanaṁ dīptaviśālanetram
dṛṣṭvā hi tvāṁ pravyathitāntarātmā
dhṛtiṁ na vindāmi śamaṁ ca viṣṇo (24)

Indeed, seeing you (your form) as one touching the heavens, effulgent, of numerous forms, open mouthed and with large brilliant eyes, O Lord Viṣṇu! I, whose mind is deeply disturbed, do not find courage or composure.

दंष्ट्राकरालानि च ते मुखानि दृष्ट्वैव कालानलसन्निभानि।
दिशो न जाने न लभे च शर्म प्रसीद देवेश जगन्निवास॥ २५॥

daṁṣṭrākarālāni ca te mukhāni
dṛṣṭvaiva kālānalasannibhāni
diśo na jāne na labhe ca śarma
prasīda deveśa jagannivāsa (25)

Indeed, seeing your mouths, which have protruding canines and are equivalent to the fire of dissolution, I do not know the directions and I have no peace. Be pleased, Lord of all Gods! Lord in whom the world exists!

अमी च त्वां धृतराष्ट्रस्य पुत्राः सर्वे सहैवावनिपालसङ्घैः।
भीष्मो द्रोणः सूतपुत्रस्तथासौ सहास्मदीयैरपि योधमुख्यैः॥ २६॥
वक्त्राणि ते त्वरमाणा विशन्ति दंष्ट्राकरालानि भयानकानि
केचिद्विलग्ना दशनान्तरेषु सन्दृश्यन्ते चूर्णितैरुत्तमाङ्गैः॥ २७॥

amī ca tvāṁ dhṛtarāṣṭrasya putrāḥ
sarve sahaivāvanipālasaṅghaiḥ
bhīṣmo droṇaḥ sūtaputrastathāsau
sahāsmadīyairapi yodhamukhyaiḥ (26)
vaktrāṇi te tvaramāṇā viśanti
daṁṣṭrākarālāni bhayānakāni
kecid vilaghnā daśanāntareṣu
sandṛśyante cūrṇitairuttamāṅgaiḥ (27)

And all these sons of Dhṛtarāṣṭra, along with hosts of kings, as well as Bhīṣma, Droṇa and that charioteer's son (Karṇa) along with our most important fighters hurriedly enter your frightening mouths with projecting canines. Some are seen sticking between the teeth with their heads crushed.

यथा नदीनां बहवोऽम्बुवेगाः समुद्रमेवाभिमुखा द्रवन्ति ।
तथा तवामी नरलोकवीराः विशन्ति वक्त्राण्यभिविज्वलन्ति ॥ २८ ॥

yathā nadīnāṁ bahavo'mbuvegāḥ
samudram evābhimukhā dravanti
tathā tavāmī naralokavīrāḥ
viśanti vaktrāṇyabhivijvalanti (28)

Just as many torrents of rivers flow towards the ocean alone, so too, these heroes in the world of men enter your flaming mouths.

यथा प्रदीप्तं ज्वलनं पतङ्गाः विशन्ति नाशाय समृद्धवेगाः ।
तथैव नाशाय विशन्ति लोकास्तवापि वक्त्राणि समृद्धवेगाः ॥ २९ ॥

yathā pradīptaṁ jvalanaṁ pataṅgāḥ
viśanti nāśāya samṛddhavegāḥ
tathaiva nāśāya viśanti lokās-
tavāpi vaktrāṇi samṛddhavegāḥ (29)

Just as moths enter a glowing fire at full speed for their destruction, so too, indeed, people also enter your mouths with great speed for their destruction.

लेलिह्यसे ग्रसमानः समन्ताल्लोकान्समग्रान्वदनैर्ज्वलद्भिः ।
तेजोभिरापूर्य जगत्समग्रं भासस्तवोग्राः प्रतपन्ति विष्णो ॥ ३० ॥

lelihyase grasamānaḥ samantā-
llokān samagrān vadanairjvaladbhiḥ
tejobhirāpūrya jagat samagraṁ
bhāsastavogrāḥ pratapanti viṣṇo (30)

Completely swallowing all the people with your effulgent flaming mouths, you lick again and again. Filling up the entire world with brilliance, your fierce flames burn, O Lord Viṣṇu!

आख्याहि मे को भवानुग्ररूपो नमोऽस्तु ते देववर प्रसीद ।
विज्ञातुमिच्छामि भवन्तमाद्यं न हि प्रजानामि तव प्रवृत्तिम् ॥ ३१ ॥

ākhyāhi me ko bhavān ugrarūpo
namo'stu te devavara prasīda
vijñātum icchāmi bhavantam ādyaṁ
na hi prajānāmi tava pravṛttim (31)

Salutations to you O Lord, the exalted among all Gods! Please tell (me), for my sake, who you are, having (this) terrible form? Be gracious. I wish to know you, the cause, because I do not understand at all your actions.

श्रीभगवानुवाच ।
कालोऽस्मि लोकक्षयकृत्प्रवृद्धो
लोकान् समाहर्तुमिह प्रवृत्तः ।
ऋतेऽपि त्वां न भविष्यन्ति सर्वे
येऽवस्थिताः प्रत्यनीकेषु योधाः ॥ ३२ ॥

śrībhagavān uvāca
kālo'smi lokakṣayakṛt pravṛddho
lokān samāhartum iha pravṛttaḥ
ṛte'pi tvāṁ na bhaviṣyanti sarve
ye'vasthitāḥ pratyanīkeṣu yodhāḥ (32)

Śrī Bhagavān said:
I am time, the destroyer of people, the one who is all over, whose activity is to make people age and die here. Even without you, all these warriors who have assembled in the opposing armies will cease to exist.

तस्मात्त्वमुत्तिष्ठ यशो लभस्व जित्वा शत्रून्भुङ्क्ष्व राज्यं समृद्धम्।
मयैवेते निहताः पूर्वमेव निमित्तमात्रं भव सव्यसाचिन्॥ ३३॥

tasmāt tvam uttiṣṭha yaśo labhasva
jitvā śatrūn bhuṅkṣva rājyaṁ samṛddham
mayaivete nihatāḥ pūrvam eva
nimittamātraṁ bhava savyasācin (33)

Therefore, get up and gain fame. Conquering the enemies, enjoy the prosperous kingdom. These (people) have already been destroyed by Me. May you be merely an instrument, Savyasācin[42] (Arjuna)!

द्रोणं च भीष्मं च जयद्रथं च
कर्णं तथान्यानपि योधवीरान्।
मया हतांस्त्वं जहि मा व्यथिष्ठाः
युध्यस्व जेतासि रणे सपत्नान्॥ ३४॥

droṇaṁ ca bhīṣmaṁ ca jayadrathaṁ ca
karṇaṁ tathānyān api yodhavīrān
mayā hatāṁstvaṁ jahi mā vyathiṣṭhāḥ
yudhyasva jetāsi raṇe sapatnān (34)

May you destroy Droṇa, Bhīṣma, Jayadratha, and Karṇa as well as other heroic warriors who are (already) destroyed by Me. Do not hesitate; fight. You will conquer the enemies in battle.

सञ्जय उवाच ।
एतच्छ्रुत्वा वचनं केशवस्य कृताञ्जलिर्वेपमानः किरीटी ।
नमस्कृत्वा भूय एवाह कृष्णं सगद्गदं भीतभीतः प्रणम्य ॥ ३५ ॥

sañjaya uvāca
etacchrutvā vacanaṁ keśavasya
kṛtāñjalirvepamānaḥ kirīṭī
namaskṛtvā bhūya evāha kṛṣṇaṁ
sagadgadaṁ bhītabhītaḥ praṇamya (35)

Sañjaya said:
Hearing these words of Kṛṣṇa, Arjuna, the crowned-one, with folded hands (and) trembling, saluting Lord Kṛṣṇa, overwhelmed with fear, and saluting (repeatedly), spoke again in a faltering voice.

अर्जुन उवाच ।
स्थाने हृषीकेश तव प्रकीर्त्या
जगत्प्रहृष्यत्यनुरज्यते च ।
रक्षांसि भीतानि दिशो द्रवन्ति
सर्वे नमस्यन्ति च सिद्धसङ्घाः ॥ ३६ ॥

arjuna uvāca
sthāne hṛṣīkeśa tava prakīrtyā
jagat prahṛṣyatyanurajyate ca
rakṣāṁsi bhītāni diśo dravanti
sarve namasyanti ca siddhasaṅghāḥ (36)

Arjuna said:
It is proper, Hṛṣīkeśa (Kṛṣṇa)! that by singing your praises the world rejoices and is devoted (to you), the frightened *rākṣasa*s run in all directions and all the hosts of *siddha*s salute (you).

कस्माच्च ते न नमेरन्महात्मन् गरीयसे ब्रह्मणोऽप्यादिकर्त्रे ।
अनन्त देवेश जगन्निवास त्वमक्षरं सदसत्तत्परं यत् ॥ ३७ ॥

kasmācca te na nameran mahātman
garīyase brahmaṇo'pyādikartre
ananta deveśa jagannivāsa
tvam akṣaraṁ sadasattatparaṁ yat (37)

O Lord, the limitless one! The Lord of all Gods! The one in whom the world exists! Why will they not salute you who is greater (than other Gods), who is the primal creator of even Brahmā? You are that eternal, limitless (*vastu*), which is both cause and effect.

त्वमादिदेवः पुरुषः पुराणस्त्वमस्य विश्वस्य परं निधानम् ।
वेत्तासि वेद्यं च परं च धाम त्वया ततं विश्वमनन्तरूप ॥ ३८ ॥

tvam ādidevaḥ puruṣaḥ purāṇas-
tvam asya viśvasya paraṁ nidhānam
vettāsi vedyaṁ ca paraṁ ca dhāma
tvayā tataṁ viśvam anantarūpa (38)

You are the first among Gods, the one who was there even before, the one who fills up everything. You are the ultimate place of resolution of this world; you are the knower and also what is to be known and you are the ultimate abode. The world is pervaded by you O Lord, the one whose forms are endless!

वायुर्यमोऽग्निर्वरुणः शशाङ्कः प्रजापतिस्त्वं प्रपितामहश्च
नमो नमस्तेऽस्तु सहस्रकृत्वः पुनश्च भूयोऽपि नमो नमस्ते ॥ ३९ ॥

vāyuryamo'gnirvaruṇaḥ śaśāṅkaḥ
prajāpatistvaṁ prapitāmahaśca
namo namaste'stu sahasrakṛtvaḥ
punaśca bhūyo'pi namo namaste (39)

You are the Lord of air, Lord Death, Lord of fire, Lord of water, presiding deity of the moon, Prajāpati, and the ultimate great grandfather, the Creator. One thousand repeated salutations to you. Again and again indeed, repeated salutations to you.

नमः पुरस्तादथ पृष्ठतस्ते नमोऽस्तु ते सर्वत एव सर्व ।
अनन्तवीर्यामितविक्रमस्त्वं सर्वं समाप्नोषि ततोऽसि सर्वः ॥ ४० ॥

namaḥ purastād atha pṛṣṭhataste
namo'stu te sarvata eva sarva
anantavīryāmitavikramastvaṁ
sarvaṁ samāpnoṣi tato'si sarvaḥ (40)

Salutations to you in the front (in the east), salutations to you at the back (in the west), indeed (salutations) to you in all directions, O Lord, the one who is everything! You are the one of infinite strength and immeasurable prowess and you completely pervade everything. Therefore, you are everything.

सखेति मत्वा प्रसभं यदुक्तं हे कृष्ण हे यादव हे सखेति ।
अजानता महिमानं तवेदं मया प्रमादात्प्रणयेन वापि ॥ ४१ ॥
यच्चावहासार्थमसत्कृतोऽसि विहारशय्यासनभोजनेषु ।
एकोऽथवाप्यच्युत तत्समक्षं तत्क्षामये त्वामहमप्रमेयम् ॥ ४२ ॥

sakheti matvā prasabhaṁ yad uktaṁ
he kṛṣṇa he yādava he sakheti
ajānatā mahimānaṁ tavedaṁ
mayā pramādāt praṇayena vāpi (41)
yaccāvahāsārtham asatkṛto'si
vihāraśayyāsanabhojaneṣu
eko'thavāpyacyuta tatsamakṣaṁ
tatkṣāmaye tvām aham aprameyam (42)

Ignorant of this glory of yours, thinking of you as a (mere) friend, whatever that was said lightly by me, as 'O Kṛṣṇa! O Yādava! O Friend!' out of carelessness or, out of intimacy, and further...
...out of jest you have been slighted, Acyuta (Kṛṣṇa)! while walking, lying down, sitting and eating, alone or even in public. For (all) that, may I ask pardon of you, the one who cannot be known?

पितासि लोकस्य चराचरस्य
त्वमस्य पूज्यश्च गुरुर्गरीयान्।
न त्वत्समोऽस्त्यभ्यधिकः कुतोऽन्यो
लोकत्रयेऽप्यप्रतिमप्रभाव ॥ ४३ ॥

pitāsi lokasya carācarasya
tvam asya pūjyaśca gururgarīyān
na tvatsamo'styabhyadhikaḥ kuto'nyo
lokatraye'pyapratimaprabhāva (43)

Lord, the one whose glories are unparalleled! You are the father of this world of sentient beings and insentient objects and you are the most worshipful of it (and its) first teacher. Even in the three worlds, there is no one equal to you, how can there be another who is superior?

तस्मात्प्रणम्य प्रणिधाय कायं प्रसादये त्वामहमीशमीड्यम् ।
पितेव पुत्रस्य सखेव सख्युः प्रियः प्रियायार्हसि देव सोढुम् ॥ ४४ ॥

tasmāt praṇamya praṇidhāya kāyaṁ
prasādaye tvām aham īśam īḍyam
piteva putrasya sakheva sakhyuḥ
priyaḥ priyāyārhasi deva soḍhum (44)

Therefore, saluting, properly laying down my body, I seek the blessing of you who are the worshipful Lord. O Lord! You should forgive (my mistakes) as a father would (the mistakes) of a son, as a friend of a friend, and as a beloved of (his) beloved.

अदृष्टपूर्वं हृषितोऽस्मि दृष्ट्वा भयेन च प्रव्यथितं मनो मे ।
तदेव मे दर्शय देव रूपं प्रसीद देवेश जगन्निवास ॥ ४५ ॥

adṛṣṭapūrvaṁ hṛṣito'smi dṛṣṭvā
bhayena ca pravyathitaṁ mano me
tad eva me darśaya deva rūpaṁ
prasīda deveśa jagannivāsa (45)

O Lord! Seeing what was not seen hitherto, I am happy; and (yet) my mind is afflicted with fear also. Please show me only that (original) form. Be pleased, O Lord of the Gods! The one in whom the world exists!

किरीटिनं गदिनं चक्रहस्तमिच्छामि त्वां द्रष्टुमहं तथैव ।
तेनैव रूपेण चतुर्भुजेन सहस्रबाहो भव विश्वमूर्ते ॥ ४६ ॥

kirīṭinaṁ gadinaṁ cakrahastam
icchāmi tvāṁ draṣṭum ahaṁ tathaiva
tenaiva rūpeṇa caturbhujena
sahasrabāho bhava viśvamūrte (46)

So too, I wish to see you as one with a crown, a mace and a disc in hand. Lord of a thousand arms! The one who is in the form of the world! May you become that form alone, which has four hands.

श्रीभगवानुवाच ।
मया प्रसन्नेन तवार्जुनेदं रूपं परं दर्शितमात्मयोगात् ।
तेजोमयं विश्वमनन्तमाद्यं यन्मे त्वदन्येन न दृष्टपूर्वम् ॥ ४७ ॥

śrībhagavān uvāca
mayā prasannena tavārjunedaṁ
rūpaṁ paraṁ darśitam ātmayogāt
tejomayaṁ viśvam anantam ādyaṁ
yanme tvadanyena na dṛṣṭapūrvam (47)

Śrī Bhagavān said:
Arjuna! By Me, who is pleased, this cosmic form was shown to you through My power—a form which is limitless, full of brilliance, includes everything and is without end. That (form) of Mine was never before seen by anyone other than you.

न वेदयज्ञाध्ययनैर्न दानैर्न च क्रियाभिर्न तपोभिरुग्रैः ।
एवंरूपः शक्य अहं नृलोके द्रष्टुं त्वदन्येन कुरुप्रवीर ॥ ४८ ॥

na vedayajñādhyayanairna dānair-
na ca kriyābhirna tapobhirugraiḥ
evaṁrūpaḥ śakya ahaṁ nṛloke
draṣṭuṁ tvadanyena kurupravīra (48)

Not by the study of the Vedas and rituals, not by charity, not by performing rituals, nor by severe austerities can I, in this form, be seen, in the world of men, by anyone other than you, Arjuna, the bravest of the Kurus!

मा ते व्यथा मा च विमूढभावो दृष्ट्वा रूपं घोरमीदृङ् ममेदम्।
व्यपेतभीः प्रीतमनाः पुनस्त्वं तदेव मे रूपमिदं प्रपश्य॥ ४९॥

mā te vyathā mā ca vimūḍhabhāvo
dṛṣṭvā rūpaṁ ghoram īdṛṅ mamedam
vyapetabhīḥ prītamanāḥ punastvaṁ
tadeva me rūpam idaṁ prapaśya (49)

May you not have fear and may you not be confused seeing this frightening form of Mine. Being free from fear and pleased again, may you see that (particular) form of Mine.

सञ्जय उवाच।
इत्यर्जुनं वासुदेवस्तथोक्त्वा स्वकं रूपं दर्शयामास भूयः।
आश्वासयामास च भीतमेनं भूत्वा पुनः सौम्यवपुर्महात्मा॥५०॥

sañjaya uvāca
ityarjunaṁ vāsudevastathoktvā
svakaṁ rūpaṁ darśayāmāsa bhūyaḥ
āśvāsayāmāsa ca bhītam enaṁ
bhūtvā punaḥ saumyavapurmahātmā (50)

Sañjaya said:
Having thus spoken to Arjuna in this way, the son of Vasudeva (Kṛṣṇa), again showed his own form and consoled him, who was frightened, having once more become the Lord with a pleasing form.

अर्जुन उवाच।
दृष्ट्वेदं मानुषं रूपं तव सौम्यं जनार्दन।
इदानीमस्मि संवृत्तः सचेताः प्रकृतिं गतः॥ ५१॥

arjuna uvāca
dṛṣṭvedaṁ mānuṣaṁ rūpaṁ tava saumyaṁ janārdana
idānīm asmi saṁvṛttaḥ sacetāḥ prakṛtiṁ gataḥ (51)

Arjuna said:
Seeing this pleasing human form of yours, Janārdana (Kṛṣṇa)! now I have become cheerful and restored to (my) original nature.

श्रीभगवानुवाच ।
सुदुर्दर्शमिदं रूपं दृष्टवानसि यन्मम ।
देवा अप्यस्य रूपस्य नित्यं दर्शनकाङ्क्षिणः ॥ ५२ ॥

śrībhagavān uvāca
sudurdarśam idaṁ rūpaṁ dṛṣṭavān asi yanmama
devā apyasya rūpasya nityaṁ darśanakāṅkṣiṇaḥ (52)

Śrī Bhagavān said:
You have seen this form of Mine, which is very difficult to see. Even the Gods always (remain) desirous of seeing this form.

नाहं वेदैर्न तपसा न दानेन न चेज्यया ।
शक्य एवंविधो द्रष्टुं दृष्टवानसि मां यथा ॥ ५३ ॥

nāhaṁ vedairna tapasā na dānena na cejyayā
śakya evaṁvidho draṣṭuṁ dṛṣṭavān asi māṁ yathā (53)

I cannot be seen in this form by (study of) the Vedas, nor by ascetic practices, nor by charity, nor by worship. You are the one who has seen Me in this way.

भक्त्या त्वनन्यया शक्य अहमेवंविधोऽर्जुन ।
ज्ञातुं द्रष्टुं च तत्त्वेन प्रवेष्टुं च परन्तप ॥ ५४ ॥

bhaktyā tvananyayā śakya aham evaṁvidho'rjuna
jñātuṁ draṣṭuṁ ca tattvena praveṣṭuṁ ca parantapa (54)

Whereas, Arjuna, the scorcher of enemies! with devotion, in which there is no other, it is possible that I can be known and seen in this form, and in reality can be entered into.

मत्कर्मकृत्मत्परमो मद्भक्तः सङ्गवर्जितः ।
निर्वैरः सर्वभूतेषु यः स मामेति पाण्डव ॥ ५५ ॥

matkarmakṛt matparamo madbhaktaḥ saṅgavarjitaḥ
nirvairaḥ sarvabhūteṣu yaḥ sa mām eti pāṇḍava (55)

The one who does all actions for My sake, for whom I am paramount, who is devoted to Me, free from attachment and free from enmity towards all beings, comes to Me, Pāṇḍava (Arjuna)!

ॐतत्सत् ।
इति श्रीमद्भगवद्गीतासूपनिषत्सु ब्रह्मविद्यायां योगशास्त्रे श्रीकृष्णार्जुन-संवादे विश्वरूप-दर्शन-योगो नाम एकादशोऽध्यायः ॥ ११ ॥

omtatsat.
iti śrīmadbhagavadgītāsūpaniṣatsu brahma-vidyāyāṁ yoga-śāstre śrīkṛṣṇārjunasaṁvāde viśvarūpa-darśana-yogo nāma ekādaśo'dhyāyaḥ (11)

Om, Brahman, is the only reality. Thus ends the eleventh chapter called *viśvarūpa-darśana-yoga*—having the topic of the vision of Cosmic Person—in the *Bhagavadgītā* which is in the form of a dialogue between Śrī Kṛṣṇa and Arjuna, which is the essence of the *Upaniṣads*, whose subject matter is both the knowledge of Brahman and *yoga*.

Chapter 12
भक्ति-योगः
Bhakti-yogaḥ
Topic of devotion

अर्जुन उवाच ।
एवं सततयुक्ता ये भक्तास्त्वां पर्युपासते ।
ये चाप्यक्षरमव्यक्तं तेषां के योगवित्तमाः ॥ १ ॥

arjuna uvāca
evaṁ satatayuktā ye bhaktāstvāṁ paryupāsate
ye cāpyakṣaram avyaktaṁ teṣāṁ ke yogavittamāḥ (1)

Arjuna said:
In this manner[43], (there are) those devotees who, abidingly committed, meditate upon you and also (there are) those who seek you as one who is not subject to decline and not available for objectification. Who among them are the greatest knowers of *yoga*?

श्रीभगवानुवाच ।
मय्यावेश्य मनो ये मां नित्ययुक्ता उपासते ।
श्रद्धया परयोपेतास्ते मे युक्ततमा मताः ॥ २ ॥

śrībhagavān uvāca
mayyāveśya mano ye māṁ nityayuktā upāsate
śraddhayā parayopetāste me yuktatamā matāḥ (2)

Śrī Bhagavān said:
Endowed with unflinching faith, their minds committed to Me, being ever united (with Me), those who meditate upon Me are considered by Me as the most exalted.

ये त्वक्षरमनिर्देश्यमव्यक्तं पर्युपासते।
सर्वत्रगमचिन्त्यं च कूटस्थमचलं ध्रुवम्॥ ३॥
सन्नियम्येन्द्रियग्रामं सर्वत्र समबुद्धयः।
ते प्राप्नुवन्ति मामेव सर्वभूतहिते रताः॥ ४॥

ye tvakṣaram anirdeśyam avyaktaṁ paryupāsate
sarvatragamacintyaṁ ca kūṭastham acalaṁ dhruvam (3)
sanniyamyendriyagrāmaṁ sarvatra samabuddhayaḥ
te prāpnuvanti mām eva sarvabhūtahite ratāḥ (4)

However, those who contemplate upon that which is not subject to decline, indefinable, not available for objectification, all pervasive, not an object of thought, which abides in *māyā,* does not move and is eternal...

...those who have complete mastery over the group of sense organs, who are always equal minded and take delight in the welfare of all beings, gain Me.

क्लेशोऽधिकतरस्तेषामव्यक्तासक्तचेतसाम्।
अव्यक्ता हि गतिर्दुःखं देहवद्भिरवाप्यते॥ ५॥

kleśo'dhikatarasteṣām avyaktāsaktacetasām
avyaktā hi gatirduḥkhaṁ dehavadbhiravāpyate (5)

Greater is the affliction for those whose minds are committed to what cannot be objectified, for, an end which cannot be objectified is reached with difficulty by those who are identified with the body.

ये तु सर्वाणि कर्माणि मयि संन्यस्य मत्पराः।
अनन्येनैव योगेन मां ध्यायन्त उपासते॥ ६॥
तेषामहं समुद्धर्ता मृत्युसंसारसागरात्।
भवामि न चिरात् पार्थ मय्यावेशितचेतसाम्॥ ७॥

ye tu sarvāṇi karmāṇi mayi sannyasya matparāḥ
ananyenaiva yogena māṁ dhyāyanta upāsate (6)
teṣām ahaṁ samuddhartā mṛtyusaṁsārasāgarāt
bhavāmi na cirāt pārtha mayyāveśitacetasām (7)

However, those who worship Me, keeping me as the ultimate end, giving up all actions unto Me, meditating upon Me with a commitment in which there is indeed no other...
...for them, whose minds are absorbed in Me, Pārtha (Arjuna)! before long I become the liberator from the ocean of *saṁsāra* that is fraught with death.

मय्येव मन आधत्स्व मयि बुद्धिं निवेशय ।
निवसिष्यसि मय्येव अत ऊर्ध्वं न संशयः ॥ ८ ॥

mayyeva mana ādhatsva mayi buddhiṁ niveśaya
nivasiṣyasi mayyeva ata ūrdhvaṁ na saṁśayaḥ (8)

In me alone may you place the mind; in me may you place the intellect. Thereafter, there is no doubt that you will abide in me alone.

अथ चित्तं समाधातुं न शक्नोषि मयि स्थिरम् ।
अभ्यासयोगेन ततो मामिच्छाप्तुं धनञ्जय ॥ ९ ॥

atha cittaṁ samādhātuṁ na śaknoṣi mayi sthiram
abhyāsayogena tato mām icchāptuṁ dhanañjaya (9)

If you are not able to absorb your mind steadily in Me, Dhanañjaya (Arjuna)! then through the practice of *yoga* may you seek to reach Me.

अभ्यासेऽप्यसमर्थोऽसि मत्कर्मपरमो भव ।
मदर्थमपि कर्माणि कुर्वन्सिद्धिमवाप्स्यसि ॥ १० ॥

abhyāse'pyasamartho'si matkarmaparamo bhava
madartham api karmāṇi kurvan siddhim avāpsyasi (10)

If you do not have the capacity for the practice (of this *yoga*) either, may you become one for whom action dedicated to Me is paramount. Even doing actions for my sake you will gain success.

अथैतदप्यशक्तोऽसि कर्तुं मद्योगमाश्रितः ।
सर्वकर्मफलत्यागं ततः कुरु यतात्मवान् ॥ ११ ॥

athaitadapyaśakto'si kartuṁ madyogam āśritaḥ
sarvakarmaphalatyāgaṁ tataḥ kuru yatātmavān (11)

If you are not able to do even this, being one whose commitment is dedicating all actions to Me, then, with a disciplined mind, give up the results of all actions (to Me).

श्रेयो हि ज्ञानमभ्यासाज्ज्ञानाद्ध्यानं विशिष्यते ।
ध्यानात्कर्मफलत्यागस्त्यागाच्छान्तिरनन्तरम् ॥ १२ ॥

śreyo hi jñānam abhyāsājjñānāddhyānaṁ viśiṣyate
dhyānāt karmaphalatyāgastyāgācchāntiranantaram (12)

Knowledge is better indeed than the practice of *yoga*; meditation is superior to knowledge; renunciation of the results of actions (is better) than meditation. Because of renunciation (there is) peace immediately.

अद्वेष्टा सर्वभूतानां मैत्रः करुण एव च ।
निर्ममो निरहङ्कारः समदुःखसुखः क्षमी ॥ १३ ॥

adveṣṭā sarvabhūtānāṁ maitraḥ karuṇa eva ca
nirmamo nirahaṅkāraḥ samaduḥkhasukhaḥ kṣamī (13)

The one who has no hatred for all beings, who has the disposition of a friend, who is compassionate, free from possessiveness, free from doership, equal in pleasant and unpleasant (situations), and indeed, one who is naturally accommodative...

सन्तुष्टः सततं योगी यतात्मा दृढनिश्चयः ।
मय्यर्पितमनोबुद्धिर्यो मद्भक्तः स मे प्रियः ॥ १४ ॥

santuṣṭaḥ satataṁ yogī yatātmā dṛḍhaniścayaḥ
mayyarpitamanobuddhiryo madbhaktaḥ sa me priyaḥ (14)

...the one who is completely satisfied, who is always united, who has mastery over his mind, whose ascertainment is firm, whose mind and intellect are resolved in Me, who is My devotee, is beloved to Me.

यस्मान्नोद्विजते लोको लोकान्नोद्विजते च यः ।
हर्षामर्षभयोद्वेगैर्मुक्तो यः स च मे प्रियः ॥ १५ ॥

yasmānnodvijate loko lokānnodvijate ca yaḥ
harṣāmarṣabhayodvegairmukto yaḥ sa ca me priyaḥ (15)

The one because of whom people do not get disturbed and who does not get disturbed by people, and who is free from elation, intolerance, fear and anxiety, he is beloved to Me.

अनपेक्षः शुचिर्दक्ष उदासीनो गतव्यथः ।
सर्वारम्भपरित्यागी यो मद्भक्तः स मे प्रियः ॥ १६ ॥

anapekṣaḥ śucirdakṣa udāsīno gatavyathaḥ
sarvārambhaparityāgī yo madbhaktaḥ sa me priyaḥ (16)

The one who has no dependence, is clean, able, and neutral, from whom fear has gone, who has completely given up all initiation (of actions), and who is My devotee is beloved to Me.

योो न हृष्यति न द्वेष्टि न शोचति न काङ्क्षति ।
शुभाशुभपरित्यागी भक्तिमान् यः स मे प्रियः ॥ १७ ॥

yo na hṛṣyati na dveṣṭi na śocati na kāṅkṣati
śubhāśubhaparityāgī bhaktimān yaḥ sa me priyaḥ (17)

The one who does not get elated, is not hostile, does not grieve, does not desire, who has completely given up good and bad (*karma*), who has devotion, is beloved to Me.

समः शत्रौ च मित्रे च तथा मानापमानयोः ।
शीतोष्णसुखदुःखेषु समः सङ्गविवर्जितः ॥ १८ ॥

samaḥ śatrau ca mitre ca tathā mānāpamānayoḥ
śītoṣṇasukhaduḥkheṣu samaḥ saṅgavivarjitaḥ (18)

The one who is the same with reference to an enemy and a friend, so too, honour and disgrace; the same with reference to cold, heat, pleasure and pain (and) free from attachment...

तुल्यनिन्दास्तुतिर्मौनी सन्तुष्टो येन केनचित् ।
अनिकेतः स्थिरमतिर्भक्तिमान्मे प्रियो नरः ॥ १९ ॥

tulyanindāstutirmaunī santuṣṭo yena kenacit
aniketaḥ sthiramatirbhaktimān me priyo naraḥ (19)

...the one who is equal to censure and praise, disciplined in speech, satisfied by whatever (he gets), who has no place to call his own, whose knowledge is firm, and who has devotion is beloved to Me.

ये तु धर्म्यामृतमिदं यथोक्तं पर्युपासते ।
श्रद्दधाना मत्परमा भक्तास्तेऽतीव मे प्रियाः ॥ २० ॥

ye tu dharmyāmṛtam idaṁ yathoktaṁ paryupāsate
śraddadhānā matparamā bhaktāste'tīva me priyāḥ (20)

However, those who follow this life that is in keeping with *dharma* leading to immortality, as was told, who are endowed with *śraddhā* and for whom I am the ultimate, those devotees are exceedingly beloved to Me.

ॐतत्सत्।
इति श्रीमद्भगवद्गीतासूपनिषत्सु ब्रह्मविद्यायां योगशास्त्रे श्रीकृष्णार्जुन-संवादे भक्ति-योगो नाम द्वादशोऽध्यायः ॥ १२ ॥

omtatsat.
iti śrīmadbhagavadgītāsūpaniṣatsu brahma-vidyāyāṁ yoga-śāstre śrīkṛṣṇārjunasaṁvāde bhakti-yogo nāma dvādaśo'dhyāyaḥ (12)

Om, Brahman, is the only reality. Thus ends the twelfth chapter called *bhakti-yoga*—having the topic of devotion—in the *Bhagavadgītā* which is in the form of a dialogue between Śrī Kṛṣṇa and Arjuna, which is the essence of the *Upaniṣads*, whose subject matter is both the knowledge of Brahman and *yoga*.

Chapter 13
क्षेत्र-क्षेत्रज्ञ-विभाग-योगः
Kṣetra-kṣetrajña-vibhāga-yogaḥ

Topic of the known and the knower

अर्जुन उवाच ।
प्रकृतिं पुरुषं चैव क्षेत्रं क्षेत्रज्ञमेव च ।
एतद्वेदितुमिच्छामि ज्ञानं ज्ञेयं च केशव[४४] ॥

arjuna uvāca
prakṛtiṁ puruṣaṁ caiva kṣetraṁ kṣetrajñam eva ca
etad veditum icchāmi jñānaṁ jñeyaṁ ca keśava

Arjuna said:
I wish to know this, Keśava (Kṛṣṇa)! *prakṛti* and *puruṣa*; the field and the knower of the field; the means of knowledge and what is to be known.

श्रीभगवानुवाच ।
इदं शरीरं कौन्तेय क्षेत्रमित्यभिधीयते ।
एतद्यो वेत्ति तं प्राहुः क्षेत्रज्ञ इति तद्विदः ॥ १ ॥

śrībhagavān uvāca
idaṁ śarīraṁ kaunteya kṣetram ityabhidhīyate
etadyo vetti taṁ prāhuḥ kṣetrajña iti tadvidaḥ (1)

Śrī Bhagavān said:
Kaunteya (Arjuna)! This body is called 'field.' The one who knows this (field) is 'the knower of the field;' thus say those who know that.

क्षेत्रज्ञं चापि मां विद्धि सर्वक्षेत्रेषु भारत ।
क्षेत्रक्षेत्रज्ञयोर्ज्ञानं यत्तज्ज्ञानं मतं मम ॥ २ ॥

kṣetrajñaṁ cāpi māṁ viddhi sarvakṣetreṣu bhārata
kṣetrakṣetrajñayorjñānaṁ yattajjñānaṁ mataṁ mama (2)

Bhārata (Arjuna)! May you know Me as the knower of the body in all the bodies. That (which is) knowledge of the body and of the knower of the body, is (truly) the knowledge. (This is) My vision.

तत्क्षेत्रं यच्च यादृक् च यद्विकारि यतश्च यत् ।
स च यो यत्प्रभावश्च तत्समासेन मे शृणु ॥ ३ ॥

tat kṣetraṁ yacca yādṛk ca yadvikāri yataśca yat
sa ca yo yatprabhāvaśca tat samāsena me śṛṇu (3)

What is that *kṣetra*, of what nature (it is), what are its modifications, from what has it come and who is the *kṣetrajña* and what is (his) glory—(for) that, listen to me in brief.

ऋषिभिर्बहुधा गीतं छन्दोभिर्विविधैः पृथक् ।
ब्रह्मसूत्रपदैश्चैव हेतुमद्भिर्विनिश्चितैः ॥ ४ ॥

ṛṣibhirbahudhā gītaṁ chandobhirvividhaiḥ pṛthak
brahmasūtrapadaiścaiva hetumadbhirviniścitaiḥ (4)

In many ways it is sung by the *ṛṣis*. It is also sung by the sentences of the Vedas as something that is varied and also as something that is distinct. And it is indeed explained by the sentences of the Veda, which reveal Brahman, without doubt, by implication, and with reasoning.

महाभूतान्यहङ्कारो बुद्धिरव्यक्तमेव च।
इन्द्रियाणि दशैकं च पञ्च चेन्द्रियगोचराः॥ ५॥
इच्छा द्वेषः सुखं दुःखं सङ्घातश्चेतना धृतिः।
एतत् क्षेत्रं समासेन सविकारमुदाहृतम्॥ ६॥

mahābhūtānyahaṅkāro buddhiravyaktam eva ca
indriyāṇi daśaikaṁ ca pañca cendriyagocarāḥ (5)
icchā dveṣaḥ sukhaṁ duḥkhaṁ saṅghātaścetanā dhṛtiḥ
etat kṣetraṁ samāsena savikāram udāhṛtam (6)

The (five) subtle elements, the *hiraṇyagarbha*, the *samaṣṭi-buddhi*, the unmanifest cause (*māyā*), the ten organs[45] and one (mind), the five sense objects, desire, aversion, pleasure, pain, the physical body, cognition, fortitude—(all) this is *kṣetra*, which is stated briefly along with its modifications.

अमानित्वमदम्भित्वमहिंसा क्षान्तिरार्जवम्।
आचार्योपासनं शौचं स्थैर्यमात्मविनिग्रहः॥ ७॥

amānitvam adambhitvam ahiṁsā kṣāntirārjavam
ācāryopāsanaṁ śaucaṁ sthairyam ātmavinigrahaḥ (7)

Absence of conceit, absence of pretension, not hurting, accommodation, straightforwardness, service to the teacher, cleanliness, steadfastness, mastery over the mind ...

इन्द्रियार्थेषु वैराग्यमनहङ्कार एव च।
जन्ममृत्युजराव्याधिदुःखदोषानुदर्शनम्॥ ८॥

indriyārtheṣu vairāgyam anahaṅkāra eva ca
janmamṛtyujarāvyādhiduḥkhadoṣānudarśanam (8)

...dispassion towards the sense objects, absence of pride and seeing clearly the defects of pain in birth, death, old age and disease...

असक्तिरनभिष्वङ्गः पुत्रदारगृहादिषु ।
नित्यं च समचित्तत्वमिष्टानिष्टोपपत्तिषु ॥ ९ ॥

asaktiranabhiṣvaṅgaḥ putradāragṛhādiṣu
nityaṁ ca samacittatvam iṣṭāniṣṭopapattiṣu (9)

...absence of sense of ownership, absence of obsession towards son, wife, house and the like, and constant evenness of mind regarding the gain of the desired and not desired...

मयि चानन्ययोगेन भक्तिरव्यभिचारिणी ।
विविक्तदेशसेवित्वमरतिर्जनसंसदि ॥ १० ॥

mayi cānanyayogena bhaktiravyabhicāriṇī
viviktadeśasevitvam aratirjanasaṁsadi (10)

...an unswerving devotion to me that is not connected to anything else, the disposition of repairing to a quiet place, no longing for the company of people...

अध्यात्मज्ञाननित्यत्वं तत्त्वज्ञानार्थदर्शनम् ।
एतज्ज्ञानमिति प्रोक्तमज्ञानं यदतोऽन्यथा ॥ ११ ॥

adhyātmajñānanityatvaṁ tattvajñānārthadarśanam
etajjñānam iti proktam ajñānaṁ yadato'nyathā (11)

...always (dwelling upon) knowledge centred on the self, keeping in view the purpose of knowledge of the truth—(all) this that was told is the means to knowledge, what is opposite to this is ignorance.

ज्ञेयं यत्तत्प्रवक्ष्यामि यज्ज्ञात्वामृतमश्नुते।
अनादिमत्परं ब्रह्म न सत्तन्नासदुच्यते॥ १२॥

jñeyaṁ yattat pravakṣyāmi yajjñātvāmṛtam aśnute
anādimatparaṁ brahma na sat tannāsad ucyate (12)

What is to be known, that I will tell clearly, knowing which one gains deathlessness. That is said to be Brahman, which has no beginning, is limitless, and is neither existent (as an object) nor non existent.

सर्वतः पाणिपादं तत्सर्वतोऽक्षिशिरोमुखम्।
सर्वतः श्रुतिमल्लोके सर्वमावृत्य तिष्ठति॥ १३॥

sarvataḥ pāṇipādaṁ tat sarvato'kṣiśiromukham
sarvataḥ śrutimalloke sarvam āvṛtya tiṣṭhati (13)

That (*jñeyaṁ brahma*) has hands and feet on all sides, has eyes, heads and mouths (faces) on all sides, has ears on all sides in the (bodies) of the people, and remains pervading everything.

सर्वेन्द्रियगुणाभासं सर्वेन्द्रियविवर्जितम्।
असक्तं सर्वभृच्चैव निर्गुणं गुणभोक्तृ च॥ १४॥

sarvendriyaguṇābhāsaṁ sarvendriyavivarjitam
asaktaṁ sarvabhṛccaiva nirguṇaṁ guṇabhoktṛ ca (14)

(That *jñeyaṁ brahma*) appears as one with attributes of organs, is free from all the organs, is unattached, is the sustainer of all, is free from the (three) qualities and is the experiencer of the (three) qualities.[46]

बहिरन्तश्च भूतानामचरं चरमेव च।
सूक्ष्मत्वात्तदविज्ञेयं दूरस्थं चान्तिके च तत्॥ १५॥

bahirantaśca bhūtānām acaraṁ caram eva ca
sukṣmatvāt tad avijñeyaṁ dūrasthaṁ cāntike ca tat (15)

That (*jñeyaṁ brahma*) is outside and inside of the beings, it is that which does not move and indeed what moves. Because it is subtle, it is not known and it is far as well as near.

अविभक्तं च भूतेषु विभक्तमिव च स्थितम् ।
भूतभर्तृ च तज्ज्ञेयं ग्रसिष्णु प्रभविष्णु च ॥ १६ ॥

avibhaktaṁ ca bhūteṣu vibhaktam iva ca sthitam
bhūtabhartṛ ca tajjñeyaṁ grasiṣṇu prabhaviṣṇu ca (16)

That *jñeyam* (*brahma*) remains undivided in the beings and is seemingly divided, is the sustainer of the beings and elements, and is the devourer and the creator.

ज्योतिषामपि तज्ज्योतिस्तमसः परमुच्यते ।
ज्ञानं ज्ञेयं ज्ञानगम्यं हृदि सर्वस्य विष्ठितम् ॥ १७ ॥

jyotiṣām api tajjyotistamasaḥ param ucyate
jñānaṁ jñeyaṁ jñānagamyaṁ hṛdi sarvasya viṣṭhitam (17)

That (*jñeyaṁ brahma*), the light of lights, is said to be beyond ignorance. It is knowledge, it is that which has to be known, it is that which is arrived at by knowledge and it is present in the minds of all.

इति क्षेत्रं तथा ज्ञानं ज्ञेयं चोक्तं समासतः ।
मद्भक्त एतद्विज्ञाय मद्भावायोपपद्यते ॥ १८ ॥

iti kṣetraṁ tathā jñānaṁ jñeyaṁ coktaṁ samāsataḥ
madbhakta etad vijñāya madbhāvāyopapadyate (18)

Thus, the *kṣetra* as well as the (means of gaining) knowledge and what is to be known have been told in brief. The one who is devoted to Me, knowing this clearly, is fit to gain the condition of being Me.

प्रकृतिं पुरुषं चैव विद्ध्यनादी उभावपि
विकारांश्च गुणांश्चैव विद्धि प्रकृतिसम्भवान् ॥ १९ ॥

prakṛtiṁ puruṣaṁ caiva viddhyanādī ubhāvapi
vikārāṁśca guṇāṁścaiva viddhi prakṛtisambhavān (19)

May you know that both *prakṛti* and *puruṣa* are indeed beginningless. May you (also) know that the modifications, and the qualities are indeed born of *prakṛti.*

कार्यकरणकर्तृत्वे हेतुः प्रकृतिरुच्यते ।
पुरुषः सुखदुःखानां भोक्तृत्वे हेतुरुच्यते ॥ २० ॥

kāryakaraṇakartṛtve hetuḥ prakṛtirucyate
puruṣaḥ sukhaduḥkhānāṁ bhoktṛtve heturucyate (20)

Prakṛti is said to be the cause in the creation of the physical body and the instruments; *puruṣa* is said to be the cause with reference to the state of being the experiencer of pleasure and pain.

पुरुषः प्रकृतिस्थो हि भुङ्क्ते प्रकृतिजान्गुणान् ।
कारणं गुणसङ्गोऽस्य सदसद्योनिजन्मसु ॥ २१ ॥

puruṣaḥ prakṛtistho hi bhuṅkte prakṛtijān guṇān
kāraṇaṁ guṇasaṅgo'sya sadasadyonijanmasu (21)

Because *puruṣa* (enjoyer, *jīva*) obtains in *prakṛti,* (he) enjoys the attributes born of *prakṛti.* His attachment to the attributes is the cause for births in higher and lower wombs.

उपद्रष्टानुमन्ता च भर्ता भोक्ता महेश्वरः ।
परमात्मेति चाप्युक्तो देहेऽस्मिन् पुरुषः परः ॥ २२ ॥

upadraṣṭānumantā ca bhartā bhoktā maheśvaraḥ
paramātmeti cāpyukto dehe'smin puruṣaḥ paraḥ (22)

The ultimate seer, permitter, sustainer, enjoyer, limitless Lord (creator), and also called 'limitless self,' is the *puruṣa*, the person who is limitless, in this body.

य एवं वेत्ति पुरुषं प्रकृतिं च गुणैः सह ।
सर्वथा वर्त्तमानोऽपि न स भूयोऽभिजायते ॥ २३ ॥

ya evaṁ vetti puruṣaṁ prakṛtiṁ ca guṇaiḥ saha
sarvathā varttamāno'pi na sa bhūyo'bhijāyate (23)

The one who knows in this manner, *puruṣa* and *prakṛti* along with its attributes, even though engaged in all ways, he is not born again.

ध्यानेनात्मनि पश्यन्ति केचिदात्मानमात्मना ।
अन्ये साङ्ख्येन योगेन कर्मयोगेन चापरे ॥ २४ ॥

dhyānenātmani paśyanti kecid ātmānam ātmanā
anye sāṅkhyena yogena karmayogena cāpare (24)

By contemplation some see the self, in the self (mind), with the self (the prepared mind), others by enquiry and some others by *karma-yoga*.

अन्ये त्वेवमजानन्तः श्रुत्वान्येभ्य उपासते ।
तेऽपि चातितरन्त्येव मृत्युं श्रुतिपरायणाः ॥ २५ ॥

anye tvevam ajānantaḥ śrutvānyebhya upāsate
te'pi cātitarantyeva mṛtyuṁ śrutiparāyaṇāḥ (25)

But others, not knowing in this manner, having heard from others (their teachers), being committed to what they have heard, follow (that), and indeed, they also cross death.

यावत्सञ्जायते किञ्चित्सत्त्वं स्थावरजङ्गमम्।
क्षेत्रक्षेत्रज्ञसंयोगात्तद्विद्धि भरतर्षभ॥ २६॥

yāvat sañjāyate kiñcit sattvaṁ sthāvarajaṅgamam
kṣetrakṣetrajñasaṁyogāt tadviddhi bharatarṣabha (26)

As long as any existent thing—moving or non-moving—is born, that may you know, Arjuna, the foremost in the clan of Bharata! is because of the connection between the *kṣetra* and the *kṣetrajña*.

समं सर्वेषु भूतेषु तिष्ठन्तं परमेश्वरम्।
विनश्यत्स्वविनश्यन्तं यः पश्यति स पश्यति॥ २७॥

samaṁ sarveṣu bhūteṣu tiṣṭhantaṁ parameśvaram
vinaśyatsvavinaśyantaṁ yaḥ paśyati sa paśyati (27)

The one who sees the Lord, as remaining the same in all beings, as the one who is not being destroyed, in the things that are perishing, he alone sees.

समं पश्यन्हि सर्वत्र समवस्थितमीश्वरम्।
न हिनस्त्यात्मनात्मानं ततो याति परां गतिम्॥ २८॥

samaṁ paśyanhi sarvatra samavasthitamīśvaram
na hinastyātmanātmānaṁ tato yāti parāṁ gatim (28)

Because of seeing the Lord as the same, as the one who obtains in the same form everywhere, he does not destroy himself by himself. Therefore, he reaches the ultimate end.

प्रकृत्यैव च कर्माणि क्रियमाणानि सर्वशः ।
यः पश्यति तथात्मानमकर्तारं स पश्यति ॥ २९ ॥

prakṛtyaiva ca karmāṇi kriyamāṇāni sarvaśaḥ
yaḥ paśyati tathātmānam akartāraṁ sa paśyati (29)

He who sees that by *prakṛti* alone actions are being performed in all ways, and so too, (he who sees) the self as a non-doer, he alone sees.

यदा भूतपृथग्भावमेकस्थमनुपश्यति ।
तत एव च विस्तारं ब्रह्म सम्पद्यते तदा ॥ ३० ॥

yadā bhūtapṛthagbhāvam ekastham anupaśyati
tata eva ca vistāraṁ brahma sampadyate tadā (30)

When one sees clearly, the condition of distinction in the beings, as having its existence in one (*ātman*), and from that alone is its projection (distinctions), then he gains Brahman.

अनादित्वान्निर्गुणत्वात्परमात्मायमव्ययः ।
शरीरस्थोऽपि कौन्तेय न करोति न लिप्यते ॥ ३१ ॥

anāditvānnirguṇatvāt paramātmāyam avyayaḥ
śarīrastho'pi kaunteya na karoti na lipyate (31)

Kaunteya (Arjuna)! This limitless self, being beginningless and without attributes, is imperishable. Even though obtaining in the body, it does not perform action, and is not affected (by results of actions).

यथा सर्वगतं सौक्ष्म्यादाकाशं नोपलिप्यते ।
सर्वत्रावस्थितो देहे तथात्मा नोपलिप्यते ॥ ३२ ॥

yathā sarvagataṁ saukṣmyād ākāśaṁ nopalipyate
sarvatrāvasthito dehe tathātmā nopalipyate (32)

Just as all pervasive space, because it is subtle, is not affected, so too, the self, abiding in all states in the body is not affected.

यथा प्रकाशयत्येकः कृत्स्नं लोकमिमं रविः ।
क्षेत्रं क्षेत्री तथा कृत्स्नं प्रकाशयति भारत ॥ ३३ ॥

yathā prakāśayatyekaḥ kṛtsnaṁ lokam imaṁ raviḥ
kṣetraṁ kṣetrī tathā kṛtsnaṁ prakāśayati bhārata (33)

Bhārata (Arjuna)! Just as one sun illumines this entire world, so too, the *kṣetrī*, one who obtains in the *kṣetra*, illumines the entire *kṣetra*.

क्षेत्रक्षेत्रज्ञयोरेवमन्तरं ज्ञानचक्षुषा ।
भूतप्रकृतिमोक्षं च ये विदुर्यान्ति ते परम् ॥ ३४ ॥

kṣetrakṣetrajñayorevam antaraṁ jñānacakṣuṣā
bhūtaprakṛtimokṣaṁ ca ye viduryānti te param (34)

Those who, in this manner, know the distinction between the *kṣetra* and the *kṣetrajña* through the eye of wisdom and (know) the freedom from *prakṛti*, the cause of the beings, they go to the ultimate end.

ॐतत्सत् ।
इति श्रीमद्भगवद्गीतासूपनिषत्सु ब्रह्मविद्यायां योगशास्त्रे श्रीकृष्णार्जुन-संवादे क्षेत्र-क्षेत्रज्ञ-विभाग-योगो नाम त्रयोदशोऽध्यायः ॥ १३ ॥

omtatsat.
iti śrīmadbhagavadgītāsūpaniṣatsu brahma-vidyāyāṁ yogaśāstre śrīkṛṣṇārjunasaṁvāde kṣetra-kṣetrajña-vibhāga-yogo nāma trayodaśo'dhyāyaḥ (13)

Om, Brahman, is the only reality. Thus ends the thirteenth chapter called *kṣetra-kṣetrajña-vibhāga-yoga*—having the topic of the known and the knower—in the *Bhagavadgītā* which is in the form of a dialogue between Śrī Kṛṣṇa and Arjuna, which is the essence of the *Upaniṣads*, whose subject matter is both the knowledge of Brahman and *yoga*.

Chapter 14
गुणत्रय-विभाग-योगः
Guṇatraya-vibhāga-yogaḥ

Topic of the division of the three *guṇas*

श्रीभगवानुवाच ।
परं भूयः प्रवक्ष्यामि ज्ञानानां ज्ञानमुत्तमम् ।
यज्ज्ञात्वा मुनयः सर्वे परां सिद्धिमितो गताः ॥ १ ॥

śrībhagavān uvāca
paraṁ bhūyaḥ pravakṣyāmi jñānānāṁ jñānam uttamam
yajjñātvā munayaḥ sarve parāṁ siddhim ito gatāḥ (1)

Śrī Bhagavān said:
I shall again tell clearly the ultimate, the most exalted knowledge among all forms of knowledge, gaining which all the sages had reached the ultimate success (release) from this (body).

इदं ज्ञानमुपाश्रित्य मम साधर्म्यमागताः ।
सर्गेऽपि नोपजायन्ते प्रलये न व्यथन्ति च ॥ २ ॥

idaṁ jñānam upāśritya mama sādharmyam āgatāḥ
sarge'pi nopajāyante pralaye na vyathanti ca (2)

Resorting to this knowledge, those who have gained oneness with Me, do not come to be born even when there is creation, and they do not perish in the dissolution (of creation).

मम योनिर्महद्ब्रह्म तस्मिन्गर्भं दधाम्यहम् ।
सम्भवः सर्वभूतानां ततो भवति भारत ॥ ३ ॥

mama yonirmahadbrahma tasmingarbhaṁ dadhāmyaham
sambhavaḥ sarvabhūtānāṁ tato bhavati bhārata (3)

Bhārata (Arjuna)! My *māyā* is the primordial cause out of which (everything) grows and which sustains (everything). That I impregnate. From that occurs the manifestation of all beings.

सर्वयोनिषु कौन्तेय मूर्तयः सम्भवन्ति याः ।
तासां ब्रह्म महद्योनिरहं बीजप्रदः पिता ॥ ४ ॥

sarvayoniṣu kaunteya mūrtayaḥ sambhavanti yāḥ
tāsāṁ brahma mahadyoniraham bījapradaḥ pitā (4)

Kaunteya (Arjuna)! The great (*māyā*) is the original (material) cause for those forms which are born in all wombs. I am the one who gives the seed, the father.

सत्त्वं रजस्तम इति गुणाः प्रकृतिसम्भवाः ।
निबध्नन्ति महाबाहो देहे देहिनमव्ययम् ॥ ५ ॥

sattvaṁ rajastama iti guṇāḥ prakṛtisambhavāḥ
nibadhnanti mahābāho dehe dehinam avyayam (5)

Arjuna, the mighty armed! *Sattva, rajas,* and *tamas,* the qualities existing in *prakṛti,* bind (as though) the changeless indweller of the body, to the body.

तत्र सत्त्वं निर्मलत्वात्प्रकाशकमनामयम् ।
सुखसङ्गेन बध्नाति ज्ञानसङ्गेन चानघ ॥ ६ ॥

tatra sattvaṁ nirmalatvāt prakāśakam anāmayam
sukhasaṅgena badhnāti jñānasaṅgena cānagha (6)

Arjuna, sinless one! There (among these), *sattva,* because it is pure, is illuminating and is free from affliction.

It binds (one) by connection to (subtle form of) pleasure and connection to knowledge.

रजो रागात्मकं विद्धि तृष्णासङ्गसमुद्भवम् ।
तन्निबध्नाति कौन्तेय कर्मसङ्गेन देहिनम् ॥ ७ ॥

rajo rāgātmakaṁ viddhi tṛṣṇāsaṅgasamudbhavam
tannibadhnāti kaunteya karmasaṅgena dehinam (7)

Kaunteya (Arjuna)! *Rajas,* may you know, is in the form of a colouring (of the mind), causing longing and well-entrenched attachment. It totally binds the indweller of the body by connection with action.

तमस्त्वज्ञानजं विद्धि मोहनं सर्वदेहिनाम् ।
प्रमादालस्यनिद्राभिस्तन्निबध्नाति भारत ॥ ८ ॥

tamastvajñānajaṁ viddhi mohanaṁ sarvadehinām
pramādālasyanidrābhistannibadhnāti bhārata (8)

Bhārata (Arjuna)! *Tamas,* may you know, is born of ignorance and causes delusion for all those who have bodies. It binds (the person) completely by indifference, slothfulness and sleep.

सत्त्वं सुखे सञ्जयति रजः कर्मणि भारत ।
ज्ञानमावृत्य तु तमः प्रमादे सञ्जयत्युत ॥ ९ ॥

sattvaṁ sukhe sañjayati rajaḥ karmaṇi bhārata
jñānam āvṛtya tu tamaḥ pramāde sañjayatyuta (9)

Bhārata (Arjuna)! *Sattva* binds in the form of pleasure, and *rajas* in the form of action. *Tamas,* on the other hand, covering knowledge, binds indeed in the form of apathy.

रजस्तमश्चाभिभूय सत्त्वं भवति भारत।
रजः सत्त्वं तमश्चैव तमः सत्त्वं रजस्तथा॥ १०॥

rajastamaścābhibhūya sattvaṁ bhavati bhārata
rajaḥ sattvaṁ tamaścaiva tamaḥ sattvaṁ rajastathā (10)

Bhārata (Arjuna)! *Sattva* arises overwhelming *rajas* and *tamas*. *Raja*s indeed (arises overwhelming) *tamas* and *sattva*. So too, *tamas* (arises overwhelming) *rajas* and *sattva*.

सर्वद्वारेषु देहेऽस्मिन्प्रकाश उपजायते।
ज्ञानं यदा तदा विद्याद्विवृद्धं सत्त्वमित्युत॥ ११॥

sarvadvāreṣu dehe'smin prakāśa upajāyate
jñānaṁ yadā tadā vidyād vivṛddhaṁ sattvamityuta (11)

When illumination, that is knowledge, is born in all the sense organs, in this body, then may one know indeed that *sattva* is predominant.

लोभः प्रवृत्तिरारम्भः कर्मणामशमः स्पृहा।
रजस्येतानि जायन्ते विवृद्धे भरतर्षभ॥ १२॥

lobhaḥ pravṛttirārambhaḥ karmaṇām aśamaḥ spṛhā
rajasyetāni jāyante vivṛddhe bharatarṣabha (12)

Arjuna, the foremost in the clan of Bharata! Greed, physical restlessness, undertaking of activities, mental restlessness, longing—these are born when *rajas* has increased.

अप्रकाशोऽप्रवृत्तिश्च प्रमादो मोह एव च।
तमस्येतानि जायन्ते विवृद्धे कुरुनन्दन॥ १३॥

aprakāśo'pravṛttiśca pramādo moha eva ca
tamasyetāni jāyante vivṛddhe kurunandana (13)

Arjuna, the joy of the Kuru family! Dullness, absence of activity, indifference, and indeed delusion—these are born, when *tamas* has increased.

यदा सत्त्वे प्रवृद्धे तु प्रलयं याति देहभृत्।
तदोत्तमविदां लोकानमलान्प्रतिपद्यते ॥ १४ ॥

yadā sattve pravṛddhe tu pralayaṁ yāti dehabhṛt
tadottamavidāṁ lokān amalān pratipadyate (14)

When the embodied one dies, when *sattva* has increased, then he gains the worlds of those who know the highest, that are free from impurity.

रजसि प्रलयं गत्वा कर्मसङ्गिषु जायते।
तथा प्रलीनस्तमसि मूढयोनिषु जायते ॥ १५ ॥

rajasi pralayaṁ gatvā karmasaṅgiṣu jāyate
tathā pralīnastamasi mūḍhayoniṣu jāyate (15)

Having died with the predominance of *rajas*, he is born among those committed to *karma*; so too, the one who died with the predominance of *tamas* is born in the wombs of those who have no discriminative faculty.

कर्मणः सुकृतस्याहुः सात्त्विकं निर्मलं फलम्।
रजसस्तु फलं दुःखमज्ञानं तमसः फलम् ॥ १६ ॥

karmaṇaḥ sukṛtasyāhuḥ sāttvikaṁ nirmalaṁ phalam
rajasastu phalaṁ duḥkham ajñānaṁ tamasaḥ phalam (16)

They say, that the result for the good action done is connected to *sattva* and is pure (a result that is free from any distress). But pain is the result of *rajas* and ignorance is the result of *tamas*.

सत्त्वात्सञ्जायते ज्ञानं रजसो लोभ एव च।
प्रमादमोहौ तमसो भवतोऽज्ञानमेव च॥ १७॥

sattvāt sañjāyate jñānaṁ rajaso lobha eva ca
pramādamohau tamaso bhavato'jñānam eva ca (17)

From *sattva* is born knowledge and indeed from *rajas* is greed. Apathy and delusion are from *tamas* and so also is ignorance.

ऊर्ध्वं गच्छन्ति सत्त्वस्था मध्ये तिष्ठन्ति राजसाः।
जघन्यगुणवृत्तिस्था अधो गच्छन्ति तामसाः॥ १८॥

ūrdhvaṁ gacchanti sattvasthā madhye tiṣṭhanti rājasāḥ
jaghanyaguṇavṛttisthā adho gacchanti tāmasāḥ (18)

Those abiding in *sattva* go (to the worlds) higher up, those belonging to *rajas* remain in the middle and those belonging to *tamas*, having the nature of the lowest *guṇa*, go down.

नान्यं गुणेभ्यः कर्तारं यदा द्रष्टानुपश्यति।
गुणेभ्यश्च परं वेत्ति मद्भावं सोऽधिगच्छति॥ १९॥

nānyaṁ guṇebhyaḥ kartāraṁ yadā draṣṭānupaśyati
guṇebhyaśca paraṁ vetti madbhāvaṁ so'dhigacchati (19)

When the seer does not see an agent other than the *guṇa*s and when he knows (himself as) beyond the *guṇa*s, he gains (understands) My nature.

गुणानेतानतीत्य त्रीन्देही देहसमुद्भवान्।
जन्ममृत्युजरादुःखैर्विमुक्तोऽमृतमश्नुते॥ २०॥

guṇān etānatītya trīndehī dehasamudbhavān
janmamṛtyujarāduḥkhairvimukto'mṛtam aśnute (20)

Crossing these three *guṇa*s, that are the cause of the body, the embodied one, released from birth, death, old age and sorrow, gains immortality.

अर्जुन उवाच ।
कैर्लिङ्गैस्त्रीन्गुणानेतानतीतो भवति प्रभो ।
किमाचारः कथं चैतांस्त्रीन्गुणानतिवर्तते ॥ २१ ॥

arjuna uvāca
kairliṅgaistrīnguṇānetānatīto bhavati prabho
kimācāraḥ kathaṁ caitāṁstrīnguṇānativartate (21)

Arjuna said:
O Lord! By what characteristics does a person become (recognizable as) one who has crossed these three *guṇa*s? What is his conduct, and how does he transcend these three *guṇa*s?

श्रीभगवानुवाच ।
प्रकाशं च प्रवृतिं च मोहमेव च पाण्डव ।
न द्वेष्टि सम्प्रवृत्तानि न निवृत्तानि काङ्क्षति ॥ २२ ॥

śrībhagavān uvāca
prakāśaṁ ca pravṛttiṁ ca moham eva ca pāṇḍava
na dveṣṭi sampravṛttāni na nivṛttāni kāṅkṣati (22)

Śrī Bhagavān said:
Pāṇḍava (Arjuna)! Brightness and activity and even delusion, that have come to occur, he does not despise. Nor does he long for those that have gone away.

उदासीनवदासीनो गुणैर्यो न विचाल्यते ।
गुणा वर्तन्त इत्येव योऽवतिष्ठति नेङ्गते ॥ २३ ॥

समदुःखसुखः स्वस्थः समलोष्टाश्मकाञ्चनः ।
तुल्यप्रियाप्रियो धीरस्तुल्यनिन्दात्मसंस्तुतिः ॥ २४ ॥
मानापमानयोस्तुल्यस्तुल्यो मित्रारिपक्षयोः ।
सर्वारम्भपरित्यागी गुणातीतः स उच्यते ॥ २५ ॥

udāsīnavadāsīno guṇairyo na vicālyate
guṇā vartanta ityeva yo'vatiṣṭhati neṅgate (23)
samaduḥkhasukhaḥ svasthaḥ samaloṣṭāśmakāñcanaḥ
tulyapriyāpriyo dhīrastulyanindātmasaṁstutiḥ (24)
mānāpamānayostulyastulyo mitrāripakṣayoḥ
sarvārambhaparityāgī guṇātītaḥ sa ucyate (25)

He who, remaining as though indifferent, is not shaken by the *guṇas*; and he who abides (in himself), (thinking) that the *guṇas* alone are acting, the one who does not move (from the vision of the self) ...

... who, being wise, is the same with reference to pleasure and pain, abiding in himself, the same with reference to a clod of earth, a stone or gold, the same in pleasant and unpleasant (situations), the same with reference to censure or praise of himself ...

... who is the same towards respect and insult, the same towards the views of a friend or an enemy, who has given up all undertakings—he is called the one who is beyond the *guṇas*.

मां च योऽव्यभिचारेण भक्तियोगेन सेवते ।
स गुणान्समतीत्यैतान्ब्रह्मभूयाय कल्पते ॥ २६ ॥

māṁ ca yo'vyabhicāreṇa bhaktiyogena sevate
sa guṇān samatītyaitān brahmabhūyāya kalpate (26)

And the one who with unswerving devotion worships/ seeks Me, he is fit for being Brahman, having properly crossed these *guṇas*.

ब्रह्मणो हि प्रतिष्ठाहममृतस्याव्ययस्य च ।
शाश्वतस्य च धर्मस्य सुखस्यैकान्तिकस्य च ॥ २७ ॥

brahmaṇo hi pratiṣṭhāham amṛtasyāvyayasya ca
śāśvatasya ca dharmasya sukhasyaikāntikasya ca (27)

I am the basis indeed of Brahman which is immortal, not subject to change, the eternal *dharma*, the basis of everything, and which is of the nature of happiness that is not subject to negation.

ॐ तत्सत् ।
इति श्रीमद्भगवद्गीतासूपनिषत्सु ब्रह्मविद्यायां योगशास्त्रे श्रीकृष्णार्जुन-संवादे गुणत्रय-विभाग-योगो नाम चतुर्दशोऽध्यायः ॥ १४ ॥

omtatsat.
iti śrīmadbhagavadgītāsūpaniṣatsu brahma-vidyāyāṁ yoga-śāstre śrīkṛṣṇārjunasaṁvāde guṇatraya-vibhāga-yogo nāma caturdaśo'dhyāyaḥ (14)

Om, Brahman, is the only reality. Thus ends the fourteenth chapter called *guṇatraya-vibhāga-yoga*—having the topic of the division of the three *guṇas*— in the *Bhagavadgītā* which is in the form of a dialogue between Śrī Kṛṣṇa and Arjuna, which is the essence of the *Upaniṣads*, whose subject matter is both the knowledge of Brahman and *yoga*.

Chapter 15

पुरुषोत्तम-योगः

Puruṣottama-yogaḥ

Topic of the Whole Person

श्रीभगवानुवाच ।
ऊर्ध्वमूलमधःशाखमश्वत्थं प्राहुरव्ययम् ।
छन्दांसि यस्य पर्णानि यस्तं वेद स वेदवित् ॥ १ ॥

śrībhagavān uvāca
ūrdhvamūlam adhaḥśākham aśvatthaṁ prāhuravyayam
chandāṁsi yasya parṇāni yastaṁ veda sa vedavit (1)

Śrī Bhagavān said:
They say the imperishable *aśvattha* tree has its roots above, its branches below and the Vedas are its leaves. The one who knows that is a knower of the Veda.

अधश्चोर्ध्वं प्रसृतास्तस्य शाखाः गुणप्रवृद्धा विषयप्रवालाः ।
अधश्च मूलान्यनुसन्ततानि कर्मानुबन्धीनि मनुष्यलोके ॥ २ ॥

adhaścordhvaṁ prasṛtāstasya śākhāḥ
guṇapravṛddhā viṣayapravālāḥ
adhaśca mūlānyanusantatāni
karmānubandhīni manuṣyaloke (2)

Its branches that are nourished by the *guṇa*s, with sense objects as their shoots are spread out below and above. And below, the diffused roots are the *karma*s that bind (one) in the world of mortals.

न रूपमस्येह तथोपलभ्यते नान्तो न चादिर्न च सम्प्रतिष्ठा ।
अश्वत्थमेनं सुविरूढमूलम् असङ्गशस्त्रेण दृढेन छित्वा ॥ ३ ॥

ततः पदं तत्परिमार्गितव्यं यस्मिन्गता न निवर्तन्ति भूयः ।
तमेव चाद्यं पुरुषं प्रपद्ये यतः प्रवृत्तिः प्रसृता पुराणी ॥ ४ ॥

na rūpam asyeha tathopalabhyate
nānto na cādirna ca sampratiṣṭhā
aśvattham enaṁ suvirūḍhamūlam
asaṅgaśastreṇa dṛḍhena chitvā (3)
tataḥ padaṁ tat parimārgitavyaṁ
yasmin gatā na nivartanti bhūyaḥ
tam eva cādyaṁ puruṣaṁ prapadye
yataḥ pravṛttiḥ prasṛtā purāṇī (4)

Its form is not as it is perceived here. It has no end, no beginning, and no continuance in between. After cutting this *aśvattha* tree, whose roots are well entrenched, with the firm weapon of detachment,...

...then, that end, into which those who have gone do not return again, is to be properly inquired into (with the attitude that) I surrender to that *ādi-puruṣa* alone, from whom the primeval creation has come forth.

निर्मानमोहा जितसङ्गदोषाः अध्यात्मनित्या विनिवृत्तकामाः ।
द्वन्द्वैर्विमुक्ताः सुखदुःखसञ्ज्ञैः गच्छन्त्यमूढाः पदमव्ययं तत् ॥ ५॥

nirmānamohā jitasaṅgadoṣāḥ
adhyātmanityā vinivṛttakāmāḥ
dvandvairvimuktāḥ sukhaduḥkhasañjñaiḥ
gacchantyamūḍhāḥ padam avyayaṁ tat (5)

Those who are free from the demand for respect and from non-objectivity, who have conquered the limitation of attachment, who are always focused on the self and from whom desires have completely gone, who are totally free from the opposites known as pleasure and suffering and are not deluded, go to (gain) that imperishable end.

न तद्भासयते सूर्यो न शशाङ्को न पावकः ।
यद्गत्वा न निवर्तन्ते तद्धाम परमं मम ॥ ६ ॥

na tad bhāsayate sūryo na śaśāṅko na pāvakaḥ
yad gatvā na nivartante tad dhāma paramaṁ mama (6)

Neither the sun, nor moon, nor fire, illumines that having gone to which, they do not return. That is My limitless abode.

ममैवांशो जीवलोके जीवभूतः सनातनः ।
मनःषष्ठानीन्द्रियाणि प्रकृतिस्थानि कर्षति ॥ ७ ॥
शरीरं यदवाप्नोति यच्चाप्युत्क्रामतीश्वरः ।
गृहीत्वैतानि संयाति वायुर्गन्धानिवाशयात् ॥ ८ ॥

mamaivāṁśo jīvaloke jīvabhūtaḥ sanātanaḥ
manaḥṣaṣṭhānīndriyāṇi prakṛtisthāni karṣati (7)
śarīraṁ yad avāpnoti yaccāpyutkrāmatīśvaraḥ
gṛhītvaitāni saṁyāti vāyurgandhān ivāśayāt (8)

In the world of living beings, a part of Me alone exists as the *jīva*, which is eternal. When the one who rules (the body) departs, he draws to himself the five senses and the mind, the sixth, obtaining in the body. When he obtains a new body, he goes, taking these (the sense organs and the mind) with him just as the wind (would carry) the fragrance from their sources (the flowers).

श्रोत्रं चक्षुः स्पर्शनं च रसनं घ्राणमेव च ।
अधिष्ठाय मनश्चायं विषयानुपसेवते ॥ ९ ॥

śrotraṁ cakṣuḥ sparśanaṁ ca rasanaṁ ghrāṇam eva ca
adhiṣṭhāya manaścāyaṁ viṣayān upasevate (9)

Presiding over the ear, the eye, the senses of touch, taste, and smell, and the mind, this person (*jīva*) experiences the sense objects.

उत्क्रामन्तं स्थितं वापि भुञ्जानं वा गुणान्वितम्।
विमूढा नानुपश्यन्ति पश्यन्ति ज्ञानचक्षुसः॥ १०॥

utkrāmantaṁ sthitaṁ vāpi bhuñjānaṁ vā guṇānvitam
vimūḍhā nānupaśyanti paśyanti jñānacakṣusaḥ (10)

The deluded do not see the one who is departing (from the body) or even remaining (in this body), experiencing or endowed with the *guṇas*. Those who have the eye of wisdom, see.

यतन्तो योगिनश्चैनं पश्यन्त्यात्मन्यवस्थितम्।
यतन्तोऽप्यकृतात्मानो नैनं पश्यन्त्यचेतसः॥ ११॥

yatanto yoginaścainaṁ paśyantyātmanyavasthitam
yatanto'pyakṛtātmāno nainaṁ paśyantyacetasaḥ (11)

The *yogins*, who are making effort, see this self obtaining in the *buddhi*. Those whose minds are not mature and who do not have *viveka*, do not see this (*ātman*) even if they are making effort.

यदादित्यगतं तेजो जगद्भासयतेऽखिलम्।
यच्चन्द्रमसि यच्चाग्नौ तत्तेजो विद्धि मामकम्॥ १२॥

yad ādityagataṁ tejo jagad bhāsayate'khilam
yaccandramasi yaccāgnau tattejo viddhi māmakam (12)

May you know that the brilliance that obtains in the sun and illumines the entire world, that which is in the moon, and which is in the fire, belongs to Me.

गामाविश्य च भूतानि धारयाम्यहमोजसा।
पुष्णामि चौषधीस्सर्वाः सोमो भूत्वा रसात्मकः॥ १३॥

gām āviśya ca bhūtāni dhārayāmyaham ojasā
puṣṇāmi cauṣadhīssarvāḥ somo bhūtvā rasātmakaḥ (13)

Having entered the earth, I sustain the beings with strength, and I nourish all the vegetation, having become *soma* in the form of (their) essence.

अहं वैश्वानरो भूत्वा प्राणिनां देहमाश्रितः।
प्राणापानसमायुक्तः पचाम्यन्नं चतुर्विधम्॥ १४॥

ahaṁ vaiśvānaro bhūtvā prāṇināṁ deham āśritaḥ
prāṇāpānasamāyuktaḥ pacāmyannaṁ caturvidham (14)

Having become the digestive fire obtaining in the bodies of living beings, endowed with *prāṇa* and *apāna*, I digest the four-fold food.

सर्वस्य चाहं हृदि सन्निविष्टो मत्तः स्मृतिर्ज्ञानमपोहनं च।
वेदैश्च सर्वैरहमेव वेद्यो वेदान्तकृद्वेदविदेव चाहम्॥ १५॥

sarvasya cāhaṁ hṛdi sanniviṣṭo
mattaḥ smṛtirjñānam apohanaṁ ca
vedaiśca sarvairaham eva vedyo
vedāntakṛd vedavid eva cāham (15)

I have entered the hearts of all. From Me (have come) memory, knowledge, and forgetfulness. I alone am the one to be known by all the Vedas and I alone am the author of the Vedanta (*vedanta-sampradāya*) and the knower of the Vedas.

द्वाविमौ पुरुषौ लोके क्षरश्चाक्षर एव च।
क्षरः सर्वाणि भूतानि कूटस्थोऽक्षर उच्यते॥ १६॥

dvāvimau puruṣau loke kṣaraścākṣara eva ca
kṣaraḥ sarvāṇi bhūtāni kūṭastho'kṣara ucyate (16)

These two persons, the perishable and the imperishable, (exist) in the world. All beings and elements are called the perishable, the changeless (is called) the imperishable.

उत्तमः पुरुषस्त्वन्यः परमात्मेत्युदाहृतः ।
यो लोकत्रयमाविश्य बिभर्त्यव्यय ईश्वरः ॥ १७ ॥

uttamaḥ puruṣastvanyaḥ paramātmetyudāhṛtaḥ
yo lokatrayamāviśya bibhartyavyaya īśvaraḥ (17)

But the other superior person is called the *paramātman*, limitless self, the changeless Lord who, having entered the three worlds, sustains (them).

यस्मात्क्षरमतीतोऽहमक्षरादपि चोत्तमः ।
अतोऽस्मि लोके वेदे च प्रथितः पुरुषोत्तमः ॥ १८ ॥

yasmāt kṣaram atīto'ham akṣarād api cottamaḥ
ato'smi loke vede ca prathitaḥ puruṣottamaḥ (18)

Because I am beyond the perishable and above the imperishable too; therefore, in the world and in the Veda, I am renowned as Puruṣottama.

यो मामेवमसम्मूढो जानाति पुरुषोत्तमम् ।
स सर्वविद्भजति मां सर्वभावेन भारत ॥ १९ ॥

yo mām evam asammūḍho jānāti puruṣottamam
sa sarvavid bhajati māṁ sarvabhāvena bhārata (19)

The one who is not deluded, who knows Me in this way, he, (becoming) the knower of (that which is) all, gains Me as the self of all, Bhārata (Arjuna)!

इति गुह्यतमं शास्त्रमिदमुक्तं मयानघ ।
एतद् बुद्ध्वा बुद्धिमान्स्यात्कृतकृत्यश्च भारत ॥ २० ॥

iti guhyatamaṁ śāstram idam uktaṁ mayānagha
etad buddhvā buddhimān syāt kṛtakṛtyaśca bhārata (20)

Bhārata (Arjuna)! The sinless one! This most profound teaching has thus been said by Me. Knowing this, a person becomes (wise), one who has *buddhi*; and who has accomplished all that has to be accomplished.

ॐतत्सत् ।
इति श्रीमद्भगवद्गीतासूपनिषत्सु ब्रह्मविद्यायां योगशास्त्रे श्रीकृष्णार्जुन-संवादे पुरुषोत्तम-योगो नाम पञ्चदशोऽध्यायः ॥ १५ ॥

omtatsat.
iti śrīmadbhagavadgītāsūpaniṣatsu brahma-vidyāyāṁ yoga-śāstre śrīkṛṣṇārjunasaṁvāde puruṣottama-yogo nāma pañcadaśo'dhyāyaḥ (15)

Om, Brahman, is the only reality. Thus ends the fifteenth chapter called *puruṣottama-yoga*—having the topic of the Whole Person—in the *Bhagavadgītā* which is in the form of a dialogue between Śrī Kṛṣṇa and Arjuna, which is the essence of the *Upaniṣads*, whose subject matter is both the knowledge of Brahman and *yoga*.

Chapter 16

दैवासुर-सम्पद्-विभाग-योगः

Daivāsura-sampad-vibhāga-yogaḥ

Topic of description of becoming and unbecoming dispositions

श्रीभगवानुवाच ।
अभयं सत्त्वसंशुद्धिर्ज्ञानयोगव्यवस्थितिः ।
दानं दमश्च यज्ञश्च स्वाध्यायस्तप आर्जवम् ॥ १ ॥
अहिंसा सत्यमक्रोधस्त्यागः शान्तिरपैशुनम् ।
दया भूतेष्वलोलुप्त्वं मार्दवं ह्रीरचापलम् ॥ २ ॥
तेजः क्षमा धृतिः शौचमद्रोहो नातिमानिता ।
भवन्ति सम्पदं दैवीमभिजातस्य भारत ॥ ३ ॥

śrībhagavān uvāca
abhayaṁ sattvasaṁśuddhirjñānayogavyavasthitiḥ
dānaṁ damaśca yajñaśca svādhyāyastapa ārjavam (1)
ahiṁsā satyamakrodhastyāgaḥ śāntirapaiśunam
dayā bhūteṣvaloluptvaṁ mārdavaṁ hrīracāpalam (2)
tejaḥ kṣamā dhṛtiḥ śaucamadroho nātimānitā
bhavanti sampadaṁ daivīmabhijātasya bhārata (3)

Śrī Bhagavān said:
Bhārata (Arjuna)! Freedom from fear, purity of mind, steadiness in contemplation, charity, judicious restraint (of sense organs), performing rituals, recitation of one's own branch of the Veda, religious discipline (austerity), alignment of thought, word, and deed...
...absence of hurting, truthfulness, resolution of anger, renunciation, resolution of the mind, absence of calumny, compassion for living beings, absence of ardent longing,

softness, modesty, absence of physical agitation...
...brilliance, composure, fortitude, cleanliness, no thought of hurting, and no exaggerated self opinion—all these are there for the one who is born to the wealth of *deva*s.

दम्भो दर्पोऽभिमानश्च क्रोधः पारुष्यमेव च ।
अज्ञानं चाभिजातस्य पार्थ सम्पदमासुरीम् ॥ ४ ॥

dambho darpo'bhimānaśca krodhaḥ pāruṣyam eva ca
ajñānaṁ cābhijātasya pārtha sampadam āsurīm (4)

Pārtha (Arjuna)! The one who is born to the wealth of an *asura*, has hypocrisy with reference to *dharma*, pride, a tendency to demand respect, anger, harshness, and indeed, a lack of discrimination.

दैवी सम्पद्विमोक्षाय निबन्धायासुरी मता
मा शुचः सम्पदं दैवीमभिजातोऽसि पाण्डव ॥ ५ ॥

daivī sampadvimokṣāya nibandhāyāsurī matā
mā śucaḥ sampadaṁ daivīm abhijāto'si pāṇḍava (5)

Spiritual wealth is considered (to be) for freedom, (the wealth) of an *asura*, for bondage. Pāṇḍava (Arjuna)! Do not grieve. You are born to spiritual wealth.

द्वौ भूतसर्गौ लोकेऽस्मिन्दैव आसुर एव च ।
दैवो विस्तरशः प्रोक्त आसुरं पार्थ मे शृणु ॥ ६ ॥

dvau bhūtasargau loke'smin daiva āsura eva ca
daivo vistaraśaḥ prokta āsuraṁ pārtha me śṛṇu (6)

In this world, there are two (types of) created beings, the divine, and the adharmic. The divine have been extensively spoken of. Listen to Me, Pārtha (Arjuna)! about the characteristics belonging to the *asura*s.

प्रवृत्तिं च निवृत्तिं च जना न विदुरासुराः ।
न शौचं नापि चाचारो न सत्यं तेषु विद्यते ॥ ७ ॥

pravṛttiṁ ca nivṛttiṁ ca janā na vidurāsurāḥ
na śaucaṁ nāpi cācāro na satyaṁ teṣu vidyate (7)

People who have qualities belonging to the *asura*s do not know what is to be done and what is to be withdrawn from. There is neither inner cleanliness nor proper conduct, nor truthfulness in them.

असत्यमप्रतिष्ठं ते जगदाहुरनीश्वरम् ।
अपरस्परसम्भूतं किमन्यत्कामहैतुकम् ॥ ८ ॥

asatyam apratiṣṭhaṁ te jagad āhuranīśvaram
aparasparasambhūtaṁ kim anyatkāmahaitukam (8)

They say, this world (of people) is untruthful, without (ethical) basis, Godless, and is born of the union of male and female, is driven by passion and nothing else.

एतां दृष्टिमवष्टभ्य नष्टात्मानोऽल्पबुद्धयः ।
प्रभवन्त्युग्रकर्माणः क्षयाय जगतोऽहिताः ॥ ९ ॥

etāṁ dṛṣṭim avaṣṭabhya naṣṭātmāno'lpabuddhayaḥ
prabhavantyugrakarmāṇaḥ kṣayāya jagato'hitāḥ (9)

Having recourse to this view, (these) enemies of the world whose minds are destroyed, who are of meagre thinking and cruel actions, are there very much for the destruction of the world.

काममाश्रित्य दुष्पूरं दम्भमानमदान्विताः ।
मोहाद् गृहीत्वासद्ग्राहान् प्रवर्तन्तेऽशुचिव्रताः ॥ १० ॥

kāmam āśritya duṣpūraṁ dambhamānamadānvitāḥ
mohād gṛhītvāsadgrāhān pravartante'śucivratāḥ (10)

Resorting to desire that is difficult to fulfil, those who are riddled with pretension, demand for respect, and pride, whose pursuits are unbecoming, having adopted false purposes due to delusion, engage themselves (in various actions).

चिन्तामपरिमेयां च प्रलयान्तामुपाश्रिताः ।
कामोपभोगपरमा एतावदिति निश्चिताः ॥ ११ ॥
आशापाशशतैर्बद्धाः कामक्रोधपरायणाः ।
ईहन्ते कामभोगार्थमन्यायेनार्थसञ्चयान् ॥ १२ ॥

cintām aparimeyāṁ ca pralayāntām upāśritāḥ
kāmopabhogaparamā etāvad iti niścitāḥ (11)
āśāpāśaśatairbaddhāḥ kāmakrodhaparāyaṇāḥ
īhante kāmabhogārtham anyāyenārthasañcayān (12)

Those committed to immeasurable concern until death, intent upon enjoyment of objects of desire, having concluded, 'It (life) is this much alone,' committed to desire and anger, and bound by hundreds of fetters of hope, engage themselves in the illegitimate accumulation of wealth for the enjoyment of objects of desire.

इदमद्य मया लब्धमिमं प्राप्स्ये मनोरथम् ।
इदमस्तीदमपि मे भविष्यति पुनर्धनम् ॥ १३ ॥

idamadya mayā labdham imaṁ prāpsye manoratham
idam astīdam api me bhaviṣyati punardhanam (13)

Today, this is gained by me. I will gain this (also) which is pleasing to the mind. This (much) wealth I have; this wealth also I will have later. (So they think).

असौ मया हतः शत्रुर्हनिष्ये चापरानपि ।
ईश्वरोऽहमहं भोगी सिद्धोऽहं बलवान् सुखी ॥ १४ ॥

asau mayā hataḥ śatrurhaniṣye cāparān api
īśvaro'ham ahaṁ bhogī siddho'haṁ balavān sukhī (14)

This enemy is destroyed by me and I will destroy others also; I am the ruler; I am the enjoyer; I am successful, powerful, and happy.

आढ्योऽभिजनवानस्मि कोऽन्योऽस्ति सदृशो मया ।
यक्ष्ये दास्यामि मोदिष्य इत्यज्ञानविमोहिताः ॥ १५ ॥

āḍhyo'bhijanavān asmi ko'nyo'sti sadṛśo mayā
yakṣye dāsyāmi modiṣya ityajñānavimohitāḥ (15)

Those who are totally deluded due to lack of discrimination say, 'I have wealth. I was born in a very good family. Who else is there who is equal to me? I will perform rituals. I will give. I will enjoy.'

अनेकचित्तविभ्रान्ता मोहजालसमावृताः ।
प्रसक्ताः कामभोगेषु पतन्ति नरकेऽशुचौ ॥ १६ ॥

anekacittavibhrāntā mohajālasamāvṛtāḥ
prasaktāḥ kāmabhogeṣu patanti narake'śucau (16)

Those who are completely deluded by many types of thoughts, covered by the net of delusion (lack of discrimination), and totally committed to the enjoyment of desirable objects, (they) fall into the unclean places of pain.

आत्मसम्भाविताः स्तब्धा धनमानमदान्विताः ।
यजन्ते नामयज्ञैस्ते दम्भेनाविधिपूर्वकम् ॥ १७ ॥

ātmasambhāvitāḥ stabdhā dhanamānamadānvitāḥ
yajante nāmayajñaiste dambhenāvidhipūrvakam (17)

Those who are self-glorifying, vain (conceited), filled with pride and arrogance because of their wealth, perform rituals that are rituals in name only, not according to stipulations (but) out of pretension.

अहङ्कारं बलं दर्पं कामं क्रोधं च संश्रिताः ।
मामात्मपरदेहेषु प्रद्विषन्तोऽभ्यसूयकाः ॥ १८ ॥
तानहं द्विषतः क्रूरान्संसारेषु नराधमान् ।
क्षिपाम्यजस्रमशुभानासुरीष्वेव योनिषु ॥ १९ ॥

ahaṅkāraṁ balaṁ darpaṁ kāmaṁ krodhaṁ ca saṁśritāḥ
mām ātmaparadeheṣu pradviṣanto'bhyasūyakāḥ (18)
tān ahaṁ dviṣataḥ krūrān saṁsāreṣu narādhamān
kṣipāmyajasram aśubhān āsurīṣveva yoniṣu (19)

Those who are completely given to egoism, (brute) strength, insolence, enjoyment, and anger, who despise Me in their own and others' bodies, who are great cavillers...

...who are hateful and cruel, who are the lowest of men, who are wrongdoers, I despatch them repeatedly into a life of transmigration only in *āsurī* wombs.

आसुरीं योनिमापन्ना मूढा जन्मनि जन्मनि ।
मामप्राप्यैव कौन्तेय ततो यान्त्यधमां गतिम् ॥ २० ॥

āsurīṁ yonim āpannā mūḍhā janmani janmani
māmaprāpyaiva kaunteya tato yāntyadhamāṁ gatim (20)

Kaunteya (Arjuna)! Those, who lack discrimination, obtaining the womb of an *asura* in every birth, certainly not reaching Me, go to an end that is even lower than that.

त्रिविधं नरकस्येदं द्वारं नाशनमात्मनः ।
कामः क्रोधस्तथा लोभस्तस्मादेतत्त्रयं त्यजेत् ॥ २१ ॥

trividhaṁ narakasyedaṁ dvāraṁ nāśanam ātmanaḥ
kāmaḥ krodhastathā lobhastasmād etattrayaṁ tyajet (21)

This doorway to painful experience, that destroys a person, is three-fold—desire, anger, and greed. Therefore, one should give up this triad.

एतैर्विमुक्तः कौन्तेय तमोद्वारैस्त्रिभिर्नरः ।
आचरत्यात्मनः श्रेयस्ततो याति परां गतिम् ॥ २२ ॥

etairvimuktaḥ kaunteya tamodvāraistribhirnaraḥ
ācaratyātmanaḥ śreyastato yāti parāṁ gatim (22)

A man who is free from these three gates to darkness, Kaunteya (Arjuna)! follows what is good for himself. Because of that, he reaches the higher end.

यः शास्त्रविधिमुत्सृज्य वर्तते कामकारतः ।
न स सिद्धिमवाप्नोति न सुखं न परां गतिम् ॥ २३ ॥

yaḥ śāstravidhim utsṛjya vartate kāmakārataḥ
na sa siddhim avāpnoti na sukhaṁ na parāṁ gatim (23)

The one who, being impelled by binding desire, engages oneself casting away the injunctions of the *śāstra*, gains neither maturity, nor happiness (here), much less a higher end.

तस्माच्छास्त्रं प्रमाणं ते कार्याकार्यव्यवस्थितौ ।
ज्ञात्वा शास्त्रविधानोक्तं कर्मकर्तुमिहार्हसि ॥ २४ ॥

tasmācchāstraṁ pramāṇaṁ te kāryākāryavyavasthitau
jñātvā śāstravidhānoktaṁ karma kartum ihārhasi (24)

Therefore, *śāstra* is the means of knowledge for you (Arjuna,) in the determination of what is to be done and what is not to be done. Knowing what is said by the mandates of the *śāstra*, you are obliged to perform action here (in this world).

ॐतत्सत् ।
इति श्रीमद्भगवद्गीतासूपनिषत्सु ब्रह्मविद्यायां योगशास्त्रे श्रीकृष्णार्जुन-संवादे दैवासुर-सम्पद्-विभाग-योगो नाम षोडशोऽध्यायः ॥ १६ ॥

omtatsat.
iti śrīmadbhagavadgītāsūpaniṣatsu brahma-vidyāyāṁ yoga-śāstre śrīkṛṣṇārjunasaṁvāde daivāsura-sampad-vibhāga-yogo nāma ṣoḍaśo'dhyāyaḥ (16)

Om, Brahman, is the only reality. Thus ends the sixteenth chapter called *daivāsura-sampad-vibhāga-yoga*—having the topic of the description of becoming and unbecoming dispositions—in the *Bhagavadgītā* which is in the form of a dialogue between Śrī Kṛṣṇa and Arjuna, which is the essence of the *Upaniṣads*, whose subject matter is both the knowledge of Brahman and *yoga.*

Chapter 17

श्रद्धात्रय-विभाग-योगः

Śraddhātraya-vibhāga-yogaḥ

Topic of the description of the three types of *śraddhā*

अर्जुन उवाच ।
ये शास्त्रविधिमुत्सृज्य यजन्ते श्रद्धयान्विताः ।
तेषां निष्ठा तु का कृष्ण सत्त्वमाहो रजस्तमः ॥ १ ॥

arjuna uvāca
ye śāstravidhim utsṛjya yajante śraddhayānvitāḥ
teṣāṁ niṣṭhā tu kā kṛṣṇa sattvam āho rajastamaḥ (1)

Arjuna said:
Kṛṣṇa! Those who perform a ritual giving up what is stipulated by the *śāstra*, but endowed with *śraddhā*, what is their basis? Is it *sattva* or *rajas* or *tamas*?

श्रीभगवानुवाच ।
त्रिविधा भवति श्रद्धा देहिनां सा स्वभावजा ।
सात्त्विकी राजसी चैव तामसी चेति तां शृणु ॥ २ ॥

śrībhagavān uvāca
trividhā bhavati śraddhā dehināṁ sā svabhāvajā
sāttvikī rājasī caiva tāmasī ceti tāṁ śṛṇu (2)

Śrī Bhagavān said:
The *śraddhā* of the embodied beings is born of the nature of the mind. It is three-fold as *sāttvika*, *rājasika*, and *tāmasika*. Listen to that (three-fold *śraddhā*).

सत्त्वानुरूपा सर्वस्य श्रद्धा भवति भारत।
श्रद्धामयोऽयं पुरुषो यो यच्छ्रद्धः स एव सः॥ ३॥

sattvānurūpā sarvasya śraddhā bhavati bhārata
śraddhāmayo'yaṁ puruṣo yo yacchraddhaḥ sa eva saḥ (3)

Bhārata (Arjuna)! *Śraddhā* of everyone is in keeping with his mind. This person is permeated by *śraddhā*. Whatever is his *śraddhā*, he conforms to that *śraddhā*.

यजन्ते सात्त्विका देवान्यक्षरक्षांसि राजसाः।
प्रेतान्भूतगणांश्चान्ये यजन्ते तामसा जनाः॥ ४॥

yajante sāttvikā devān yakṣarakṣāṁsi rājasāḥ
pretān bhūtagaṇāṁścānye yajante tāmasā janāḥ (4)

The *sāttvika* people worship the *deva*s; the *rājasika* (people) worship the *yakṣa-rakṣas*, (and) the other, *tāmasika* (people), worship ghosts and *bhūta-gaṇa*s.

अशास्त्रविहितं घोरं तप्यन्ते ये तपो जनाः।
दम्भाहङ्कारसंयुक्ताः कामरागबलान्विताः॥ ५॥
कर्शयन्तः शरीरस्थं भूतग्राममचेतसः।
मां चैवान्तःशरीरस्थं तान्विद्ध्यासुरनिश्चयान्॥ ६॥

aśāstravihitaṁ ghoraṁ tapyante ye tapo janāḥ
dambhāhaṅkārasaṁyuktāḥ kāmarāgabalānvitāḥ (5)
karśayantaḥ śarīrasthaṁ bhūtagrāmam acetasaḥ
māṁ caivāntaḥśarīrasthaṁ tān viddhyāsuraniścayān (6)

Those people who are riddled with pretension and egoity, who lack in discrimination, endowed with strong passion and longing who perform terrible religious disciplines not enjoined by the *śāstra*, emaciating the sense organs obtaining in the body, and Me as well, who obtains within the body—may you know them (to be) of *āsura* conviction.

आहारस्त्वपि सर्वस्य त्रिविधो भवति प्रियः ।
यज्ञस्तपस्तथा दानं तेषां भेदमिमं शृणु ॥ ७ ॥

āhārastvapi sarvasya trividho bhavati priyaḥ
yajñastapastathā dānaṁ teṣāṁ bhedam imaṁ śṛṇu (7)

And, for everyone, the food that is liked also is three-fold, so too, are ritual, religious discipline, and charity. Listen to this difference of theirs.

आयुःसत्त्वबलारोग्यसुखप्रीतिविवर्धनाः ।
रस्याः स्निग्धाः स्थिरा हृद्या आहाराः सात्त्विकप्रियाः ॥ ८ ॥

āyuḥsattvabalārogyasukhaprītivivardhanāḥ
rasyāḥ snigdhāḥ sthirā hṛdyā āhārāḥ sāttvikapriyāḥ (8)

Succulent, creamy, fortifying and pleasing foods, which increase longevity, mental clarity, strength, health, pleasure in taste and aesthetic pleasure, are loved by *sāttvika* people.

कट्वम्ललवणात्युष्णतीक्ष्णरूक्षविदाहिनः ।
आहारा राजसस्येष्टा दुःखशोकामयप्रदाः ॥ ९ ॥

kaṭvamlalavaṇātyuṣṇatīkṣṇarūkṣavidāhinaḥ
āhārā rājasyeṣṭā duḥkhaśokāmayapradāḥ (9)

Foods that are bitter, sour, salty, excessively hot, pungent, astringent, and burning, that give pain, sorrow and ill health are highly desired by *rājasika* people.

यातयामं गतरसं पूति पर्युषितं च यत्।
उच्छिष्टमपि चामेध्यं भोजनं तामसप्रियम्॥ १०॥

yātayāmaṁ gatarasaṁ pūti paryuṣitaṁ ca yat
ucchiṣṭam api cāmedhyaṁ bhojanaṁ tāmasapriyam (10)

Food which is stale or inadequately cooked, from which the essence has gone, which is putrid, over-night, refuse, and also unfit as an offering, is beloved to a *tāmasika* person.

अफलाकाङ्क्षिभिर्यज्ञो विधिदृष्टो य इज्यते।
यष्टव्यमेवेति मनः समाधाय स सात्त्विकः॥ ११॥

aphalākāṅkṣibhiryajño vidhidṛṣṭo ya ijyate
yaṣṭavyameveti manaḥ samādhāya sa sāttvikaḥ (11)

That ritual, which is known through the *śāstra*, which is performed by those who do not expect a result (other than *antaḥkaraṇa-śuddhi*), by making up the mind, 'This ritual is just to be performed,' is *sāttvika*.

अभिसन्धाय तु फलं दम्भार्थमपि चैव यत्।
इज्यते भरतश्रेष्ठ तं यज्ञं विद्धि राजसम्॥ १२॥

abhisandhāya tu phalaṁ dambhārthamapi caiva yat
ijyate bharataśreṣṭha taṁ yajñaṁ viddhi rājasam (12)

On the other hand, may you know that ritual which is performed keeping a result in view, and also just to proclaim one's own religiosity, is *rājasika*, Arjuna, the greatest among the descendants of Bharata!

विधिहीनमसृष्टान्नं मन्त्रहीनमदक्षिणम्।
श्रद्धाविरहितं यज्ञं तामसं परिचक्षते॥ १३॥

vidhihīnam asṛṣṭānnaṁ mantrahīnam adakṣiṇam
śraddhāvirahitaṁ yajñaṁ tāmasaṁ paricakṣate (13)

They say that a ritual, which is bereft of the stipulations of *śāstra*, without distribution of food, without proper recitation of *mantras*, without distribution of wealth and without *śraddhā*, is *tāmasika*.

देवद्विजगुरुप्राज्ञपूजनं शौचमार्जवम्।
ब्रह्मचर्यमहिंसा च शारीरं तप उच्यते॥ १४॥

devadvijaguruprājñapūjanaṁ śaucam ārjavam
brahmacaryam ahiṁsā ca śārīraṁ tapa ucyate (14)

Worshipping deities, *brāhmaṇas*, teachers and wise people, external cleanliness, straightforwardness, self discipline, and not physically hurting are (collectively) called discipline of the physical body.

अनुद्वेगकरं वाक्यं सत्यं प्रियहितं च यत्।
स्वाध्यायाभ्यसनं चैव वाङ्मयं तप उच्यते॥ १५॥

anudvegakaraṁ vākyaṁ satyaṁ priyahitaṁ ca yat
svādhyāyābhyasanaṁ caiva vāṅmayaṁ tapa ucyate (15)

Speech, which does not cause agitation, which is true, pleasing and beneficial, and daily repetition of one's own Veda, are (collectively) called discipline of speech.

मनःप्रसादः सौम्यत्वं मौनमात्मविनिग्रहः।
भावसंशुद्धिरित्येतत्तपो मानसमुच्यते॥ १६॥

manaḥprasādaḥ saumyatvaṁ maunam ātmavinigrahaḥ
bhāvasaṁśuddhirityetat tapo mānasam ucyate (16)

Mental cheerfulness, cheerfulness in expression, absence of pressure to talk, mastery over the mind, clean intent—this (these together) is called mental discipline.

श्रद्धया परया तप्तं तपस्तत्त्रिविधं नरैः ।
अफलाकाङ्क्षिभिर्युक्तैः सात्त्विकं परिचक्षते ॥ १७ ॥

śraddhayā parayā taptaṁ tapastat trividhaṁ naraiḥ
aphalākāṅkṣibhiryuktaiḥ sāttvikaṁ paricakṣate (17)

That three-fold *tapas*, observed with total *śraddhā* by people who have no expectation of results (other than mental purity) and who are composed, is called *sāttvika*.

सत्कारमानपूजार्थं तपो दम्भेन चैव यत् ।
क्रियते तदिह प्रोक्तं राजसं चलमध्रुवम् ॥ १८ ॥

satkāramānapūjārthaṁ tapo dambhena caiva yat
kriyate tadiha proktaṁ rājasaṁ calam adhruvam (18)

That *tapas*, which is done for the sake of (receiving) honour, respect, and worship and with ostentation, which is unsteady and not lasting, is called here *rājasika*.

मूढग्राहेणात्मनो यत्पीडया क्रियते तपः ।
परस्योत्सादनार्थं वा तत्तामसमुदाहृतम् ॥ १९ ॥

mūḍhagrāheṇātmano yat pīḍayā kriyate tapaḥ
parasyotsādanārthaṁ vā tat tāmasam udāhṛtam (19)

That *tapas*, which is done due to deluded understanding, by afflicting one's body or for the sake of destroying another, is called *tāmasika*.

दातव्यमिति यद्दानं दीयतेऽनुपकारिणे ।
देशे काले च पात्रे च तद्दानं सात्त्विकं स्मृतम् ॥ २० ॥

dātavyam iti yaddānaṁ dīyate'nupakāriṇe
deśe kāle ca pātre ca taddānaṁ sāttvikaṁ smṛtam (20)

That charity, which is given to one from whom one does not expect a return, in the proper place, at the proper time, and to a worthy recipient, thinking, 'It is to be given,' is considered *sāttvika* charity.

यत्तु प्रत्युपकारार्थं फलमुद्दिश्य वा पुनः ।
दीयते च परिक्लिष्टं तद्दानं राजसं स्मृतम् ॥ २१ ॥

yattu pratyupakārārthaṁ phalam uddiśya vā punaḥ
dīyate ca parikliṣṭaṁ taddānaṁ rājasaṁ smṛtam (21)

On the other hand, that charity, which is given for the sake of being helped in return, or keeping in view, a result (*puṇya*) to be gained later, and that which is fraught with pain, is considered *rājasika*.

अदेशकाले यद्दानमपात्रेभ्यश्च दीयते ।
असत्कृतमवज्ञातं तत्तामसमुदाहृतम् ॥ २२ ॥

adeśakāle yaddānam apātrebhyaśca dīyate
asatkṛtam avajñātaṁ tattāmasam udāhṛtam (22)

That charity, which is given without respect (improperly), and contemptuously at the wrong place and wrong time, and to unworthy recipients, is called *tāmasika*.

ॐ तत्सदिति निर्देशो ब्रह्मणस्त्रिविधः स्मृतः ।
ब्राह्मणास्तेन वेदाश्च यज्ञाश्च विहिताः पुरा ॥ २३ ॥

oṁ tatsaditi nirdeśo brahmaṇastrividhaḥ smṛtaḥ
brāhmaṇāstena vedāśca yajñāśca vihitāḥ purā (23)

'*Oṁ tat sat,*' is the three-fold expression of Brahman. By that, the *brāhmaṇas*, the (four) Vedas, and rituals were created in the beginning.

तस्मादोमित्युदाहृत्य यज्ञदानतपःक्रियाः ।
प्रवर्तन्ते विधानोक्ताः सततं ब्रह्मवादिनाम् ॥ २४ ॥

tasmād omityudāhṛtya yajñadānatapaḥkriyāḥ
pravartante vidhānoktāḥ satataṁ brahmavādinām (24)

Therefore, for those who know the Vedas, the activities such as rituals, charities, and religious disciplines, mentioned by injunctions (of the Veda), always commence after uttering '*Om*'.

तदित्यनभिसन्धाय फलं यज्ञतपःक्रियाः ।
दानक्रियाश्च विविधाः क्रियन्ते मोक्षकाङ्क्षिभिः ॥ २५ ॥

tadityanabhisandhāya phalaṁ yajñatapaḥkriyāḥ
dānakriyāśca vividhāḥ kriyante mokṣakāṅkṣibhiḥ (25)

Saying '*tat*,' various activities (such as) rituals, religious disciplines and charities are performed by those who want *mokṣa*, without expecting a result (other than *antaḥkaraṇa-śuddhi*).

सद्भावे साधुभावे च सदित्येतत्प्रयुज्यते ।
प्रशस्ते कर्मणि तथा सच्छब्दः पार्थ युज्यते ॥ २६ ॥

sadbhāve sādhubhāve ca sadityetat prayujyate
praśaste karmaṇi tathā sacchabdaḥ pārtha yujyate (26)

The word '*sat*' is used with reference to bringing (something) into existence and (with reference to) a righteous life; so too, Pārtha (Arjuna)! the word '*sat*' is used for a sanctifying *karma*.

यज्ञे तपसि दाने च स्थितिः सदिति चोच्यते ।
कर्म चैव तदर्थीयं सदित्येवाभिधीयते ॥ २७ ॥

yajñe tapasi dāne ca sthitiḥ saditi cocyate
karma caiva tadarthīyaṁ sadityevābhidhīyate (27)

A commitment with reference to a ritual, a religious discipline, and giving is called '*sat*', and a *karma* for their sake (or for the sake of Īśvara) is also called '*sat*'.

अश्रद्धया हुतं दत्तं तपस्तप्तं कृतं च यत्।
असदित्युच्यते पार्थ न च तत्प्रेत्य नो इह॥ २८॥

aśraddhayā hutaṁ dattaṁ tapastaptaṁ kṛtaṁ ca yat
asadityucyate pārtha na ca tatpretya no iha (28)

That which is, without *śraddhā*, offered (in a religious ritual), given (as charity), performed as a religious discipline, and that (*karma*) which is done, is called *asat*, that which does not serve its purpose, Pārtha (Arjuna)! That is not (fruitful) after death and indeed not here.

ॐतत्सत्।
इति श्रीमद्भगवद्गीतासूपनिषत्सु ब्रह्मविद्यायां योगशास्त्रे श्रीकृष्णार्जुन-संवादे श्रद्धात्रय-विभाग-योगो नाम सप्तदशोऽध्यायः॥ १७॥

omtatsat.
iti śrīmadbhagavadgītāsūpaniṣatsu brahma-vidyāyāṁ yoga-śāstre śrīkṛṣṇārjunasaṁvāde śraddhātraya-vibhāga-yogo nāma saptadaśo'dhyāyaḥ (17)

Om, Brahman, is the only reality. Thus ends the seventeenth chapter called *śraddhātraya-vibhāga-yoga*—having the topic of the description of the three types of *śraddhā*—in the *Bhagavadgītā* which is in the form of a dialogue between Śrī Kṛṣṇa and Arjuna, which is the essence of the *Upaniṣads*, whose subject matter is both the knowledge of Brahman and *yoga*.

Chapter 18

मोक्ष-संन्यास-योगः

Mokṣa-sannyāsa-yogaḥ

Topic of freedom and renunciation

अर्जुन उवाच।
संन्यासस्य महाबाहो तत्त्वमिच्छामि वेदितुम्।
त्यागस्य च हृषीकेश पृथक्केशिनिषूदन॥ १॥

arjuna uvāca
sanyāsasya mahābāho tattvam icchāmi veditum
tyāgasya ca hṛṣīkeśa pṛthak keśiniṣūdana (1)

Arjuna said:
Hṛṣīkeśa (Kṛṣṇa)! The slayer of Keśī! The mighty armed! I want to know distinctly the truth of *sannyāsa* and *tyāga*.

श्रीभगवानुवाच।
काम्यानां कर्मणां न्यासं संन्यासं कवयो विदुः।
सर्वकर्मफलत्यागं प्राहुस्त्यागं विचक्षणाः॥ २॥

śrībhagavān uvāca
kāmyānāṁ karmaṇāṁ nyāsaṁ sannyāsaṁ kavayo viduḥ
sarvakarmaphalatyāgaṁ prāhustyāgaṁ vicakṣaṇāḥ (2)

Śrī Bhagavān said:
The wise know *sannyāsa* as renunciation of actions for desired objects; the learned people say renunciation of the results of all actions is *tyāga*.

त्याज्यं दोषवदित्येके कर्म प्राहुर्मनीषिणः।
यज्ञदानतपःकर्म न त्याज्यमिति चापरे॥ ३॥

tyājyaṁ doṣavad ityeke karma prāhurmanīṣiṇaḥ
yajñadānatapaḥkarma na tyājyam iti cāpare (3)

Some wise men say that action, which is (inherently) defective, is to be given up, and others say that an action, which is a ritual, charity, or religious discipline should not be given up.

निश्चयं शृणु मे तत्र त्यागे भरतसत्तम ।
त्यागो हि पुरुषव्याघ्र त्रिविधः सम्प्रकीर्तितः ॥ ४ ॥

niścayaṁ śṛṇu me tatra tyāge bharatasattama
tyāgo hi puruṣavyāghra trividhaḥ samprakīrtitaḥ (4)

Arjuna, the most mature among the Bharata family! The tiger among men! Listen to My ascertained opinion about this renunciation. Renunciation is well stated as three-fold.

यज्ञदानतपःकर्म न त्याज्यं कार्यमेव तत् ।
यज्ञो दानं तपश्चैव पावनानि मनीषिणाम् ॥ ५ ॥

yajñadānatapaḥkarma na tyājyaṁ kāryameva tat
yajño dānaṁ tapaścaiva pāvanāni manīṣiṇām (5)

An action that is a ritual, charity, or religious discipline is not to be given up; that is indeed to be done. Ritual, charity, and religious discipline are indeed purifying for those who are discriminative.

एतान्यपि तु कर्माणि सङ्गं त्यक्त्वा फलानि च
कर्तव्यानीति मे पार्थ निश्चितं मतमुत्तमम् ॥ ६ ॥

etānyapi tu karmāṇi saṅgaṁ tyaktvā phalāni ca
kartavyānīti me pārtha niścitaṁ matam uttamam (6)

Even these actions are to be done giving up the attachment and giving up the results. This is My clear, proper vision, Pārtha (Arjuna)!

नियतस्य तु संन्यासः कर्मणो नोपपद्यते।
मोहात्तस्य परित्यागस्तामसः परिकीर्तितः॥ ७॥

niyatasya tu sannyāsaḥ karmaṇo nopapadyate
mohāt tasya parityāgastāmasaḥ parikīrtitaḥ (7)

Renunciation of enjoined action is not proper. Renunciation of it (enjoined action), out of delusion, is called *tāmasika*.

दुःखमित्येव यत्कर्म कायक्लेशभयात्त्यजेत्।
स कृत्वा राजसं त्यागं नैव त्यागफलं लभेत्॥ ८ ॥

duḥkham ityeva yatkarma kāyakleśabhyāt tyajet
sa kṛtvā rājasaṁ tyāgaṁ naiva tyāgaphalaṁ labhet (8)

One may give up the *karma* as indeed painful out of fear of affliction to one's physical body. Having done that *rājasika* renunciation, one would certainly not gain the result of renunciation.

कार्यमित्येव यत्कर्म नियतं क्रियतेऽर्जुन।
सङ्गं त्यक्त्वा फलं चैव स त्यागः सात्त्विको मतः॥ ९॥

kāryam ityeva yatkarma niyataṁ kriyate'rjuna
saṅgaṁ tyaktvā phalaṁ caiva sa tyāgaḥ sāttviko mataḥ (9)

'It is to be done,' thinking thus when only the enjoined *karma* is done, giving up attachment and result, Arjuna! it is considered to be a *sāttvika* renunciation.

न द्वेष्ट्यकुशलं कर्म कुशले नानुषज्जते ।
त्यागी सत्त्वसमाविष्टो मेधावी छिन्नसंशयः ॥ १० ॥

na dveṣṭyakuśalaṁ karma kuśale nānuṣajjate
tyāgī sattvasamāviṣṭo medhāvī chinnasaṁśayaḥ (10)

The renunciate (of the results of actions), (being) the one who is endowed with a pure mind, (thereafter being) the one who has discriminative knowledge and whose doubts are gone, does not despise unpleasant (to be done) *karma*, nor does he cling to auspicious *karma*.

न हि देहभृता शक्यं त्यक्तुं कर्माण्यशेषतः ।
यस्तु कर्मफलत्यागी स त्यागीत्यभिधीयते ॥ ११ ॥

na hi dehabhṛtā śakyaṁ tyaktuṁ karmāṇyaśeṣataḥ
yastu karmaphalatyāgī sa tyāgītyabhidhīyate (11)

Indeed actions cannot be given up completely by the one who sustains a body; but the one who is a renunciate of the results of action is called a *tyāgin*.

अनिष्टमिष्टं मिश्रं च त्रिविधं कर्मणः फलम् ।
भवत्यत्यागिनां प्रेत्य न तु संन्यासिनां क्वचित् ॥ १२ ॥

aniṣṭam iṣṭaṁ miśraṁ ca trividhaṁ karmaṇaḥ phalam
bhavatyatyāginām̐ pretya na tu sannyāsinām̐ kvacit (12)

The three-fold result of action—undesirable, desirable, and a mixture—exists after death for the non-renunciates, but never for the renunciates.

पञ्चैतानि महाबाहो कारणानि निबोध मे ।
साङ्ख्ये कृतान्ते प्रोक्तानि सिद्धये सर्वकर्मणाम् ॥ १३ ॥

pañcaitāni mahābāho kāraṇāni nibodha me
sāṅkhye kṛtānte proktāni siddhaye sarvakarmaṇām (13)

Understand from Me, Arjuna, the mighty armed! these five causes for the accomplishment of all *karmas* are told in the *śāstra* at the end of the Veda (that is, Vedanta) which is the point of culmination of all *karma*.

अधिष्ठानं तथा कर्ता करणं च पृथग्विधम्।
विविधाश्च पृथक् चेष्टा दैवं चैवात्र पञ्चमम्॥ १४॥

adhiṣṭhānaṁ tathā kartā karaṇaṁ ca pṛthagvidham
vividhāśca pṛthak ceṣṭā daivaṁ caivātra pañcamam (14)

(They are) the physical body, the agent, the manifold means (of action)[47], the distinct and diverse activities (of the *prāṇas*), and indeed, *daiva* (the presiding deities) is the fifth here.

शरीरवाङ्मनोभिर्यत्कर्म प्रारभते नरः।
न्याय्यं वा विपरीतं वा पञ्चैते तस्य हेतवः॥ १५॥

śarīravāṅmanobhiryat karma prārabhate naraḥ
nyāyyaṁ vā viparītaṁ vā pañcaite tasya hetavaḥ (15)

That *karma*, whether proper or the opposite (improper), which a man undertakes with body, speech or mind, has these five causes.

तत्रैवं सति कर्तारमात्मानं केवलं[४८] तु यः।
पश्यत्यकृतबुद्धित्वान्न स पश्यति दुर्मतिः॥ १६॥

tatraivaṁ sati kartāram ātmānaṁ kevalaṁ tu yaḥ
paśyatyakṛtabuddhitvānna sa paśyati durmatiḥ (16)

When this is so, the one who sees, on the other hand, the self, which is 'pure,' as the agent, because of an immature mind, that person whose thinking is distorted does not see (the truth).

यस्य नाहंकृतो भावो बुद्धिर्यस्य न लिप्यते ।
हत्वापि स इमाँल्लोकान्न हन्ति न निबध्यते ॥ १७ ॥

yasya nāhaṅkṛto bhāvo buddhiryasya na lipyate
hatvāpi sa imām̐llokānna hanti na nibadhyate (17)

The one who has no doership, the one whose mind is not affected, he, even killing these people, does not kill, nor is he bound.

ज्ञानं ज्ञेयं परिज्ञाता त्रिविधा कर्मचोदना ।
करणं कर्म कर्तेति त्रिविधः कर्मसङ्ग्रहः ॥ १८ ॥

jñānaṁ jñeyaṁ parijñātā trividhā karmacodanā
karaṇaṁ karma karteti trividhaḥ karmasaṅgrahaḥ (18)

Knowledge (the thought corresponding to an object), the object of knowledge, (and) the knower are the three-fold impellers of action. The means of doing (instrument), the object of the action, and the agent are the three-fold constituents of action.

ज्ञानं कर्म च कर्ता च त्रिधैव गुणभेदतः ।
प्रोच्यते गुणसङ्ख्याने यथावच्छृणु तान्यपि ॥ १९ ॥

jñānaṁ karma ca kartā ca tridhaiva guṇabhedataḥ
procyate guṇasaṅkhyāne yathāvacchṛṇu tānyapi (19)

Knowledge, action and agent are only three-fold according to the differences in *guṇa*, it is said in the *śāstra* dealing with the enumeration of the *guṇa*s. Listen to those also just as it is (unfolded).

सर्वभूतेषु येनैकं भावमव्ययमीक्षते ।
अविभक्तं विभक्तेषु तज्ज्ञानं विद्धि सात्त्विकम् ॥ २० ॥

sarvabhūteṣu yenaikaṁ bhāvam avyayam īkṣate
avibhaktaṁ vibhakteṣu tajjñānaṁ viddhi sāttvikam (20)

Know that to be *sāttvika* knowledge by which one knows one changeless existence in all things (and beings) and the undivided among the divided.

पृथक्त्वेन तु यज्ज्ञानं नानाभावान्पृथग्विधान् ।
वेत्ति सर्वेषु भूतेषु तज्ज्ञानं विद्धि राजसम् ॥ २१ ॥

pṛthaktvena tu yajjñānaṁ nānābhāvān pṛthagvidhān
vetti sarveṣu bhūteṣu tajjñānaṁ viddhi rājasam (21)

On the other hand, may you know that knowledge by which one knows distinctly the manifold nature of different kinds of beings, as *rājasa*.

यत्तु कृत्स्नवदेकस्मिन्कार्ये सक्तमहैतुकम् ।
अतत्त्वार्थवदल्पं च तत्तामसमुदाहृतम् ॥ २२ ॥

yattu kṛtsnavad ekasmin kārye saktam ahaitukam
atattvārthavad alpaṁ ca tat tāmasam udāhṛtam (22)

Whereas that (knowledge by) which (one is) committed to one object, as though it is everything (and) which is illogical, without truth, and very limited, that (knowledge) is called *tāmasa*.

नियतं सङ्गरहितमरागद्वेषतः कृतम् ।
अफलप्रेप्सुना कर्म यत्तत्सात्त्विकमुच्यते ॥ २३ ॥

niyataṁ saṅgarahitam arāgadveṣataḥ kṛtam
aphalaprepsunā karma yattat sāttvikam ucyate (23)

That action, which is enjoined and which is done without attachment, without being impelled by likes and dislikes, by a person without a (binding) desire for result, is called *sāttvika*.

यत्तु कामेप्सुना कर्म साहंकारेण वा पुनः ।
क्रियते बहुलायासं तद्राजसमुदाहृतम् ॥ २४ ॥

yattu kāmepsunā karma sāhaṅkāreṇa vā punaḥ
kriyate bahulāyāsaṁ tad rājasam udāhṛtam (24)

But that *karma* which is done by one who has a (pronounced) desire for the result or again with arrogance (and) a lot of exertion is called *rājasa*.

अनुबन्धं क्षयं हिंसामनवेक्ष्य च पौरुषम् ।
मोहादारभ्यते कर्म यत्तत्तामसमुच्यते ॥ २५ ॥

anubandhaṁ kṣayaṁ hiṁsām anavekṣya ca pauruṣam
mohād ārabhyate karma yattat tāmasam ucyate (25)

That action, which is begun not taking into account the natural consequence, loss, injury (to others), and one's own capacity because of delusion is called *tāmasa*.

मुक्तसङ्गोऽनहंवादी धृत्युत्साहसमन्वितः ।
सिद्ध्यसिद्ध्योर्निर्विकारः कर्ता सात्त्विक उच्यते ॥ २६ ॥

muktasaṅgo'nahaṁvādī dhṛtyutsāhasamanvitaḥ
siddhyasiddhyornirvikāraḥ kartā sāttvika ucyate (26)

The one who is free from attachment, who has no egotism, who is endowed with resolve and enthusiasm and is unperturbed in success and failure, is called a *sāttvika* doer.

रागी कर्मफलप्रेप्सुर्लुब्धो हिंसात्मकोऽशुचिः ।
हर्षशोकान्वितः कर्ता राजसः परिकीर्तितः ॥ २७ ॥

rāgī karmaphalaprepsurlubdho hiṁsātmako'śuciḥ
harṣaśokānvitaḥ kartā rājasaḥ parikīrtitaḥ (27)

The one who has a predominance of *rāga* and a predominant desire for the result of action, who is greedy, whose nature is to hurt, who is not clean and who is subject to elation and depression is called a *rājasa* doer.

अयुक्तः प्राकृतः स्तब्धः शठो नैष्कृतिकोऽलसः ।
विषादी दीर्घसूत्री च कर्ता तामस उच्यते ॥ २८ ॥

ayuktaḥ prākṛtaḥ stabdhaḥ śaṭho naiṣkṛtiko'lasaḥ
viṣādī dīrghasūtrī ca kartā tāmasa ucyate (28)

The one who is disturbed, immature, irreverent, deceptive, cruel, lazy, given to sadness, and a procrastinator is called a *tāmasa* doer.

बुद्धेर्भेदं धृतेश्चैव गुणतस्त्रिविधं शृणु ।
प्रोच्यमानमशेषेण पृथक्त्वेन धनञ्जय ॥ २९ ॥

buddherbhedaṁ dhṛteścaiva guṇatastrividhaṁ śṛṇu
procyamānam aśeṣeṇa pṛthaktvena dhanañjaya (29)

Dhanañjaya (Arjuna)! Please listen to the three-fold difference of the mind and of the resolve, according to *guṇa*, that is being told completely and severally.

प्रवृत्तिं च निवृत्तिं च कार्याकार्ये भयाभये ।
बन्धं मोक्षं च या वेत्ति बुद्धिः सा पार्थ सात्त्विकी ॥ ३० ॥

pravṛttiṁ ca nivṛttiṁ ca kāryākārye bhayābhaye
bandhaṁ mokṣaṁ ca yā vetti buddhiḥ sā pārtha sāttvikī 30)

The mind, which knows the pursuit of *karma* and renunciation, what is to be done and what is not to be done, what is to be feared and what is not to be feared, and bondage and freedom, that (mind), Pārtha (Arjuna)! is *sāttvikī*.

यया धर्ममधर्मं च कार्यं चाकार्यमेव च ।
अयथावत्प्रजानाति बुद्धिः सा पार्थ राजसी ॥ ३१ ॥

yayā dharmam adharmaṁ ca kāryaṁ cākāryam eva ca
ayathāvat prajānāti buddhiḥ sā pārtha rājasī (31)

That mind, with which one wrongly knows what is proper and improper, what is to be done and what is not to be done, Pārtha (Arjuna)! is *rājasī*.

अधर्मं धर्ममिति या मन्यते तमसावृता ।
सर्वार्थान्विपरीतांश्च बुद्धिः सा पार्थ तामसी ॥ ३२ ॥

adharmaṁ dharmam iti yā manyate tamasāvṛtā
sarvārthān viparītāṁśca buddhiḥ sā pārtha tāmasī (32)

The mind, which covered with ignorance considers what is improper as proper, and all things the reverse (of what they are), that (mind), Pārtha (Arjuna)! is *tāmasī*.

धृत्या यया धारयते मनःप्राणेन्द्रियक्रियाः ।
योगेनाव्यभिचारिण्या धृतिः सा पार्थ सात्त्विकी ॥ ३३ ॥

dhṛtyā yayā dhārayate manaḥprāṇendriyakriyāḥ
yogenāvyabhicāriṇyā dhṛtiḥ sā pārtha sāttvikī (33)

The unflinching resolve, with which one sustains, by practice, the activities of the mind, *prāṇa*, and organs of action and knowledge, (that resolve) is *sāttvikī*, Pārtha (Arjuna)!

यया तु धर्मकामार्थान्धृत्या धारयतेऽर्जुन ।
प्रसङ्गेन फलाकाङ्क्षी धृतिः सा पार्थ राजसी ॥ ३४ ॥

yayā tu dharmakāmārthān dhṛtyā dhārayate'rjuna
prasaṅgena phalākāṅkṣī dhṛtiḥ sā pārtha rājasī (34)

Whereas, the resolve, with which the one who has a longing for result as the occasion arises, sustains (activities for) religious merit, pleasure, and security, (that resolve) is *rājasī*, Pārtha (Arjuna)!

यया स्वप्नं भयं शोकं विषादं मदमेव च ।
न विमुञ्चति दुर्मेधा धृतिः सा पार्थ तामसी ॥ ३५ ॥

yayā svapnaṁ bhayaṁ śokaṁ viṣādaṁ madam eva ca
na vimuñcati durmedhā dhṛtiḥ sā pārtha tāmasī (35)

That resolve, by which the one whose thinking is improper, does not give up (excess) sleep, fear, sorrow, depression and intoxication, is *tāmasī*, Pārtha (Arjuna)!

सुखं त्विदानीं त्रिविधं शृणु मे भरतर्षभ ।
अभ्यासाद्रमते यत्र दुःखान्तं च निगच्छति ॥ ३६ ॥
यत्तदग्रे विषमिव परिणामेऽमृतोपमम् ।
तत्सुखं सात्त्विकं प्रोक्तमात्मबुद्धिप्रसादजम् ॥ ३७ ॥

sukhaṁ tvidānīṁ trividhaṁ śṛṇu me bharatarṣabha
abhyāsād ramate yatra duḥkhāntaṁ ca nigacchati (36)
yattadagre viṣam iva pariṇāme'mṛtopamam
tatsukhaṁ sāttvikaṁ proktamātmabuddhiprasādajam (37)

Listen to Me now, Arjuna, the foremost in the clan of Bharata! about the three-fold happiness. That in which one discovers joy by repeated practice (of meditation) and gains the end of sorrow...

...which in the beginning is like poison (and) when there is transformation, is like nectar, that happiness is called *sāttvika*, born of the clarity of self-knowledge.

विषयेन्द्रियसंयोगाद्यत्तदग्रेऽमृतोपमम्।
परिणामे विषमिव तत्सुखं राजसं स्मृतम्॥ ३८॥

viṣayendriyasaṁyogād yattad agre'mṛtopamam
pariṇāme viṣam iva tat sukhaṁ rājasaṁ smṛtam (38)

That happiness (arising) from the contact of a sense organ with its object, which in the beginning is like nectar and when it changes is like poison, is considered *rājasa*.

यदग्रे चानुबन्धे च सुखं मोहनमात्मनः।
निद्रालस्यप्रमादोत्थं तत्तामसमुदाहृतम्॥ ३९॥

yadagre cānubandhe ca sukhaṁ mohanam ātmanaḥ
nidrālasyapramādotthaṁ tattāmasam udāhṛtam (39)

That happiness, which in the beginning and at the end, is self deluding, (and) born of sleep, laziness, and indifference, is called *tāmasa*.

न तदस्ति पृथिव्यां वा दिवि देवेषु वा पुनः।
सत्त्वं प्रकृतिजैर्मुक्तं यदेभिः स्यात् त्रिभिर्गुणैः॥ ४०॥

na tadasti pṛthivyāṁ vā divi deveṣu vā punaḥ
sattvaṁ prakṛtijairmuktaṁ yadebhiḥ syāt tribhirguṇaiḥ (40)

There is no existent being either on the earth or, furthermore, in heaven among the Gods, who is free from these three *guṇa*s born of *prakṛti* (nature).

ब्राह्मणक्षत्रियविशां शूद्राणां च परन्तप।
कर्माणि प्रविभक्तानि स्वभावप्रभवैर्गुणैः॥ ४१॥

brāhmaṇakṣatriyaviśāṁ śūdrāṇāṁ ca parantapa
karmāṇi pravibhaktāni svabhāvaprabhavairguṇaiḥ (41)

The duties of the *brāhmaṇas, kṣatriyas, vaiśyas*, and *śūdras*, Arjuna, the scorcher of foes! are divided according to qualities born of *svabhāva* (Īśvara's *māyā*, one's nature and one's *karma*).

शमो दमस्तपः शौचं क्षान्तिरार्जवमेव च।
ज्ञानं विज्ञानमास्तिक्यं ब्रह्मकर्म स्वभावजम्॥ ४२॥

śamo damastapaḥ śaucaṁ kṣāntirārjavam eva ca
jñānaṁ vijñānamāstikyaṁ brahmakarma svabhāvajam (42)

Composure, restraint, religious discipline, (inner and external) cleanliness, accommodation, rectitude, knowledge, assimilated knowledge, and accepting the veracity of the Vedas, are (collectively) the duties, born of nature, of a *brāhmaṇa*.

शौर्यं तेजो धृतिर्दाक्ष्यं युद्धे चाप्यपलायनम्।
दानमीश्वरभावश्च क्षात्रं कर्म स्वभावजम्॥ ४३॥

śauryaṁ tejo dhṛtirdākṣyaṁ yuddhe cāpyapalāyanam
dānam īśvarabhāvaśca kṣātraṁ karma svabhāvajam (43)

Valour, self-confidence, resolve, adroitness, not running (away) from conflict, giving, and overlordship (leadership) are the naturally born duties and disposition of a *kṣatriya*.

कृषिगौरक्ष्यवाणिज्यं वैश्यकर्म स्वभावजम्।
परिचर्यात्मकं कर्म शूद्रस्यापि स्वभावजम्॥ ४४॥

kṛṣigaurakṣyavāṇijyaṁ vaiśyakarma svabhāvajam
paricaryātmakaṁ karma śūdrasyāpi svabhāvajam (44)

Agriculture, tending cattle, and commerce are the natural duties of a *vaiśya*. The natural duty of a *śūdra* is in the form of service.

स्वे स्वे कर्मण्यभिरतः संसिद्धिं लभते नरः।
स्वकर्मनिरतः सिद्धिं यथा विन्दति तच्छृणु॥ ४५॥

sve sve karmaṇyabhirataḥ saṁsiddhiṁ labhate naraḥ
svakarmanirataḥ siddhiṁ yathā vindati tacchṛṇu (45)

A man who delights in his own duty gains success. Listen to how one devoted to his own duty, finds success.

यतः प्रवृत्तिर्भूतानां येन सर्वमिदं ततम्।
स्वकर्मणा तमभ्यर्च्य सिद्धिं विन्दति मानवः॥ ४६॥

yataḥ pravṛttirbhūtānāṁ yena sarvam idaṁ tatam
svakarmaṇā tamabhyarcya siddhiṁ vindati mānavaḥ (46)

Through one's duty, worshipping Him from whom is the creation of the beings, by whom all this is pervaded, a human being gains success.

श्रेयान् स्वधर्मो विगुणः परधर्मात्स्वनुष्ठितात्।
स्वभावनियतं कर्म कुर्वन्नाप्नोति किल्बिषम्॥ ४७॥

śreyān svadharmo viguṇaḥ paradharmāt svanuṣṭhitāt
svabhāvaniyataṁ karma kurvannāpnoti kilbiṣam (47)

One's own duty, devoid of merit, is better than the duty of another, well donc. Doing action enjoined according to one's nature, one does not gain any blemish.

सहजं कर्म कौन्तेय सदोषमपि न त्यजेत्।
सर्वारम्भा हि दोषेण धूमेनाग्निरिवावृताः ॥ ४८ ॥

sahajaṁ karma kaunteya sadoṣam api na tyajet
sarvārambhā hi doṣeṇa dhūmenāgnirivāvṛtāḥ (48)

The *karma* that is natural (according to one's birth), Kaunteya (Arjuna)! though defective, one should not give up, because all undertakings are covered with fault, like fire (is covered) with smoke.

असक्तबुद्धिः सर्वत्र जितात्मा विगतस्पृहः।
नैष्कर्म्यसिद्धिं परमां संन्यासेनाधिगच्छति ॥ ४९ ॥

asaktabuddhiḥ sarvatra jitātmā vigataspṛhaḥ
naiṣkarmyasiddhiṁ paramāṁ sannyāsenādhigacchati (49)

The one whose mind is free from attachment everywhere, who has self mastery, and from whom longing has gone, gains the most exalted accomplishment of actionlessness by renunciation.

सिद्धिं प्राप्तो यथा ब्रह्म तथाप्नोति निबोध मे।
समासेनैव कौन्तेय निष्ठा ज्ञानस्य या परा ॥ ५० ॥

siddhiṁ prāpto yathā brahma tathāpnoti nibodha me
samāsenaiva kaunteya niṣṭhā jñānasya yā parā (50)

Learn from Me in brief, Kaunteya (Arjuna)! how the one who has gained the accomplishment (of *antaḥkaraṇa-śuddhi*) gains the ultimate certainty of the knowledge that is Brahman.

बुद्ध्या विशुद्धया युक्तो धृत्यात्मानं नियम्य च ।
शब्दादीन्विषयांस्त्यक्त्वा रागद्वेषौ व्युदस्य च ॥ ५१ ॥
विविक्तसेवी लघ्वाशी यतवाक्कायमानसः ।
ध्यानयोगपरो नित्यं वैराग्यं समुपाश्रितः ॥ ५२ ॥
अहङ्कारं बलं दर्पं कामं क्रोधं परिग्रहम् ।
विमुच्य निर्ममः शान्तो ब्रह्मभूयाय कल्पते ॥ ५३ ॥

buddhyā viśuddhayā yukto dhṛtyātmānaṁ niyamya ca
śabdādīn viṣayāṁstyaktvā rāgadveṣau vyudasya ca (51)
viviktasevī laghvāśī yatavākkāyamānasaḥ
dhyānayogaparo nityaṁ vairāgyaṁ samupāśritaḥ (52)
ahaṅkāraṁ balaṁ darpaṁ kāmaṁ krodhaṁ parigraham
vimucya nirmamaḥ śānto brahmabhūyāya kalpate (53)

The one who endowed with a mind that is very clear, mastering the body-mind-sense-complex with a firm resolve, giving up the sense objects such as sound, etc., and giving up likes and dislikes...

...who lives in a quiet place, who eats lightly, whose speech, body and mind are mastered, who is always committed to contemplation, who has completely resorted to freedom from longing...

...giving up misplaced 'I sense', power, vainfulness, binding desire, anger, ownership (of external things), the one who has no sense of ownership (of his own body, etc.), and who is tranquil, is fit to gain abidance in the knowledge of Brahman being oneself.

ब्रह्मभूतः प्रसन्नात्मा न शोचति न काङ्क्षति ।
समः सर्वेषु भूतेषु मद्भक्तिं लभते पराम् ॥ ५४ ॥

brahmabhūtaḥ prasannātmā na śocati na kāṅkṣati
samaḥ sarveṣu bhūteṣu madbhaktiṁ labhate parām (54)

The one who has 'become' Brahman (has recognised oneself as Brahman), whose mind is cheerful, does not grieve or long for anything. That person for whom all beings are the same (as himself) gains the highest devotion to Me.

भक्त्या मामभिजानाति यावान् यश्चास्मि तत्त्वतः ।
ततो मां तत्त्वतो ज्ञात्वा विशते तदनन्तरम् ॥ ५५ ॥

bhaktyā mām abhijānāti yāvān yaścāsmi tattvataḥ
tato māṁ tattvato jñātvā viśate tadanantaram (55)

By *bhakti* (knowledge), he knows Me properly as to how much I am and who I am in reality. Thereafter, knowing Me in reality, he enters (Me) soon after that (knowing).

सर्वकर्माण्यपि सदा कुर्वाणो मद्व्यपाश्रयः ।
मत्प्रसादादवाप्नोति शाश्वतं पदमव्ययम् ॥ ५६ ॥

sarvakarmāṇyapi sadā kurvāṇo madvyapāśrayaḥ
matprasādād avāpnoti śāśvataṁ padam avyayam (56)

The one who is always doing all (proper) actions, whose basis (for all actions and results) is Myself, gains the end, which is eternal and imperishable, because of My grace.

चेतसा सर्वकर्माणि मयि संन्यस्य मत्परः ।
बुद्धियोगमुपाश्रित्य मच्चित्तः सततं भव ॥ ५७ ॥

cetasā sarvakarmāṇi mayi sannyasya matparaḥ
buddhiyogam upāśritya maccittaḥ satataṁ bhava (57)

Being one whose (only) end is Myself, mentally renouncing all actions unto Me, resorting to a life of *karma-yoga*, may you become one whose mind is always in Me.

मच्चित्तः सर्वदुर्गाणि मत्प्रसादात्तरिष्यसि ।
अथ चेत्त्वमहङ्कारान्न श्रोष्यसि विनङ्क्ष्यसि ॥ ५८ ॥

maccittaḥ sarvadurgāṇi matprasādāt tariṣyasi
atha cet tvam ahaṅkārānna śroṣyasi vinaṅkṣyasi (58)

Being one whose mind is always in Me, you will cross all difficulties because of My grace. If, because of egotism, you do not listen (to Me), you will perish.

यदहङ्कारमाश्रित्य न योत्स्य इति मन्यसे ।
मिथ्यैष व्यवसायस्ते प्रकृतिस्त्वां नियोक्ष्यति ॥ ५९ ॥

yadahaṅkāram āśritya na yotsya iti manyase
mithyaiṣa vyavasāyaste prakṛtistvāṁ niyokṣyati (59)

Resorting to egotism, you think, 'I will not fight.' This resolve of yours is false. Your disposition will impel you.

स्वभावजेन कौन्तेय निबद्धः स्वेन कर्मणा ।
कर्तुं नेच्छसि यन्मोहात्करिष्यस्यवशोऽपि तत् ॥ ६० ॥

svabhāvajena kaunteya nibaddhaḥ svena karmaṇā
kartuṁ necchasi yanmohāt kariṣyasyavaśo'pi tat (60)

Kaunteya (Arjuna)! Out of delusion, being definitely bound by your own action, which is born of your natural disposition, you will helplessly do just what you do not wish to do.

ईश्वरः सर्वभूतानां हृद्देशेऽर्जुन तिष्ठति ।
भ्रामयन् सर्वभूतानि यन्त्रारूढानि मायया ॥ ६१ ॥

īśvaraḥ sarvabhūtānāṁ hṛddeśe'rjuna tiṣṭhati
bhrāmayan sarvabhūtāni yantrārūḍhāni māyayā (61)

The Lord remains at the seat of the intellect of all beings, Arjuna! causing all beings to move, revolve, by (the magic of his) *māyā*, (like) those (figures) which are mounted on a machine (are made to revolve).

तमेव शरणं गच्छ सर्वभावेन भारत।
तत्प्रसादात्परां शान्तिं स्थानं प्राप्स्यसि शाश्वतम्॥ ६२ ॥

tameva śaraṇaṁ gaccha sarvabhāvena bhārata
tatprasādātparāṁ śāntiṁ sthānaṁ prāpsyasi śāśvatam (62)

Surrender to Him alone with your whole heart, Bhārata (Arjuna)! By His grace you will gain absolute peace, the eternal abode.

इति ते ज्ञानमाख्यातं गुह्याद्गुह्यतरं मया।
विमृश्यैतदशेषेण यथेच्छसि तथा कुरु॥ ६३॥

iti te jñānam ākhyātaṁ guhyād guhyataraṁ mayā
vimṛśyaitad aśeṣeṇa yathecchasi tathā kuru (63)

Thus, the knowledge that is more secret than any secret was told by Me to you. Considering this thoroughly, you may do just as you wish.

सर्वगुह्यतमं भूयः शृणु मे परमं वचः।
इष्टोऽसि मे दृढमिति ततो वक्ष्यामि ते हितम्॥ ६४॥

sarvaguhyatamaṁ bhūyaḥ śṛṇu me paramaṁ vacaḥ
iṣṭo'si me dṛḍham iti tato vakṣyāmi te hitam (64)

Again, listen to My ultimate statement, which is the most secret of all. You are definitely beloved to Me, therefore, I will tell you, what is good.

मन्मना भव मद्भक्तो मद्याजी मां नमस्कुरु ।
मामेवैष्यसि सत्यं ते प्रतिजाने प्रियोऽसि मे ॥ ६५ ॥

manmanā bhava madbhakto madyājī māṁ namaskuru
māmevaiṣyasi satyaṁ te pratijāne priyo'si me (65)

Become one whose mind is offered to Me, one whose devotion is to Me, one whose worship is to Me; do salutations to Me. You will reach Me alone. I truly promise you. (Because) you are dear to Me.

सर्वधर्मान् परित्यज्य मामेकं शरणं व्रज ।
अहं त्वा सर्वपापेभ्यो मोक्षयिष्यामि मा शुचः ॥ ६६ ॥

sarvadharmān parityajya mām ekaṁ śaraṇaṁ vraja
ahaṁ tvā sarvapāpebhyo mokṣayiṣyāmi mā śucaḥ (66)

Giving up all *karmas*, take refuge in Me alone. I will release you from all *karmas*; do not grieve.

इदं ते नातपस्काय नाभक्ताय कदाचन ।
न चाशुश्रूषवे वाच्यं न च मां योऽभ्यसूयति ॥ ६७ ॥

idaṁ te nātapaskāya nābhaktāya kadācana
na cāśuśrūṣave vācyaṁ na ca māṁ yo'bhyasūyati (67)

This (teaching which has been taught) to you is never to be taught to the one who has no religious discipline, nor to the one who has no devotion, nor to the one who is not willing to listen, nor to the one who finds fault with Me (where there is none).

य इमं परमं गुह्यं मद्भक्तेष्वभिधास्यति ।
भक्तिं मयि परां कृत्वा मामेवैष्यत्यसंशयः ॥ ६८ ॥

ya imaṁ paramaṁ guhyaṁ madbhakteṣvabhidhāsyati
bhaktiṁ mayi parāṁ kṛtvā māmevaiṣyatyasaṁśayaḥ (68)

The one who teaches this most exalted, secret (*śāstra*) to My devotees, having the highest devotion for Me, will come to Me alone. There is no doubt.

न च तस्मान्मनुष्येषु कश्चिन्मे प्रियकृत्तमः ।
भविता न च मे तस्मादन्यः प्रियतरो भुवि ॥ ६९ ॥

na ca tasmānmanuṣyeṣu kaścinme priyakṛttamaḥ
bhavitā na ca me tasmād anyaḥ priyataro bhuvi (69)

And there is no one other than him who is the best among men who do what is dear to Me, and there will not be another dearer to Me on the earth than he.

अध्येष्यते च य इमं धर्म्यं संवादमावयोः ।
ज्ञानयज्ञेन तेनाहमिष्टः स्यामिति मे मतिः ॥ ७० ॥

adhyeṣyate ca ya imaṁ dharmyaṁ saṁvādam āvayoḥ
jñānayajñena tenāham iṣṭaḥ syām iti me matiḥ (70)

The one who studies or recites this dialogue of ours, that is unopposed to *dharma*, through that ritual in the form of knowledge, I would be worshipped. This is My conclusion.

श्रद्धावाननसूयश्च शृणुयादपि यो नरः ।
सोऽपि मुक्तः शुभाँल्लोकान्प्राप्नुयात्पुण्यकर्मणाम् ॥ ७१ ॥

śraddhāvanan asūyaśca śṛṇuyād api yo naraḥ
so'pi muktaḥ śubhān lokān prāpnuyāt puṇyakarmaṇām (71)

The person who has trust (in this *śāstra*), and who does not find fault with (this *śāstra*), even if he merely listens (to this teaching), he also, being freed (from the body), would gain the auspicious worlds of those who do good *karmas*.

कच्चिदेतच्छ्रुतं पार्थ त्वयैकाग्रेण चेतसा ।
कच्चिदज्ञानसम्मोहः प्रनष्टस्ते धनञ्जय ॥ ७२ ॥

kaccid etacchrutaṁ pārtha tvayaikāgreṇa cetasā
kaccid ajñānasammohaḥ pranaṣṭaste dhanañjaya (72)

Has this been 'listened to' by you, Pārtha (Arjuna)! with a single pointed mind? Is your delusion that is caused by ignorance destroyed, Dhanañjaya (Arjuna)?

अर्जुन उवाच ।
नष्टो मोहः स्मृतिर्लब्धा त्वत्प्रसादान्मयाच्युत ।
स्थितोऽस्मि गतसन्देहः करिष्ये वचनं तव ॥ ७३ ॥

arjuna uvāca
naṣṭo mohaḥ smṛtirlabdhā tvatprasādānmayācyuta
sthito'smi gatasandehaḥ kariṣye vacanaṁ tava (73)

Arjuna said:
By your grace, (my) delusion is gone; and I have gained recognition (of myself). O Lord Acyuta (Kṛṣṇa)! I remain as one from whom all doubts have gone. I will do what you say.

सञ्जय उवाच ।
इत्यहं वासुदेवस्य पार्थस्य च महात्मनः ।
संवादमिममश्रौषमद्भुतं रोमहर्षणम् ॥ ७४ ॥

sañjaya uvāca
ityahaṁ vāsudevasya pārthasya ca mahātmanaḥ
saṁvādam imam aśrauṣam adbhutaṁ romaharṣaṇam (74)

Sañjaya said:
Thus, I have heard this dialogue between Kṛṣṇa and Arjuna, of great mind and heart, which is wonderful and makes one's hair stand on end.

व्यासप्रसादाच्छ्रुतवानेतद्गुह्यमहं परम् ।
योगं योगेश्वरात्कृष्णात्साक्षात्कथयतः स्वयम् ॥ ७५ ॥

vyāsaprasādācchrutavān etad guhyam ahaṁ param
yogaṁ yogeśvarāt kṛṣṇāt sākṣāt kathayataḥ svayam (75)

By the grace of Vyāsa, I have listened to this secret and ultimate *yoga* from Kṛṣṇa, the Lord of *yoga*, directly teaching (it) himself.

राजन्संसृत्य संसृत्य संवादमिममद्भुतम् ।
केशवार्जुनयोः पुण्यं हृष्यामि च मुहुर्मुहुः ॥ ७६ ॥

rājan saṁsṛtya saṁsṛtya saṁvādam imam adbhutam
keśavārjunayoḥ puṇyaṁ hṛṣyāmi ca muhurmuhuḥ (76)

O King! Repeatedly recalling this wondrous, auspicious, dialogue between Kṛṣṇa and Arjuna, I rejoice again and again.

तच्च संसृत्य संसृत्य रूपमत्यद्भुतं हरेः ।
विस्मयो मे महान् राजन्हृष्यामि च पुनः पुनः ॥ ७७ ॥

tacca saṁsṛtya saṁsṛtya rūpam atyadbhutaṁ hareḥ
vismayo me mahān rājan hṛṣyāmi ca punaḥ punaḥ (77)

Further, repeatedly recalling that most wondrous form of the Lord Hari, I have great amazement, O King! and I rejoice again and again.

यत्र योगेश्वरः कृष्णो यत्र पार्थो धनुर्धरः ।
तत्र श्रीर्विजयो भूतिर्ध्रुवा नीतिर्मतिर्मम ॥ ७८ ॥

yatra yogeśvaraḥ kṛṣṇo yatra pārtho dhanurdharaḥ
tatra śrīrvijayo bhūtirdhruvā nītirmatirmama (78)

Wherever there is Kṛṣṇa, the Lord of *yoga*, wherever there is Arjuna, the one who bears the bow, there wealth, victory, various riches, and definite justice are present. This is my conclusion.

ॐतत्सत् ।
इति श्रीमद्भगवद्गीतासूपनिषत्सु ब्रह्मविद्यायां योगशास्त्रे श्रीकृष्णार्जुन-संवादे मोक्ष-संन्यास-योगो नाम अष्टादशोऽध्यायः ॥ १८ ॥

omtatsat.
iti śrīmadbhagavadgītāsūpaniṣatsu brahma-vidyāyāṁ yoga-śāstre śrīkṛṣṇārjunasaṁvāde mokṣa-sannyāsa-yogo nāma aṣṭādaśo'dhyāyaḥ (18)

Om, Brahman, is the only reality. Thus ends the eighteenth chapter called *mokṣa-sannyāsa-yoga*—having the topic of the freedom and renunciation—in the *Bhagavadgītā* which is in the form of a dialogue between Śrī Kṛṣṇa and Arjuna, which is the essence of the *Upaniṣads*, whose subject matter is both the knowledge of Brahman and *yoga.*

NOTES

1 The blue lily is deceptive. It looks like a lotus but it is not one.

2 Kurukṣetra exists even today between Delhi and Ambala. The great King Kuru, the founder of the Kuru dynasty, performed big *tapas* here and established *dharma*. Therefore, it is Kurukṣetra and also called *dharmakṣetra*.

3 Sātyaki was the son of Śini, a *yādava* chieftain. He was a disciple of Arjuna and was totally devoted to Kṛṣṇa. He was counted as an *atiratha*.

4 King Virāṭa of Matsya-deśa (also known as Virāṭa-deśa) was the father of Uttarā who was given in marriage to Abhimanyu. It was in his country that the Pāṇḍavas spent their *ajñāta-vāsa*.

5 Dhṛṣṭaketu was the son of Śiśupāla, the king of Cedi.

6 Cekitāna was a *yādava* chieftain belonging to the *vṛṣṇi* clan and was the commander of one of the seven *akṣauhiṇī*s of the Pāṇḍava-army.

7 One of the brothers of Kuntī.

8 King of Kunti-deśa, who adopted Kuntī as his daughter.

9 Father of Devikā, another wife of Yudhiṣṭhira.

10 Yudhāmanyu and Uttamaujas were brothers and they were princes under the king of Pāñcāla. They fought valiantly for all the eighteen days of the war, but were killed while asleep, by Aśvatthāmā in the end.

11 Abhimanyu was the son of Arjuna and Subhadrā, sister of Kṛṣṇa. He was a great warrior who was mercilessly killed by the ganging up of all the *mahāratha*s of the Kaurava-army.

12 He was the brother of Droṇa's wife Kṛpī. He taught archery to the Kaurava and the Pāṇḍava princes before Droṇa became their master. He is counted among the *cirañjīvin*s, those who live forever.

[13] He was the son of Droṇa and is also one of the *ciranjīvins*. He was so fiercely devoted to Duryodhana that on the last day when he was sure there was no more hope for Duryodhana, he went to the Pāṇḍavas' camp at night and killed all the men there when they were asleep.

[14] A son of Dhṛtarāṣṭra, an exception among the Dhārtarāṣṭras, he was noted for his sense of justice and righteousness. He was the only one who protested against the humiliation of Draupadī in the Kaurava-sabhā.

[15] Bhūriśravā— he was the grandson of Bāhlika, older brother of Śantanu.

[16] He was the husband of Duśśalā, Duryodhana's sister and the king of Sindhu-deśa. He was instrumental in the killing of Abhimanyu by stopping the Pāṇḍavas from going to Abhimanyu's help when he was caught up inside the *cakra-vyūha*. He could do this because, earlier he had obtained a boon from Lord Śiva that he would defeat all the Pāṇḍavas together except Arjuna, single-handedly for one day. The killing of Abhimanyu by several *mahāratha*s together, led Arjuna to make a vow that, if he did not kill Jayadratha by sunset of the next day he would kill himself. The next day, Duryodhana did all he could to protect Jayadratha so that Arjuna would be forced to put an end to his own life. Again, Kṛṣṇa saved the situation by creating an artificial sunset and forcing Jayadratha come out of his hiding so that Arjuna could kill him and fulfil his vow.

[17] *Sat-cid-ānanda-lakṣaṇa-svarūpād na kadāpi cyavate iti acyutaḥ*, the one who never falls from his nature of absolute existence, knowledge and limitlessness is Acyuta.

[18] *Bharatasya gotrāpatyam*, descendant of Bharata.

[19] *Guḍākā nidrā tasyāḥ iśaḥ*, one who has mastery over sleep.

[20] *Hṛṣīkānām indriyaṇām īśaḥ*, the lord of the senses.

[21] *Pṛthāyāḥ apatyam*, son of Pṛthā (Kuntī).

[22] *Kuntyāḥ apatyam*, son of Kuntī.

23 Arjuna's compassion was born of distress because what was going to happen was destruction and all the people who would be involved were his own people.

24 *Keśi-nāmānaṁ daityaṁ vāti hinasti iti keśavaḥ*, the one who is the destroyer of the demon Keśi is Keśava.

25 *Gobhiḥ vāṇibhiḥ vedānta-vākyaiḥ vindate iti govindaḥ*, the one who is gained (known) through the words of Vedanta is Govinda.

26 *Madhu-nāmānam asuraṁ sūditavān iti Madhusūdanaḥ*, the one who is the slayer of the demon, Madhu, is Madhusūdana.

27 *Asurāṇāṁ janānāṁ narakādi-gamayitṛtvād janārdanaḥ*, the one who chastises those given to improper ways is Janārdana.

28 *Māyāḥ śriyo dhavaḥ patiḥ mādhavaḥ*, the consort of Goddess Lakṣmī is Mādhava.

29 *Vṛṣṇi-kula-prasūtaḥ vārṣṇeyaḥ*, the one who is born in the dynasty of Vṛṣṇi is Vārṣṇeya.

30 *Yoga* here in the compound '*viṣāda-yoga*' means 'topic'; one of the many meanings of the word. The same meaning is in all the following titles of chapters.

31 Here the word '*yoga*' refers to anything a person needs in terms of preparation of the mind that is needed for the assimilation of this knowledge. Since the *Gitā* discusses all these along with the *brahma-vidyā*, it is also referred to as a *yoga-śāstra*.

32 This is the general rule (*utsarga*) and every rule has exception (*apavāda*). One may die young due to many reasons.

33 *Digvijaye prabhūtaṁ dhanam ajayad iti dhanañjayaḥ*, one who acquired large wealth during his conquest tour is Dhanañjaya.

34 In the Vedas.

35 The Veda is called '*sarvagataṁ brahma*' here, because it reveals everything. ब्रह्म (वेदः) सर्वार्थप्रकाशकत्वात् सर्वगतम्। (शाङ्करभाष्यम् ३.१५)

36 The word '*guṇa*' has many meanings. In this verse, *prakṛteḥ guṇaiḥ* means, by the modifications of *prakṛti*, meaning, by the mind, senses and the physical body.

[37] The *jñānins* and the *tattva-darśins* mentioned in the previous verse.

[38] A son of Pāṇḍu.

[39] *Māyā* united with the three *guṇas*.

[40] *Puruṣebhyaḥ uttamaḥ puruṣottamaḥ*, the one who transcends all beings is Puruṣottama.

[41] Sanskrit words for fame etc., are feminine. They are valued by all.

[42] *Savyena vāmena hastena sacituṁ śarān sandhātuṁ śīlaṁ yasya saḥ*, one who can naturally place the arrows on the bow with his left hand (and shoot).

[43] As stated in the last verse of the previous chapter (11.55).

[44] In some *Gītā* manuscripts this opening verse is not found and hence it does not carry verse number.

[45] Five *jñānendriyas* and the five *karmendriyas* put together make ten. The five *jñānendriyas* are, *śrotra* - the ears, *cakṣu-* the eyes, *tvak* - the sense of touch, *rasanā* - the sense of taste, and *ghrāṇa* - the sense of smell. The five *karmendriyas* are, *vāk* - the organ of speech, *pāṇi* - the hands, *pāda* - the feet, *pāyu* - the organ of excretion, and *upastha* - the organ of reproduction.

[46] *Sattva, rajas* and *tamas*.

[47] This includes the five organs of action, the five sense organs, the mind that entertains the fancy to do a given action, and the *buddhi* that resolves to do it.

[48] Here the word '*kevala*' means 'pure,' untouched by anything.

Oṁ tat sat

Alphabetical index of verses

For a list of our other publications,
please visit the website at:
www.avrpt.com

...or contact :

ARSHA VIDYA RESEARCH
AND PUBLICATION TRUST

32 / 4 Sir Desika Road,
Mylapore Chennai 600 004
Telefax : 044 - 2499 7131
Email : avrandpt@gmail.com
Website : www.avrpt.com

ARSHA VIDYA GURUKULAM

Anaikatti P.O.
Coimbatore 641 108
Ph : 0422 - 2657001
Fax : 0422 - 2657002
Email : office@arshavidya.in
Website : www.arshavidya.in

SWAMI DAYANANDA ASHRAM

Purani Jhadi, P.B.No. 30
Rishikesh, Uttaranchal 249 201
Telefax : 0135 - 2430769
Email : ashrambookstore@yahoo.com
Website : www.dayananda.org

ARSHA VIDYA GURUKULAM

P.O. Box 1059. Pennsylvania
PA 18353, USA
Ph : 001 - 570 - 992 - 2339
Email : avp@epix.net
Website : www.arshavidya.org

Our publications are also available at all leading bookstores and downloadable through the 'Teachings of Swami Dayananda' APP for Android and Apple devices.